Introduction

by Robert P. Weeks

I

There is no shortage of Hemingway criticism: the writings which deal with his work already bulk much larger than the work itself. The main purpose of the present selection, therefore, is to assemble those approaches to his work which have proved most fruitful, and to give wider circulation to several first-rate studies not readily available. It has also seemed important to do justice to what might be called the Minority Report, for Hemingway criticism is as notable for dissension as for quantity. Few writers have had so many devoted admirers and so many vehement detractors at the same time.

From the beginning Hemingway's work was generously and perceptively received. The best of his critics recognized that though he dealt with a limited range of characters, placed them in quite similar circumstances, measured them against an unvarying code, and rendered them in a style that epitomized these other limitations, it was precisely this ruthless economy that gave his writing its power. And when Hemingway himself commented on his aims, it was clear that he knew what he was doing. He knowingly restricted himself in order to strip down, compress, and energize his writing. Prose, he once said, is not interior decoration but architecture, and the Baroque is over.[1] His best work stands as a striking application to writing of Mies van der Rohe's architectural maxim: "Less is more."

On the other hand, Hemingway's detractors, many of whom are well-qualified, have doggedly insisted—and sometimes with a certain logic—that less is simply less: Hemingway is too limited, they say. His characters are mute, insensitive, uncomplicated men; his "action" circles narrowly about the ordeals, triumphs, and defeats of the bull ring, the battlefield, the trout stream, and similar male proving grounds; his style (some deny Hemingway's writing the benefit of this term) has stripped so much away that little is left but "a group of clevernesses"; and his "code" is at best a crudely simple outlook, in no sense comparable to

[1] *Death in the Afternoon* (New York: Scribner, 1932), p. 191.

1

the richer, more profound Stoicism which it is sometimes thought to resemble.

Hemingway's narrow range of characters has been censured most vigorously by British critics. One of the earliest of these, Wyndham Lewis, in an essay entitled "The Dumb Ox: A Study of Ernest Hemingway," wrote in 1934 that the Hemingway hero is "a dull-witted, bovine, monosyllabic simpleton" who speaks with "the voice of the 'folk,' of the masses, . . . the cannon fodder, the cattle outside the slaughterhouse, serenely chewing the cud—of those to whom things are done, in contrast to those who have executive will and intelligence." [2] Both Aldous Huxley and D. S. Savage have since supported the dumb ox evaluation, Savage with his essay on Hemingway in *The Withered Branch* (1950). In it he describes the Hemingway character as "a creature without religion, morality, politics, culture, or history—without any of those aspects, that is to say, of the distinctively human existence." Hemingway's contribution lies in what Savage calls "the proletarianization of literature: the adaptation of the technical artistic conscience to the subaverage human consciousness." [3]

Sean O'Faolain takes essentially the same stand: assigning a chapter of his book, *The Vanishing Hero*, to Hemingway, he says that "his Hero is always as near as makes no matter to being brainless, has no past, no traditions, and no memories." Then he adds, "We may regret this exclusive glorification of brute courage, strength, skill and grace, but I doubt if it is literary criticism to do so." [4] And, naturally, for these critics of the Hemingway hero, his characteristic heroine is even worse. For Edmund Wilson she is "amoeba-like," for Leslie Fiedler a "mindless, soft, subservient . . . animal or thing." [5]

The critics who disparage Hemingway's characters because they lack inwardness are probably outnumbered by those who disparage his fictional situations for the narrowness of their range. It has been said that

> the world that remains most alive to Hemingway is that stretch between puberty and maturity which is strictly governed by the ephebic code: a world of mixed apprehension and bravado before the rite of passage, the baptism of fire, the introduction to sex. Afterward comes the boasting, along with such surviving ideals as Hemingway subsumes in the word *cojones*.[6]

[2] Wyndham Lewis, "The Dumb Ox: A Study of Ernest Hemingway," *The American Review*, III (June, 1934), 302, 312.

[3] D. S. Savage, *The Withered Branch* (London: Eyre, 1950), pp. 27, 31.

[4] Sean O'Faolain, *The Vanishing Hero* (Boston: Little, 1957), p. 144.

[5] Edmund Wilson, "Hemingway: Gauge of Morale," *The Wound and the Bow* (Cambridge: Houghton, 1941), p. 239. Leslie Fiedler, *Love and Death in the American Novel* (New York: Criterion 1959), pp. 304, 306. [Reprinted on pp. 86-92 of this book.]

[6] Harry Levin, "Observations on the Style of Hemingway," *Kenyon Review*, XIII (Autumn, 1951), 607. [Reprinted on pp. 72-85 of this book.]

This is not only a world of men without women, but of men without jobs, men without parents or children, men without homes or even communities. It is a world in which the soldiers desert or else operate as guerillas, for there are no lasting affiliations in this world of isolates.

One assumption underlying such criticism is that the province of the novelist is the extensive yet subtle network of human relationships that enmeshes every human being. The poet may address his own soul or examine his private relationship with the universe or with nature, but the novelist may not. *His* work must be, to some extent, *engagé,* involved in and committed to society, as in even the highly poetic and intensive novels of Joyce, Woolf, and Faulkner. And Hemingway, according to Nemi D'Agostino, "had neither the talent nor the training to create a work of art *engagé* in the deepest sense." [7] His characters go into battle, but never to the ballot box; they are constantly being tested but never in a social context. According to this view, raw physical courage is not only the supreme value in his fictive world but practically the only one.

As a direct consequence of limiting his characters to certain types and severely limiting the situations in which he places them, Hemingway works with a relatively narrow group of ethical problems. On this account, some deny that his writing has any moral sense whatever. They see in it only a "devastating . . . contempt for human values and human life, which puts killing a man on the same level of actuality as cooking an egg or blacking one's boots." [8] More generally the charge has been that although there is a code of morality underlying Hemingway's fiction it is extremely thin. "It is a morality," Delmore Schwartz wrote, "for wartime, for sport, for drinking, and for expatriates; and there are, after all, a good many other levels of existence, and on those levels the activities in question fall into place and become rather minor. Consider, for example, how irrelevant the morality would be when the subject matter was family life." [9] The adjective most commonly used to describe the Hemingway hero's moral stance is "stoical," but, according to Sean O'Faolain, this term simply serves to expose the shallowness of Hemingway's moral sensitivity. He calls it a grave injustice to Hemingway to invoke the complexity and variety of that noble philosophy with its

> effective blending of a life of useful activity in service to others with a quasi-Oriental love of contemplation. We must not invite such comparisons.

[7] Nemi D'Agostino, "The Later Hemingway," *The Sewanee Review,* LXVIII (Summer, 1960), 486. [Reprinted on pp. 152-160 of this book.]

[8] *The Withered Branch,* p. 27.

[9] Delmore Schwartz, "Ernest Hemingway's Literary Situation," *Southern Review,* III (Spring, 1938), 777.

Hemingway is not a thoughtful man. He has no evident interest in social, moral, or philosophical ideas at all.[10]

The objections to Hemingway's style, like those to his characters and situations, rest ultimately on the belief that it, too, is sterile. Too much has been stripped away, leaving the diction pale, the syntax weak, the verbs without energy, the adjectives colorless. All that remains, according to Leon Edel, is "the artful illusion of a Style . . . He has conjured up an *effect* of a Style by a process of evasion, very much as he sets up an aura of emotion—by walking directly away from emotion!" [11] Professor Edel sees the Hemingway world as one of "superficial action almost wholly without reflection." And the hollowness of this world is glossed over by the "surface writing, dressed out in prose mannerisms," [12] which passes for a style but actually is not.

The vehemence of these depreciations has not been overlooked, least of all by the author himself. For example, when several unfavorable reviews of *Men Without Women* appeared in American magazines (including one in the *Saturday Review of Literature* under the heading: "Simple Annals of the Callous"), Hemingway's response was a poem, which appeared in *The Little Review*, May 1929, dedicated to the author of the review.

Valentine

For a Mr. Lee Wilson Dodd and Any of His
    Friends Who Want It.

Sing a song of critics
pockets full of lye
four and twenty critics
hope that you will die
hope that you will peter out
hope that you will fail
so they can be the first one
be the first to hail
any happy weakening or sign of quick decay.
(All very much alike, weariness too great,
sordid small catastrophes, stack the cards on fate,
very vulgar people, annals of the callous,
dope fiends, soldiers, prostitutes,
men without a gallus) [13]

.   .   .

[10] *The Vanishing Hero*, p. 138.
[11] Leon Edel, "The Art of Evasion," *Folio*, XX (Spring, 1955), 19. [Reprinted on pp. 169-171 of this book.]
[12] *Ibid.*
[13] Ernest Hemingway, "Valentine," *Little Review*, XII (May, 1929), 42.

"Sordid little catastrophes" and "very vulgar people" are phrases that had appeared in Joseph Wood Krutch's review of the book that contained "The Killers" and "Fifty Grand." The dismissal of Ole Andresen's and Jack Brennan's ordeals as "little catastrophes" and of Nick Adams as "very vulgar" no doubt helps to explain Hemingway's feeling that the critics' pockets were full of lye. Many critics, however, had something quite different in their pockets for Hemingway.

II

Critics who defend Hemingway have never denied that in his selection of characters he prefers bullfighters, bridge blowers, lion hunters, and big-game fishermen. To dismiss these men as "heavy-footed village idiots," however, lacking in sensitivity, intellect, and feeling is, they will claim, to misjudge them grossly. As Philip Young points out in his "Adventures of Nick Adams," [14] the Hemingway hero is not the simple primitive he is mistaken for. A good deal of his primitivism is a complicated barrier made of ritual, legend, sacraments, and symbols (to use Malcolm Cowley's terms[15]), which trembles and cracks under a terror he cannot face. It is true that Hemingway's vision of life embodies itself in stories about physical activity in the outdoor world, but Professor Young argues that the real battleground in these stories is inward.

The second major objection to Hemingway's writing—that it focuses on the limited situations of battlefield and blood sports—can be embraced as an advantage. Harry Levin has done this very neatly: "That he has succeeded within limits, and with considerable strain, is less important than that he has succeeded, that a few more aspects of life have been captured for literature." [16] But the more characteristic response has been to maintain that this world—like Homer's—is less limited than it appears to be; that Hemingway has succeeded in making war—and the other forms of violence that interest him—a moral equivalent of life. The soldiers, boxers, and bullfighters are tested and found to behave under stress not as Republicans, intellectuals, Spaniards, or expatriates behave, but as men do. Seen in this light, Hemingway is a classicist. His achievement is not merely that he has rendered the here and now with the authority of a candid photograph; he has also given us a glimpse of eternal and universal truth. As Sean O'Faolain puts it,

He is, within his honestly stated limits, and despite the weaknesses and idiosyncrasies that belong to the coarser element of his mind, a writer

[14] Philip Young, *Ernest Hemingway* (New York: Rinehart, 1952), p. 27. [Reprinted on pp. 95-111 of this book.]
[15] Malcolm Cowley, Introduction, *The Portable Hemingway* (New York: Viking, 1944), p. xxii. [Reprinted on pp. 40-51 of this book.]
[16] "Observations on the Style of Hemingway," p. 605.

whose subject is *l'essence de l'homme et son tragique immuable*. I dare to say that Racine would have been shocked by his stories, but that if he were patient enough he would have come to understand and admire what Hemingway is seeking. Zola would not have been in the least shocked by him, and would never have been able to understand what he is seeking. I place Hemingway, in his own modest way, in the great and almost defunct classical tradition.[17]

No objection to Hemingway's work has been answered as profusely and spiritedly as the charge that his writing advances a trivial criticism of life. So many critics have taken up arms against this charge that a conventional battle plan has evolved: the superficial interpretation of a given short story or novel is sketched out; then the more profound view is disclosed by explicating what was implied chiefly through irony, symbolism, repetition, and juxtaposition of characters; finally, the moral code underlying this more profound view is shown to be responsible as well as broadly relevant. No one has followed this plan more skillfully than the two critics who introduced it, Robert Penn Warren and Cleanth Brooks. By examining "The Killers" with the same alert care with which one would read and re-read a subtle poem, Brooks and Warren helped to open a fruitful new chapter of Hemingway criticism. Ray B. West, Jr., Mark Spilka, and Joseph Waldmeir in their sensitive and illuminating explications of *A Farewell to Arms*, *The Sun Also Rises*, and *The Old Man and the Sea*, respectively, follow this general plan. Professor Spilka's conclusion is typical:

> Pedro is the real hero of the parable, the final moral touchstone, the man whose code gives meaning to a world where love and religion are defunct, where the proofs of manhood are difficult and scarce, and where every man must learn to define his own moral conditions and then live up to them.[18]

In much the same way that the limited world of Hemingway's fiction can be shown to imply a much broader one, his spare, economical style can be revealed as a precise instrument of implication. "The dignity of movement of an iceberg is due to only one-eighth of it being above water."[19] So Hemingway himself has written, effectively characterizing the immense power of the unsaid. In his excellent essay on Hemingway's use of this power, E. M. Halliday points to the role of irony in Hemingway's world view:

[17] *The Vanishing Hero*, p. 142.
[18] Mark Spilka, "The Death of Love in *The Sun Also Rises*," in Charles Shapiro, ed., *Twelve Original Essays on Great American Novels* (Detroit: Wayne State University Press, 1958), p. 256. [Reprinted on pp. 127-138 of this book.]
[19] *Death in the Afternoon*, p. 192.

The ironic gap between expectation and fulfillment, pretense and fact, intention and action, the message sent and the message received, the way things are thought or ought to be and the way things are—this has been Hemingway's great theme from the beginning; and it has called for an ironic method to do it artistic justice.[20]

Symbolism has also been important to Hemingway in awaking reverberations beyond his compact style, but he has employed it with characteristic restraint. Malcolm Cowley (as late as 1944) was the first to suggest that Hemingway belonged "with Poe and Hawthorne and Melville: the haunted and nocturnal writers, the men who dealt in images that were symbols of an inner world." [21]

Hemingway's style, apart from these broader strategies of irony and symbolism, has received surprisingly little attention. It has been much more widely imitated than analyzed. Robert Penn Warren discerningly compares his purgation of the language to Wordsworth's, and Claude-Edmonde Magny examines the devices by which he exalts the instant as it flies, but by far the best anatomy of his full stylistic range is Harry Levin's pleasantly discursive "Observations on Hemingway's Style." Professor Levin convincingly demonstrates that the informal syntax, the neglect of adjectives and verbs, the reliance on nouns, is part of a carefully executed plan. What Leon Edel has characterized as "a series of charming tricks," becomes under Professor Levin's scrutiny a series of interlocking strategies for communicating excitement.

III

The debate of the critics on these matters has been powerfully influenced by a force outside the writing itself: Hemingway the man. Some literature can be satisfactorily read and discussed without taking the author into account. Other literature seems inseparable from the person who created it. To an extraordinary degree Hemingway and what he has written exist in a synergetic relationship, re-enforcing and fulfilling each other; he has created a personal legend which serves as an ambiance in which we read him. Lionel Trilling has said of such writers that their work

> often seems to have its importance less in itself than as a part of the personal legend. And the same thing may be said in greater or lesser degree of most of the great figures of modern literature. Yeats, Eliot, Lawrence, Joyce, Proust, Gide, Rilke, Kafka—all have their place in the modern

[20] E. M. Halliday, "Hemingway's Ambiguity: Symbolism and Irony," *American Literature*, XXVIII (March, 1956), 15.
[21] Introduction, *The Portable Hemingway*, p. vii.

pantheon not only as writers but as personalities, as notable cultural examples.[22]

Hemingway's place in such a pantheon is secure, for his personal legend has seized our imagination as firmly as his novels and stories. Nick Adams, Jake Barnes, Frederic Henry, Francis Macomber, Harry, the writer-protagonist of "The Snows of Kilimanjaro," Colonel Cantwell, and even old Santiago are fleshed out and corroborated by the figure of Ernest Hemingway—Hemingway the soldier, seated in a wheelchair in a Milan hospital with his wounded legs propped up; the expatriate, running before the bulls at Pamplona; the hunter, grinning beside the carcass of a huge kudu bull in the Tanganyika bush; the war correspondent, chatting with Ilya Ehrenburg in the bomb-shattered Hotel Florida in Madrid, or riding in a jeep through the Huertgen Forest dressed in a field coat and steel helmet; or the fisherman, sitting in the stern of the *Pilar* buckled in deep-sea fishing harness. Ernest Hemingway is, indeed, a "unique cultural example," who inhabited our world, yet energized and gave substance to the fictive world of the Hemingway hero.

But if his personal legend has seized our imagination, it has also repelled or attracted it—for reasons that are seldom clear and never simple. Hemingway criticism is full of attempts to neutralize, measure, or somehow cope with the author's galvanic personality, and none of the efforts are wholly satisfactory. Some of the early criticism made no attempt to separate the writer from his writing: it was not fiction but autobiography. Edmund Wilson went almost to the other extreme. He described the "public" Hemingway of the mid-Thirties, whose name appeared in the gossip columns, and whose writing appeared in *Esquire*, as "certainly the worst-invented character to be found in the author's work. If he is obnoxious, the effect is somewhat mitigated by the fact that he is intrinsically incredible." [23]

The most memorable attempt to write a character sketch of Hemingway—and the most controversial—was made by Lillian Ross in the pages of *The New Yorker*. In the Preface to her book *Portrait of Hemingway*, (Simon and Schuster, 1961, p. 14) in which the Profile is reprinted, she states:

It was a sympathetic piece, covering two days Hemingway spent in New York, in which I tried to describe as precisely as possible how Hemingway, who had the nerve to be like nobody else on earth, looked and sounded when he was in action, talking, between work periods—to give a picture of the man as he was, in his uniqueness and with his vitality and his enormous spirit of fun intact. Before it was published, I sent a galley proof of it to

[22] Lionel Trilling, *A Gathering of Fugitives* (Boston: Beacon Press, 1956), p. 19.
[23] "Hemingway: Gauge of Morale," p. 226.

the Hemingways, and they returned it marked with corrections. In an accompanying letter, Hemingway said that he had found the Profile funny and good, and that he had suggested only one deletion. Then a strange and mysterious thing happened. Nothing like it had ever happened before in my writing experience, or has happened since. To the complete surprise of Hemingway and the editors of *The New Yorker* and myself, it turned out, when the Profile appeared, that what I had written was extremely controversial. Most readers took the piece for just what it was, and I trust that they enjoyed it in an uncomplicated fashion. However, a certain number of readers reacted violently, and in a very complicated fashion. . . . Some of the more devastation-minded among them called the Profile "devastating."

Hemingway, with these people in mind, wrote to Miss Ross:

About our old piece; the hell with them. Think one of the "devastating" things was that I drink a little in it and that makes them think I am a rummy. But of course if they (the devastate people) drank what I drink in that piece they would die or something. Then . . . because I have fun a lot of the time and am not really spooky and so far always get up when they count over me some people are jealous. They can't understand you being a serious writer and not be solemn.[24]

Hemingway, like his characters, can give the superficial impression of being crude and uncomplicated, but as Miss Ross and others have tried to show, whoever is satisfied with that judgment is forced to overlook much of the evidence. Harry Levin compares Hemingway's refusal to behave like a man of letters to Hotspur's professing to be a laconic Philistine and turning out, "with no little grandiloquence—to be the most poetic character in Shakespeare's play."[25]

The problem of satisfactorily relating Hemingway the man to his work is central in the three scholarly, full-length studies of Hemingway that we have. Charles Fenton's *The Apprenticeship of Ernest Hemingway: The Young Years* is a carefully documented account of Hemingway's experiences as a journalist and World War I ambulance driver and soldier. It is an indispensable book for those with a serious interest in Hemingway; yet, paradoxically, nowhere is Hemingway's presence vividly felt in the book. Mr. Fenton has collected a great many pertinent facts from Oak Park, Kansas City, Fossalta, Toronto, Paris—all the key cities in the young Hemingway's itinerary—but he never catches up with the man himself, who always seems to have moved on before Mr. Fenton arrives.

Carlos Baker's purpose in *Hemingway: the Writer as Artist* was not, he tells us in his introduction, to write the history of Hemingway's

[24] Ernest Hemingway, quoted in Lillian Ross, "The Hemingway Profile," *Correspondence, The New Republic,* CXLV (August 7, 1961), 31.
[25] "Observations on the Style of Ernest Hemingway," p. 605.

"private battles or his public wars." He gives us, instead, a responsible
and reliable account of Hemingway's work from 1920 to 1955. Apart
from Professor Baker's insistence that Hemingway's writing rests on "a
substructure of symbolic meanings which has gone unrecorded and for
the most part unobserved," [26] his critical comments are generally reasonable and helpful. But like Mr. Fenton's book, this one seldom gives us
the feeling of what Hemingway was like as a man. In a praiseworthy
effort to avoid the petty, ephemeral, and irrelevant, Professor Baker
leaves us with a figure in marble, pale and opaque, but of heroic propor-
tions, to whom he sometimes refers with embarrassing piety as *"leo
Maximus."*

Philip Young's *Ernest Hemingway* (1952) lacks the solidity of Baker's
book, but is by far the most provocative, the most intellectually ad-
venturous full-length study of Hemingway that exists. By showing the
links connecting the Nick Adams stories to each other and to Hemingway's own experiences in northern Michigan and Italy, Professor Young
sketches a compelling portrait of the Hemingway hero, the big, tough,
outdoor man, who is actually a wounded man—"a sensitive, humorless,
honest, rather passive male" [27]—sickened by too much violence. Besides
demolishing the dumb ox school of criticism as itself crude, insensitive,
and dull-witted, Professor Young's book accomplishes two other things.
It provides us with a brilliant exercise in biographical criticism, and
shows us how rewarding it can be to see Hemingway as Twain's suc-
cessor in developing the American version of a paradise lost.

It remains for some future biographer-critic to apply Professor Young's
method to Hemingway's entire career. If the Nick Adams stories illuminate Hemingway's emotional and literary situation, there is reason to
hope that a similar examination of *For Whom the Bell Tolls* and *The
Old Man and the Sea* would tell us much about the later Hemingway.
Neither the Spanish nor the Cuban novel has been satisfactorily related
to the rest of Hemingway's work or to what is virtually the same thing,
Hemingway's development as a writer. It is a commonplace of Hemingway criticism to say, as David Daiches does, that *For Whom the Bell
Tolls* "clearly represents a new beginning in Hemingway's career as a
writer," [28] and that *The Old Man and the Sea* is a triumph, a tender
fulfillment of the affirmative attitude that made its first successful appearance in *For Whom the Bell Tolls.* But for all their snow-blindness
and their doctrinal rigidity, the Marxist critics may have seen more
clearly and judged more sanely than anyone else the essential meaning

---

[26] Carlos Baker, *Hemingway: The Writer As Artist* (Princeton: Princeton University Press, 1956), p. xiv. The best analysis of Professor Baker's "substructure of
symbolic meanings" is E. M. Halliday's "Hemingway's Ambiguity: Symbolism and
Irony," which is reprinted on pp. 52-71 of this book.

[27] *Ernest Hemingway*, p. 26.

[28] David Daiches, "Ernest Hemingway," *College English*, II (May, 1941), 736.

of the Spanish novel. Alvah Bessie's review in *The New Masses* is typical:

> An astounding thing has happened that anyone who was even remotely concerned with what happened in Spain will find almost incredible: Hemingway has treated that war (in an essential way) exactly as he treated the First World War in *A Farewell to Arms*. There is a morbid concentration upon the meaning of *individual* death, *personal* happiness, *personal* misery . . . For the author of *For Whom the Bell Tolls* does not convince us, in this novel, that 'any man's death diminishes me, because I am involved in Mankinde.' He only convinces us—no matter how tenderly he may write of the love of Robert Jordan and Maria—that the imagination of his own death may yet destroy him as an artist.[29]

Similarly, one suspects that when the dust has settled, we will see Hemingway's last novel as "a late work by a tired writer. . . . It is separated by the space of a whole lifetime from the lucid movement, the fresh and crystalline clarity, the poignancy, and the shock-power of the language of the young Hemingway." [30] This is the judgment of Nemi D'Agostino, as he looks with statesmanlike purview at the last segment of Hemingway's career. The book is not an ignoble end, but it certainly does not triumphantly culminate the career of one of the finest writers of our time.

IV

For nearly forty years the value of Hemingway's fiction has been under debate. This introduction has traced the pattern of that debate so that examples from it in this collection may be seen not as isolated events but as parts of a long and continuing discussion. Central in the pattern, as we have seen, is the issue of Hemingway's limitations, and the question in each instance has been: Are these limitations a weakness or a strength? Almost equally central, however, is the strong, bright thread of Hemingway's personality, which runs through the controversy about his work as colorfully and distinctly as through the work itself.

Yet, it would be misleading to give the impression that the criticism of Hemingway has always been conducted in these orderly terms—or that it should be. Hemingway's limitations can best be defended, not in isolation, but as they actually affect us when we apprehend them *in situ* in a given work. For the power and distinctiveness of Hemingway's fiction derive from the combination of his various limitations. Considered singly, any one of them is crippling. How could one hope to write

[29] Alvah Bessie, "Hemingway's *For Whom the Bell Tolls*," *New Masses*, XXXVII (November 5, 1940), 28.
[30] "The Later Hemingway," p. 492.

serious literature about characters and situations so bare, in a style that is quite inflexible and spare, only designed, it would seem, to celebrate the virtue of the stiff upper lip? The effect of the "less is more" principle can be experienced only when one looks at the whole façade or some large feature of a building, for only then can the absence of ornamentation be apprehended as a value in itself.

The power of this effect can be demonstrated if we look at a scene in which his various limitations all work together. An ideal scene is one which Hemingway evokes again and again. It appears in "The Killers," "A Clean, Well-Lighted Place," "The Capital of the World," and several other of his finest stories, and he uses it to end five of his six novels. It is the scene in which the hero has finally been cornered, but as he gallantly suffers his defeat he is not alone; he is in the presence of others who either do not even notice him, or if they do are unaware of his ordeal and of the gallantry with which he endures it. Here, in short compass, Hemingway brings to bear his most powerful and distinctive skills, for this particular scene is obviously deeply meaningful to him.

The most recent example is found in *The Old Man and the Sea*. That novel ends with a party of tourists sitting in a cafe, the Terrace, looking down into the water, and seeing Santiago's marlin with its great long white spine and the huge tail at the end of it. One of them, a woman, asks the waiter what it is and he says "Eshark" in an effort to explain what had happened to the marlin. She then remarks:

> "I didn't know sharks had such handsome, beautifully formed tails."
> "I didn't either," her male companion said.
> Up the road, in his shack, the old man was sleeping again. He was still sleeping on his face and the boy was sitting by him watching him. The old man was dreaming about the lions.[31]

The tourists with their flat, matter-of-fact unawareness speak for the uninitiated, the insensitive majority oblivious to the suffering and the gallantry of the Hemingway hero. But the tourists are worse than unaware; they completely misconstrue the evidence available to them. The bare facts of their unawareness are stated economically and without emphasis—except for the emphasis of "placement" at the end of the story. The effect of the tourists' uncomprehending response is to intensify the poignancy of the hero's suffering and to arouse the reader's compassion and identification with him. Hemingway's fishermen, soldiers, waiters, and other limited and seemingly unpromising characters are generally elevated by this strategy to persons deserving our attention. They are not dumb oxen chewing their cuds at the door of the slaughterhouse, but gallant men enduring their suffering with grace in a cold,

[31] *The Old Man and the Sea* (New York: Scribner, 1952), p. 140.

empty universe. Occasionally they have one companion who recognizes and values their admirable stoicism, but this only emphasizes the rarity of such recognition in this world. And, anyway, it is made clear that the hero is beyond such help.

By selecting a common man like Santiago for his hero, Hemingway gives his story a classical universality. More than that, when he shows us the bravery and resolution this ordinary man can summon up in the face of defeat, we are struck with pity and awe. Here is Aristotle's dictum turned upside down: we are moved not by the fall of a great man but the elevation to heroism of what we had taken to be a little man. And the tourists, by their unawareness in the final scene, flat, unemphatic and understated as it is, underscore as nothing else could the solitary, dignified, self-sufficient valor of the old fisherman. Their unawareness of Santiago's ordeal helps to elevate it far above the sort of pathos that outsiders often *are* aware of, perhaps because they can mitigate it with their commiseration. Thus the final scene of *The Old Man and the Sea* demonstrates how skilfully Hemingway combines self-imposed limitations to stir our emotions and bring into focus the central meaning of his novel.

Essentially the same strategies are evident in the other novels. In *Across the River and Into the Trees,* while Colonel Cantwell dies of a heart attack in the back seat of his Buick staff car, $T/5$ Jackson sits unconcernedly behind the wheel. Jackson has been used throughout the novel to epitomize unawareness—he is even insensitive to the loveliness of Venice—and thus he makes a fitting non-witness to the gallant Colonel's death. In the last paragraph of *For Whom the Bell Tolls*, Lieutenant Berrendo, the sensitive and devout Fascist cavalry officer, rides through the woods with his eyes on the trail, unaware that the dying Robert Jordan is watching him and that as soon as he reaches a sunlit place up ahead he will pass before the sights of Jordan's submachine gun. (The substitution of Lieutenant Berrendo, an admirable character, for the usual insensitive, unaware character supports the view that this novel is not the partisan treatment of the Spanish Civil War some believe it to be. Whereas this scene is invariably used elsewhere in Hemingway to differentiate the initiated from the uninitiated, the ironical view of war is so powerful in *For Whom the Bell Tolls* that it dissolves partisanship and places Jordan and the enemy, Berrendo, on much the same footing: each is a good man about to die.) The same scene is dominated by the dying Harry Morgan at the end of *To Have and Have Not* as he is brought into Key West harbor alongside the yachts of the villainous well-to-do who are pointedly unaware of his heroic end.

And, finally, there is the highly effective use of the same motif at the end of *A Farewell to Arms,* which Hemingway is said to have rewritten many times before he was satisfied. Even years later he was quoted as saying that the end of that novel was unbearably poignant to him—not a usual comment for him to make. The novel ends, it will be recalled, with Catherine Barkley undergoing a Caesarean section and dying shortly after it. During the operation her lover, Frederic Henry, waits in the empty hall, where he sees two nurses hurrying to the operating room. One of them says:

> "They're going to do a Caesarean."
> The other one laughed, "We're just in time. Aren't we lucky?" [32]

Frederic takes time out from the ordeal of watching Catherine die to go to a nearby cafe for lunch, then for supper. It is a brightly lighted cafe filled with people many of whom know each other and sit together chatting, playing cards, or placidly drinking beer quite unaware that sitting among them is a man whose world is coming to an end.

The short stories contain variations on this scene so numerous that it is clearly seen to be a presiding metaphor of the author's fictive world. For example, "Old Man at the Bridge," originally a news dispatch filed by Hemingway from Spain, but reclassified by him as a short story and placed in *The Fifth Column and the First Forty-Nine Short Stories*, deals with an old man sitting by the side of the road near the front during the Spanish Civil War. The old man tells the narrator he was the last person to leave the town of San Carlos before the Fascist army arrived. He had stayed behind to take care of his two goats, one cat, and four pairs of pigeons.

> "And you have no family?" I asked, watching the far end of the bridge where a few last carts were hurrying down the slope of the bank.
> "No . . . only the animals I stated. The cat, of course, will be all right. A cat can look out for itself, but I cannot think what will become of the others."
> "What politics have you?" I asked.
> "I am without politics," he said. "I am seventy-six years old. I have come twelve kilometers now and I think I can go no further."
> "This is not a good place to stop," I said. "If you can make it, there are trucks up the road where it forks for Tortosa."
> "I will wait a while," he said, "and then I will go. Where do the trucks go?"
> "Towards Barcelona," I told him.
> "I know no one in that direction," he said, "but thank you very much. Thank you again very much."

> .   .   .

> There was nothing to do about him. It was Easter Sunday and the Fascists were advancing toward the Ebro. It was a gray overcast day with a

[32] *A Farewell to Arms* (New York: Scribner, 1929), p. 335.

low ceiling so their planes were not up. That and the fact that cats know how to look after themselves was all the good luck that old man would ever have.[33]

In this brief episode Hemingway has written a concise yet moving parable of our time. The effort to find meaning and purpose in our cats and goats in the face of what seems to be an inexorable and unspeakable holocaust, the desolateness of knowing no one in the direction of Barcelona—these have been experienced by millions in this century and may yet be experienced by millions more before the century ends. The situation and the old man have no particular pungency in themselves; the style likewise is spare and unemphatic; yet the combination of these elements with the narrator's relative indifference transmutes the materials into art.

Hemingway understood suffering, like the Old Masters in Auden's poem "Musée des Beaux Arts"—that it occurs "while someone else is eating or opening a window or just walking dully along"—or watching carts hurrying down a slope. In "The Killers," to take another example, after Nick warns Ole Andresen that the killers are lying in wait for him, Nick encounters Mrs. Bell, the woman who runs the rooming house Ole lives in. Mrs. Bell is utterly unaware of Ole's situation. She thinks he has stayed in all day because "he don't feel well." She plays in this story the same function as the torturer's horse in the renaissance painting of the crucifixion described in Auden's poem. While the martydom is running its bloody course, the horse "scratches its innocent behind on a tree." Again, in the superb story "The Capital of the World," the boy Paco is mortally wounded while practicing a bull-fighting maneuver in the Madrid *pension* where he works as a waiter. Paco bleeds to death in the deserted dining room after calmly instructing a fellow waiter, "Advise one of the priests," and meanwhile his two older sisters sit in a nearby theater watching Greta Garbo in *Anna Christie*. The story ends with the comment that the Garbo movie "disappointed all Madrid for a week." Even in "A Clean, Well-Lighted Place," the burden of the story is carried by the contrast between a young, unaware waiter who has no feeling for a desperate old man who dreads leaving the clean, well-lighted cafe, and a middle-aged waiter who knows what it is to experience the horror of nothingness. The older waiter describes the contrast in terms that apply as well to Mrs. Bell, the tourists in *The Old Man and the Sea*, and the other impervious characters so essential to Hemingway's view of the world: "Some lived in it and never felt it but he knew it was all nada."

With consummate art in these works and stories—art so unobtrusive as to elicit the charge of not being art at all—Hemingway confers on a

[33] "Old Man at the Bridge," *The Fifth Column and the First Forty-Nine Stories* (New York: Scribner, 1938), pp. 177-178.

seemingly routine experience affecting ordinary people a cosmic significance. And his style, far from being a series of surface mannerisms,
reveals itself to be a way of looking at the world and expressing an
attitude of tense resignation in the face of inevitable suffering and
defeat. In the characters that do not share the secret, either because they
are insensitive like the narrator in "Old Man at the Bridge," or have
no way of knowing it, like Mrs. Bell in "The Killers," Hemingway
mirrors man's fate as he sees it and shows us that suffering and death,
even when heroically endured, are a lonely and personal affair.

These evaluations are but another way of saying that Hemingway's
art does lack a broad base. He has won his reputation as an artist
of the first rank by operating within limits that would have stifled a
lesser writer. But within and because of these limits, he has in his
best work uttered a lyric cry that—although it may not resemble the
full orchestra of Tolstoy or the organ tones of Melville—is nonetheless a
moving and finely wrought response to our times.

How Do You Like It Now, Gentlemen?

by Lillian Ross

Ernest Hemingway, who may well be the greatest American novelist and short-story writer of our day, rarely came to New York. For many years, he spent most of his time on a farm, the Finca Vigia, nine miles outside Havana, with his wife, a domestic staff of nine, fifty-two cats, sixteen dogs, a couple of hundred pigeons, and three cows. When he did come to New York, it was only because he had to pass through it on his way somewhere else. Late in 1949, on his way to Europe, he stopped in New York for a few days. I had written to him asking if I might see him when he came to town, and he had sent me a typewritten letter saying that would be fine and suggesting that I meet his plane at the airport. "I don't want to see anybody I don't like, nor have publicity, nor be tied up all the time," he went on. "Want to go to the Bronx Zoo, Metropolitan Museum, Museum of Modern Art, ditto of Natural History, and see a fight. Want to see the good Breughel at the Met, the one, no two, fine Goyas and Mr. El Greco's Toledo. Don't want to go to Toots Shor's. Am going to try to get into town and out without having to shoot my mouth off. I want to give the joints a miss. Not seeing news people is not a pose. It is only to have time to see your friends." In pencil, he added, "Time is the least thing we have of."

Time did not seem to be pressing Hemingway the day he flew in from Havana. He was to arrive at Idlewild late in the afternoon, and I went out to meet him. His plane had landed by the time I got there, and I found him standing at a gate waiting for his luggage and for his wife, who had gone to attend to it. He had one arm around a scuffed, dilapidated briefcase pasted up with travel stickers. He had the other around a wiry little man whose forehead was covered with enormous beads of perspiration. Hemingway had on a red plaid wool shirt, a figured wool necktie, a tan wool sweater-vest, a brown tweed jacket tight across the back and with sleeves too short for his arms, gray flannel slacks, Argyle socks, and loafers, and he looked bearish, cordial, and constricted. His hair, which was very long in back, was gray, except at the temples, where it was white; his mustache was white, and he had a ragged, half-inch, full white beard. There was a bump about the size of a walnut over his left eye. He had on steel-rimmed spectacles, with a piece of paper under the nosepiece. He was in no hurry to get into Manhattan. He crooked the arm around the briefcase into a tight hug and said that inside was the unfinished manuscript of his new book, "Across the River and Into the Trees." He crooked the arm around the wiry little man into a tight hug and said he had been his seat companion on the flight. The man's name, as I got it in a mumbled introduction, was Myers, and he was returning from a business trip to Cuba. Myers made a slight attempt to dislodge himself from the embrace, but Hemingway held on to him affectionately.

"He read book all way up on plane," Hemingway said. He spoke with a perceptible Midwestern accent, despite the Indian talk. "He liked book, I think," he added, giving Myers a little shake and beaming down at him.

"Whew!" said Myers.

"Book too much for him," Hemingway said. "Book start slow, then increase in pace till it becomes impossible to stand. I bring emotion up to where you can't stand it, then we level off, so we won't have to provide oxygen tents for the readers. Book is like engine. We have to slack her off gradually."

"Whew!" said Myers.

Hemingway released him. "Not trying for no-hit game in book," he said. "Going to win maybe twelve to nothing or maybe twelve to eleven."

Myers looked puzzled.

"She's better book than 'Farewell,' " Hemingway said. "I think this is best one, but you are always prejudiced, I guess. Especially if you want to be champion." He shook Myers' hand. Thanks for reading book," he said.

"Pleasure," Myers said, and walked off unsteadily.

Hemingway watched him go, and then turned to me. "After you finish a book, you know, you're dead," he said moodily. "But no one knows you're dead. All they see is the irresponsibility that comes in after the terrible responsibility of writing." He said he felt tired but was in good shape physically; he had brought his weight down to two hundred and eight, and his blood pressure was down, too. He had considerable rewriting to do on his book, and he was determined to keep at it until he was absolutely satisfied. "They can't yank novelist like they can pitcher," he said. "Novelist has to go the full nine, even if it kills him."

We were joined by Hemingway's wife, Mary, a small, energetic, cheerful woman with close-cropped blond hair, who was wearing a long, belted mink coat. A porter pushing a cart heaped with luggage followed her. "Papa, everything is here," she said to Hemingway. "Now we ought to get going, Papa." He assumed the air of a man who was not going to be rushed. Slowly, he counted the pieces of luggage. There were fourteen, half of them, Mrs. Hemingway told me, extra-large Valpaks designed by her husband and bearing their *hierro*, also designed by him. When Hemingway had finished counting, his wife suggested that he tell the porter where to put the luggage. Hemingway told the porter to stay right there and watch it; then he turned to his wife and said, "Let's not crowd, honey. Order of the day is to have a drink first."

We went into the airport cocktail lounge and stood at the bar. Hemingway put his briefcase down on a chromium stool and pulled the stool close to him. He ordered bourbon and water. Mrs. Hemingway said she would have the same, and I ordered a cup of coffee. Hemingway told the bartender to bring double bourbons. He waited for the drinks with impatience, holding on to the bar with both hands and humming an unrecognizable tune. Mrs. Hemingway said she hoped it wouldn't be dark by the time they got to New York. Hemingway said it wouldn't make any difference to him, because New York was a rough town, a phony town, a town that was the same in the dark as it was in the light, and he was not exactly overjoyed to be going there anyway. What he was looking forward to, he said, was Venice. "Where I like it is out West in Wyoming, Montana, and Idaho, and I like Cuba and Paris and around Venice," he said. "Westport gives me the horrors." Mrs. Hemingway lit a cigarette and handed me the pack. I passed it along to him, but he said he didn't smoke. Smoking ruined his sense of smell, a sense he found completely indispensable for hunting. "Cigarettes smell so awful to you when you have a nose that can truly smell," he said, and laughed, hunching his shoulders and raising the back of his fist to his face, as though he expected somebody to hit him. Then he enumerated elk, deer, possum, and coon as some of the things he could truly smell.

The bartender brought the drinks. Hemingway took several large swallows and said he got along fine with animals, sometimes better than with human beings. In Montana, once, he lived with a bear, and the bear slept with him, got drunk with him, and was a close friend. He asked me whether there were still bears at the Bronx Zoo, and I said I didn't know, but I was pretty sure there were bears at the Central Park Zoo. "I always used to go to the Bronx Zoo with Granny Rice," he said. "I love to go to the zoo. But not on Sunday. I don't like to see the people making fun of the animals, when it should be the other way around." Mrs. Hemingway took a small notebook out of her purse and opened it; she told me she had made a list of chores she and her husband had to do before their boat sailed. They included buying a hot-water-bottle cover, an elementary Italian grammar, a short history of Italy, and for Hemingway, four woolen undershirts, four pairs of cotton underpants, two pairs of woolen underpants, bedroom slippers, a belt, and a coat. "Papa has never had a coat," she said. "We've got to buy Papa a coat." Hemingway grunted and leaned against the bar. "A nice, rainproof coat," Mrs. Hemingway said. "And he's got to get his glasses fixed. He needs some good soft padding for the nose-piece. It cuts him up brutally. He's had that same piece of paper under the nosepiece for weeks. When he really wants to get cleaned up, he changes the paper." Hemingway grunted again.

The bartender came up, and Hemingway asked him to bring another round of drinks. Then he said, "First thing we do, Mary, as soon as we hit hotel, is call up the Kraut." "The Kraut," he told me, with that same fist-to-the-face laugh, was his affectionate term for Marlene Dietrich, an old friend, and was part of a large vocabulary of special code terms and speech mannerisms indigenous to the Finca Vigia. "We have a lot of fun talking a sort of joke language," he said.

"First we call Marlene, and then we order caviar and champagne, Papa," Mrs. Hemingway said. "I've been waiting months for that caviar and champagne."

"The Kraut, caviar, and champagne," Hemingway said slowly, as though he were memorizing a difficult set of military orders. He finished his drink and gave the bartender a repeat nod, and then he turned to me. "You want to go with me to buy coat?" he asked.

"Buy coat and get glasses fixed," Mrs. Hemingway said.

I said I would be happy to help him do both, and then I reminded him that he said he wanted to see a fight. The only fight that week, I had learned from a friend who knows all about fights, was at the St. Nicholas Arena that night. I said that my friend had four tickets and would like to take all of us. Hemingway wanted to know who was fighting. When I told him, he said they were bums. Bums, Mrs. Hemingway repeated, and added that they had better fighters in Cuba. Hemingway gave me a long, reproachful look. "Daughter, you've got to learn that a bad fight is worse than no fight," he said. We would all go to a fight when he got back from Europe, he said, because it was absolutely necessary to go to several good fights a year. "If you quit going for too long a time, then you never go near them," he said. "That would be very dangerous." He was interrupted by a brief fit of coughing. "Finally," he concluded, "you end up in one room and won't move."

After dallying at the bar a while longer, the Hemingways asked me to go with them to their hotel. Hemingway ordered the luggage loaded into one taxi, and the three of us got into another. It was dark now. As we drove along the boulevard, Hemingway watched the road carefully. Mrs. Hemingway told me that he always watched the road, usually from the front seat. It was a habit he got into during the First World War. I asked them what they planned to do in Europe. They said they were going to stay a week or so in Paris, and then drive to Venice.

"I love to go back to Paris," Hemingway said, his eyes still fixed on the road. "Am going in the back door and have no interviews and no publicity and never get a haircut, like in the old days. Want to go to cafés where I know no one but one waiter and his replacement, see all the new pictures and the old ones, go to the bike races and the fights, and see the new riders and fighters. Find good, cheap restaurants where you can keep your own napkin. Walk all over the town and see where we made our mistakes and where we had our few bright ideas. And learn the form and try and pick winners in the blue, smoky afternoons, and then go out the next day to play them at Auteuil and Enghien."

"Papa is a good handicapper," Mrs. Hemingway said.

"When I know the form," he said.

We were crossing the Queensboro Bridge, and we had a good view of the Manhattan skyline. The lights were on in the tall office buildings. Hemingway did not seem to be impressed. "This ain't my town," he said. "It's a town you come to for a short time. It's murder." Paris was like another home to him, he said. "I am as lonesome and as happy as I can be in that town we lived in and worked and learned and grew up in, and then fought our way back into." Venice was another of his home towns. The last time he and his wife were in Italy, they had lived for four months in Venice and the Cortina Valley, and he had gone hunting, and now he had put the locale and some of the people in the book he was writing. "Italy was so damned wonderful," he said. "It was sort of like having died and gone to Heaven, a place you'd figured never to see."

Mrs. Hemingway said that she had broken her right ankle skiing there but that she planned to go skiing there again. Hemingway was hospitalized in Padua with an eye infection, which developed into erysipelas, but he wanted to go back to Italy and wanted to see his many good friends there. He was looking forward to seeing the gondoliers on a windy day, the Gritti Palace hotel, where they had stayed during their last visit, and the Locanda Cipriani, which was an old inn on Torcello, an island in the lagoon northeast of Venice where some of the original Venetians lived before they built Venice. Now about seventy people lived on Torcello, and the men were professional duck hunters. While there, Hemingway had gone duck-hunting a lot with the gardener of the old inn. "We'd go around through the canals and jump-shoot, and I'd walk the prairies at low tide for snipe," he said. "It was a big fly route for ducks that came all the way down from the Pripet Marshes. I shot good and thus became a respected local character. They have some sort of little bird that comes through, after eating grapes in the north, on his way to eat grapes in the south. The local characters sometimes shot them sitting, and I occasionally shot them flying. Once, I shot two high doubles, rights and lefts, in a row, and the gardener cried with emotion. Coming home, I shot a high duck against the rising moon and dropped him in the canal. That precipitated an emotional crisis I thought I would never get him out of but did, with about a pint of Chianti. We each took a pint out with us. I drank mine to keep warm coming home. He drank his when overcome by emotion." We were silent for a while, and then Hemingway said, "Venice was lovely."

The Hemingways were stopping at the Sherry-Netherland. Hemingway registered and told the room clerk that he did not want any announcement made of his arrival and did not want any visitors, or any telephone calls, either, except for Miss Dietrich. Then we went up to the suite—living room, bedroom, and serving pantry—that had been reserved for them. Hemingway paused at the entrance and scouted the living room. It was large, decorated in garish colors, and furnished with imitation-Chippendale furniture and an imitation fireplace containing imitation coals.

"Joint looks O.K.," he said. "Guess they call this the Chinese Gothic Room." He moved in and took the room.

Mrs. Hemingway went over to a bookcase and examined its contents. "Look, Papa," she said. "They're phony. They're pasteboard backs, Papa. They're not real books."

Hemingway put his briefcase down on a bright-red couch and advanced on the bookcase, then slowly, with expression, read the titles aloud— "Elementary Economics," "Government of the United States," "Sweden, the Land and the People," and "Sleep in Peace," by Phyllis Bentley. "I think we are an outfit headed for extinction," he said, starting to take off his necktie.

After getting his necktie off, and then his jacket, Hemingway handed them to his wife, who went into the bedroom, saying she was going to unpack. He unbuttoned his collar and went over to the telephone. "Got to call the Kraut," he said. He telephoned the Plaza and asked for Miss Dietrich. She was out, and he left word for her to come over for supper. Then he called room service and ordered caviar and a couple of bottles of Perrier-Jouët, *brut*.

Hemingway went back to the bookcase and stood there stiffly, as though he could not decide what to do with himself. He looked at the pasteboard backs again and said, "Phony, just like the town." I said that there was a tremendous amount of talk about him these days in literary circles—that the critics seemed to be talking and writing definitively not only about the work he had done but about the work he was going to do. He said that, of all the people he did not wish to see in New York, the people he wished least to see were the critics.

"They are like those people who go to ball games and can't tell the players without a score card," he said. "I am not worried about what anybody I do not like might do. What the hell! If they can do you harm, let them do it. It is like being a third baseman and protesting because they hit line drives to you. Line drives are regrettable, but to be expected." The closest competitors of the critics among those he wished least to see, he said, were certain writers who wrote books about the war when they had not seen anything of war at first hand. "They are just like an outfielder who will drop a fly on you when you have pitched to have the batter hit a high fly to that outfielder, or when they're pitching they try to strike everybody out." When he pitched, he said, he never struck anybody out, except under extreme necessity. "I knew I had only so many fast balls in that arm," he said. "Would make them pop to short instead, or fly out, or hit it on the ground, bouncing."

A waiter arrived with the caviar and champagne, and Hemingway told him to open one of the bottles. Mrs. Hemingway came in from the bedroom and said she couldn't find his toothbrush. He said that he didn't know where it was but that he could easily buy another. Mrs. Hemingway said all right, and went back into the bedroom. Hemingway poured two glasses of champagne, gave one to me, and picked up the other one and took a sip. The waiter watched him anxiously. Hemingway hunched his shoulders and said something in Spanish to the waiter. They both laughed, and the waiter left. Hemingway took his glass over to the red couch and sat down, and I sat in a chair opposite him.

"I can remember feeling so awful about the first war that I couldn't write about it for ten years," he said, suddenly very angry. "The wound combat makes in you, as a writer, is a very slow-healing one. I wrote three stories about it in the old days—'In Another Country,' 'A Way You'll Never Be,' and 'Now I Lay Me.'" He mentioned a war writer who, he said, was apparently thinking of himself as Tolstoy, but who'd be able to play Tolstoy only on the Bryn Mawr field-hockey team. "He never hears a shot fired in anger, and he sets out to beat who? Tolstoy, an artillery officer who fought at Sevastopol, who knew his stuff, who was a hell of a man anywhere you put him—bed, bar, in an empty room where he had to think. I started out very quiet and I beat Mr. Turgenev. Then I trained hard and I beat Mr. de Maupassant. I've fought two draws with Mr. Stendhal, and I think I had an edge in the last one. But nobody's going to get me in any ring with Mr. Tolstoy unless I'm crazy or I keep getting better."

He had begun his new book as a short story. "Then I couldn't stop it. It went straight on into a novel," he said. "That's the way all my novels got started. When I was twenty-five, I read novels by Somersault Maugham and Stephen St. Vixen Benét." He laughed hoarsely. "They had written novels, and I was ashamed because I had not written any novels. So I wrote 'The Sun' when I was twenty-seven, and I wrote it in six weeks, starting on my birthday, July 21st, in Valencia, and finishing it September 6th, in Paris. But it was really lousy and the rewriting took nearly five months. Maybe that will encourage young writers so they won't have to go get advice from their psychoanalysts. Analyst once wrote me, What did I learn from psychoanalysts? I answered, Very little but hope they had learned as much as they were able to understand from my published works. You never saw a counter-puncher who was punchy. Never lead against a hitter unless you can outhit him. Crowd a boxer, and take everything he has, to get inside. Duck a swing. Block a hook. And counter a jab with everything you own. Papa's delivery of hard-learned facts of life."

Hemingway poured himself another glass of champagne. He liked to write in longhand, he said, but he had recently bought a tape recorder and was trying to get up the courage to use it. "I'd like to learn talk machine," he said. "You just tell talk machine anything you want and get secretary to type it out." He wrote without facility, except for dialogue. "When the people are talking, I can hardly write it fast enough or keep up with it, but with an almost unbearable high manifold pleasure. I put more inches on than she will take, and then fly her as near as I know to how she should be flown, only flying as crazy as really good pilots fly crazy sometimes. Most of the time flying conservatively but with an awfully fast airplane that makes up for the conservatism. That way, you live longer. I mean your writing lives longer. How do you like it now, gentlemen?" The question seemed to have some special significance for him, but he did not bother to explain it.

I wanted to know whether, in his opinion, the new book was different from his others, and he gave me another long, reproachful look. "What do you think?" he said after a moment. "You don't expect me to write 'The Farewell to Arms Boys in Addis Ababa,' do you? Or 'The Farewell to Arms Boys Take a Gunboat'?" The book was about the command level in the Second World War. "I am not interested in the G.I. who wasn't one," he said, suddenly angry again. "Or the injustices done to *me*, with a capital 'M.' I am interested in the goddam sad science of war." The new novel had a good deal of profanity in it. "That's because in war they talk profane, although I always try to talk gently," he said. "I think I've got 'Farewell' beat in this one," he went on. He touched his briefcase. "It hasn't got the youth and the ignorance." Then he asked wearily, "How do you like it now, gentlemen?"

There was a knock at the door, and Hemingway got up quickly and opened it. It was Miss Dietrich. Their reunion was a happy one. Mrs. Hemingway came out of the bedroom and greeted the guest enthusiastically. Miss Dietrich stood back from Hemingway and looked at him with approval. "Papa, you look wonderful," she said slowly.

"I sure missed you, daughter," said Hemingway. He raised his fist to his face, and his shoulders shook as he laughed silently.

Miss Dietrich was wearing a mink coat. She sighed loudly, took off the coat, and handed it to Mrs. Hemingway. Then she sighed again and sat down in an overstuffed chair. Hemingway poured a glass of champagne, took it to her, and refilled the other glasses.

"The Kraut's the best that ever came into the ring," he said as he handed me my glass. Then he pulled a chair up beside Miss Dietrich's, and they compared notes on friends and on themselves. They talked about theatre and motion-picture people, one of whom, a man, Hemingway referred to as a "sea heel."

Miss Dietrich wanted to know what a "sea heel" was.

"The sea is bigger than the land," he told her.

Mrs. Hemingway went into the serving pantry and came out in a few minutes with caviar spread on toast.

"Mary, I am telling Papa how I have to behave because I am a grandmother," Miss Dietrich said, taking a piece of toast. "I have to think always of the children. You know, Papa?"

Hemingway gave a sympathetic grunt, and Miss Dietrich took from her purse some snapshots of her grandson and passed them around. He was eighteen months old, she told us. Hemingway said that he looked like a winner, and that he would be proud to own a piece of him if he ever got into the ring.

Miss Dietrich said that her daughter was going to have another child soon. "I'll be a grandmother *again,* Papa," she said.

Hemingway gave her a bleak look. "I'm going to be a grandfather in a few months," he said. "My son Bumby's wife."

Mrs. Hemingway told me that Bumby was the nickname of her husband's eldest son, John, an Army captain stationed in Berlin. His two other sons, she said, were Patrick, known as Mouse, who was a twenty-one-year-old sophomore at Harvard, and was planning to get married in June, and Gregory, known as Gigi, who was eighteen and a freshman at St. John's, at Annapolis. In addition to the present Mrs. Hemingway, Patrick was going to invite to his wedding his and Gigi's mother Pauline Pfeiffer, who was Hemingway's second wife. Bumby's mother and Hemingway's first wife was Hadley Richardson, now Mrs. Paul Scott Mowrer, and Hemingway's third wife was Martha Gellhorn.

"Everything you do, you do for the sake of the children," Miss Dietrich said.

"Everything for the children," Hemingway said. He refilled Miss Dietrich's glass.

"Thank you, Papa," she said, and sighed. She lived at the Plaza, she told him, but spent a good deal of her time at the apartment of her daughter, who lived on Third Avenue. "Papa, you should see me when

they go out," she said, and took a sip of champagne. "I'm the baby-sitter.
As soon as they leave the house, I go around and look in all the corners
and straighten the drawers and clean up. I can't stand a house that isn't
neat and clean. I go around in all the corners with towels I bring with
me from the Plaza, and I clean up the whole house. Then they come
home at one or two in the morning, and I take the dirty towels and
some of the baby's things that need washing, and, with my bundle over
my shoulder, I go out and get a taxi, and the driver, he thinks I am this
old washerwoman from Third Avenue, and he takes me in the taxi
and talks to me with sympathy, so I am afraid to let him take me to
the Plaza. I get out a block away from the Plaza and I walk home with
my bundle and I wash the baby's things, and then I go to sleep."

"Daughter, you're hitting them with the bases loaded," Hemingway
said earnestly.

There was a ring at the door, and a bellboy brought in a florist's box.
Mrs. Hemingway opened it and took out some green orchids, which
were from her mother. Mrs. Hemingway put the flowers in a vase and
said it was time to order supper.

As we ate, the Hemingways and Miss Dietrich talked about the war.
All three had seen it at first hand. Mrs. Hemingway, who, as Mary
Welsh, was a *Time* correspondent in London, met Hemingway there
during the war, and both saw a good deal of Miss Dietrich there and,
later on, in Paris. Miss Dietrich was a U.S.O. entertainer, and performed
on almost every front in the European theatre. She grew a little sad
as she talked about the war. She had loved entertaining the troops, and
the spirit overseas, she said, was the best she had ever found in people
anywhere. "Everybody was the way people should be all the time," she
continued. "Not mean and afraid but good to each other."

Hemingway raised his glass in a toast to her.

"I've finally figured out why Papa sometimes gets mean now that the
war is over," Mrs. Hemingway said. "It's because there is no occasion for
him to be valorous in peacetime."

"It was different in the war," Miss Dietrich said. "People were not so
selfish and they helped each other."

Hemingway asked her about some recordings she had made, during
the war, of popular American songs with lyrics translated into German,
and said he'd like to have them. "I'll give you manuscript of new book
for recordings if you want to trade even, daughter," he told her.

"Papa, I don't trade with you. I love you," said Miss Dietrich.

"You're the best that ever came into the ring," Hemingway said.

Late the next morning, I was awakened by a telephone call from
Hemingway, who asked me to come right over to the hotel. He sounded
urgent. I had a fast cup of coffee, and when I turned up at the suite,
I found the door open and walked in. Hemingway was talking on the

telephone. He was wearing an orange plaid bathrobe that looked too small for him, and he had a glass of champagne in one hand. His beard looked more scraggly than it had the day before. "My boy Patrick is coming down from Harvard and I'd like to reserve a room for him," he was saying into the telephone. " 'P,' as in 'Patrick.' " He paused and took a sip of champagne. "Much obliged. He'll be down from Harvard."

Hemingway hung up, and from his bathrobe pocket took a box of pills. He shook two of them into the palm of his hand, and downed them with a mouthful of champagne. He told me that he had been up since six, that his wife was still asleep, and that he had done enough work for that morning and wanted to talk, an activity he found relaxing. He always woke at daybreak, he explained, because his eyelids were especially thin and his eyes especially sensitive to light. "I have seen all the sunrises there have been in my life, and that's half a hundred years," he said. He had done considerable revision that morning on the manuscript. "I wake up in the morning and my mind starts making sentences, and I have to get rid of them fast—talk them or write them down," he said. "How did you like the Kraut?"

Very much, I said.

"I love the Kraut and I love Ingrid," he said. "If I weren't married to Miss Mary and didn't love Miss Mary, I would try to hook up with either of them. Each one has what the other hasn't. And what each has, I love very much." For a moment, he looked bewildered, and then he said quickly, "Would never marry an actress, on account they have their careers and they work bad hours."

I asked him whether he still wanted to buy a coat, and he said sure but he didn't want to be rushed or crowded and it was cold outside. On a serving table near the couch were two champagne coolers, each containing ice and a bottle. He carried his glass over there and held up one of the bottles and squinted at it. It was empty. He put it back in the cooler, head down. Then he opened the other bottle, and as he poured some champagne into his glass, he sang, " ' So feed me am-mu-ni-tion, keep me in the Third Division, your dog-face soldier boy's O.K.' " Breaking off, he said, "Song of the Third Infantry Division. I like this song when I need music inside myself to go on. I love all music, even opera. But I have no talent for it and cannot sing. I have a perfect goddam ear for music, but I can't play any instrument by ear—not even the piano. My mother used to make me play the cello. She took me out of school one year to learn the cello, when I wanted to be out in the fresh air playing football. She wanted to have chamber music in the house."

His briefcase was lying open on a chair near the desk, and the manuscript pages were protruding from it; someone seemed to have stuffed them into the briefcase without much care. Hemingway told me that he had been cutting the manuscript. "The test of a book is how much good stuff you can throw away," he said. "When I'm writing it, I'm just as

proud as a goddam lion. I use the oldest words in the English language.
People think I'm an ignorant bastard who doesn't know the ten-dollar
words. I know the ten-dollar words. There are older and better words
which if you arrange them in the proper combination you make it stick.
Remember, anybody who pulls his erudition or education on you hasn't
any. Also, daughter, remember that I never carried Teddy bears to bed
with me since I was four. Now, with seventy-eight-year-old grandmothers
taking advantage of loopholes in the G.I. Bill of Rights whereby a gold-
star mother can receive her son's education, I thought of establishing a
scholarship and sending myself to Harvard, because my Aunt Arabelle
has always felt very bad that I am the only Hemingway boy that never
went to college. But I have been so busy I have not got around to it.
I only went to high school and a couple of military cram courses, and
never took French. I began to learn to read French by reading the A.P.
story in the French paper after reading the American A.P. story, and
finally learned to read it by reading accounts of things I had seen—*les
événements sportifs*—and from that and *les crimes* it was only a jump to
Dr. de Maupassant, who wrote about things I had seen or could understand. Dumas, Daudet, Stendhal, who when I read him I knew that was
the way I wanted to be able to write. Mr. Flaubert, who always threw
them perfectly straight, hard, high, and inside. Then Mr. Baudelaire,
that I learned my knuckle ball from, and Mr. Rimbaud, who never
threw a fast ball in his life. Mr. Gide and Mr. Valéry I couldn't learn
from. I think Mr Valéry was too smart for me. Like Jack Britton and
Benny Leonard."

Jack Britton, he continued, was a fighter he admired very much.
"Jack Britton kept on his toes and moved around and never let them hit
him solid," he said. "I like to keep on my toes and never let them hit
me solid. Never lead against a hitter unless you can outhit him. Crowd
a boxer," he said, assuming a boxing stance and holding his right hand,
which was grasping the champagne glass, close to his chest. With his
left hand, he punched at the air, saying, "Remember. Duck a swing.
Block a hook. And counter a jab with everything you own." He
straightened up and looked thoughtfully at his glass. Then he said, "One
time, I asked Jack, speaking of a fight with Benny Leonard, 'How did you
handle Benny so easy, Jack?' 'Ernie,' he said, 'Benny is an awfully smart
boxer. All the time he's boxing, he's thinking. All the time he was thinking, I was hitting him.'" Hemingway gave a hoarse laugh, as though he
had heard the story for the first time. "Jack moved very geometrically
pure, never one-hundredth of an inch too much. No one ever got a solid
shot at him. Wasn't anybody he couldn't hit any time he wanted to." He
laughed again. "'All the time he was thinking, I was hitting him.'"
The anecdote, he told me, had been in the original version of his
short story "Fifty Grand," but Scott Fitzgerald had persuaded him to
take it out. "Scott thought everybody knew about it, when only Jack

Britton and I knew about it, because Jack told it to me," he said. "So Scott told me to take it out. I didn't want to, but Scott was a successful writer and a writer I respected, so I listened to him and took it out."

Hemingway sat down on the couch and nodded his head up and down sharply a couple of times to get my attention. "As you get older, it is harder to have heroes, but it is sort of necessary," he said. "I have a cat named Boise, who wants to be a human being," he went on slowly, lowering his voice to a kind of grumble. "So Boise eats everything that human beings eat. He chews Vitamin B Complex capsules, which are as bitter as aloes. He thinks I am holding out on him because I won't give him blood-pressure tablets, and because I let him go to sleep without Seconal." He gave a short, rumbling laugh. "I am a strange old man," he said. "How do you like it now, gentlemen?"

Fifty, Hemingway said, on reconsideration, is not supposed to be old. "It is sort of fun to be fifty and feel you are going to defend the title again," he said. "I won it in the twenties and defended it in the thirties and the forties, and I don't mind at all defending it in the fifties."

After a while, Mrs. Hemingway came into the room. She was wearing gray flannel slacks and a white blouse, and she said she felt wonderful, because she had had her first hot bath in six months. Then she said she was going out to do her errands, and suggested that Hemingway get dressed and go out and do his. He said that it was lunchtime and that if they went out then, they would have to stop someplace for lunch, whereas if they had lunch sent up to the room, they might save time. Mrs. Hemingway said she would order lunch while he got dressed. Still holding his glass, he reluctantly got up from the couch. Then he finished his drink and went into the bedroom. By the time he came out—wearing the same outfit as the day before, except for a blue shirt with a button-down collar—a waiter had set the table for our lunch. We couldn't have lunch without a bottle of Tavel, Hemingway said, and we waited until the waiter had brought it before starting to eat.

Hemingway began with oysters, and he chewed each one very thoroughly. "Eat good and digest good," he told us.

"Papa, please get glasses fixed," Mrs. Hemingway said.

He nodded. Then he nodded a few times at me—a repetition of the sign for attention. "What I want to be when I am old is a wise old man who won't bore," he said, then paused while the waiter set a plate of asparagus and an artichoke before him and poured the Tavel. Hemingway tasted the wine and gave the waiter a nod. "I'd like to see all the new fighters, horses, ballets, bike riders, dames, bullfighters, painters, airplanes, sons of bitches, café characters, big international whores, restaurants, years of wine, newsreels, and never have to write a line about any of it," he said. "I'd like to write lots of letters to my friends and get back letters. Would like to be able to make love good until I was eighty-five, the way Clemenceau could. And what I would like to be is not Bernie Baruch. I wouldn't sit on park benches, although I might go around the park once in a while to feed the pigeons, and also I wouldn't have any long beard, so there could be an old man didn't look like Shaw." He stopped and ran the back of his hand along his beard, and looked around the room reflectively. "Have never met Mr. Shaw," he said. "Never been to Niagara Falls, either. Anyway, I would take up harness racing. You aren't up near the top at that until you're over seventy-five. Then I could get me a good young ball club, maybe, like Mr. Mack. Only I wouldn't signal with a program, so as to break the pattern. Haven't figured out yet what I would signal with. And when that's over, I'll make the prettiest corpse since Pretty Boy Floyd. Only suckers worry about saving their souls. Who the hell should care about saving his soul when it is a man's duty to lose it intelligently, the way you would sell a position you were defending, if you could not hold it, as expensively as possible, trying to make it the most expensive position that was ever sold. It isn't hard to die." He opened his mouth and laughed, at first soundlessly and then loudly. "No more worries," he said. He picked up a long spear of asparagus with his fingers and looked at it without enthusiasm. "It takes a pretty good man to make any sense when he's dying," he said.

Mrs. Hemingway had finished eating, and she quickly finished her wine. Hemingway slowly finished his. I looked at my wristwatch, and found that it was almost three. The waiter started clearing the table, and we all got up. Hemingway stood looking sadly at the bottle of champagne, which was not yet empty. Mrs. Hemingway put on her coat, and I put on mine.

"The half bottle of champagne is the enemy of man," Hemingway said. We all sat down again.

"If I have any money, I can't think of any better way of spending money than on champagne," Hemingway said, pouring some.

When the champagne was gone, we left the suite. Downstairs, Mrs. Hemingway told us to remember to get glasses fixed, and scooted away.

Hemingway balked for a moment in front of the hotel. It was a cool, cloudy day. This was not good weather for him to be out in, he said sulkily, adding that his throat felt kind of sore. I asked him if he wanted to see a doctor. He said no. "I never trust a doctor I have to pay," he said, and started across Fifth Avenue. A flock of pigeons flew by. He stopped, looked up, and aimed an imaginary rifle at them. He pulled the trigger, and then looked disappointed. "Very difficult shot," he said. He turned quickly and pretended to shoot again. "Easy shot," he said. "Look!" He pointed to a spot on the pavement. He seemed to be feeling better, but not much better.

I asked him if he wanted to stop first at his optician's. He said no. I mentioned the coat. He shrugged. Mrs. Hemingway had suggested that

he look for a coat at Abercrombie & Fitch, so I mentioned Abercrombie
& Fitch. He shrugged again and lumbered slowly over to a taxi, and
we started down Fifth Avenue in the afternoon traffic. At the corner of
Fifty-fourth, we stopped on a signal from the traffic cop. Hemingway
growled. "I love to see an Irish cop being cold," he said. "Give you eight
to one he was an M.P. in the war. Very skillful cop. Feints and fakes
good. Cops are not like they are in the Hellinger movies. Only once in
a while." We started up again, and he showed me where he once walked
across Fifth Avenue with Scott Fitzgerald. "Scott wasn't at Princeton any
more, but he was still talking football," he said, without animation.
"The ambition of Scott's life was to be on the football team. I said,
'Scott, why don't you cut out this football?' I said, 'Come on, boy.'
He said, 'You're crazy.' That's the end of that story. If you can't get
through traffic, how the hell are you gonna get through the line? But
I am not Thomas Mann," he added. "Get another opinion."

By the time we reached Abercrombie's, Hemingway was moody again.
He got out of the taxi reluctantly and reluctantly entered the store. I
asked him whether he wanted to look at a coat first or something else.

"Coat," he said unhappily.

In the elevator, Hemingway looked even bigger and bulkier than he
had before, and his face had the expression of a man who is being forcibly
subjected to the worst kind of misery. A middle-aged woman standing
next to him stared at his scraggly white beard with obvious alarm and
disapproval. "Good Christ!" Hemingway said suddenly, in the silence of
the elevator, and the middle-aged woman looked down at her feet.

The doors opened at our floor, and we got out and headed for a
rack of topcoats. A tall, dapper clerk approached us, and Hemingway
shoved his hands into his pants pockets and crouched forward. "I think
I still have credit in this joint," he said to the clerk.

The clerk cleared his throat. "Yes, sir," he said.

"Want to see coat," Hemingway said menacingly.

"Yes, sir," said the clerk. "What kind of coat did you wish to see, sir?"

"That one." He pointed to a straight-hanging, beltless tan gabardine
coat on the rack. The clerk helped him into it, and gently drew him over
to a full-length mirror. "Hangs like a shroud," Hemingway said, tearing
the coat off. "I'm tall on top. Got any other coat?" he asked, as though
he expected the answer to be no. He edged impatiently toward the
elevators.

"How about this one, sir, with a removable lining, sir?" the clerk said.
This one had a belt. Hemingway tried it on, studied himself in the
mirror, and then raised his arms as though he were aiming a rifle.
"You're going to use it for *shooting*, sir?" the clerk asked. Hemingway
grunted, and said he would take the coat. He gave the clerk his name,
and the clerk snapped his fingers. "Of course!" he said. "There was

something . . ." Hemingway looked embarrassed and said to send the coat to him at the Sherry-Netherland, and then said he'd like to look at a belt.

"What kind of belt, Mr. Hemingway?" the clerk asked.

"Guess a brown one," Hemingway said.

We moved over to the belt counter, and another clerk appeared.

"Will you show Mr. Hemingway a belt?" the first clerk said, and stepped back and thoughtfully watched Hemingway.

The second clerk took a tape measure from his pocket, saying he thought Hemingway was a size 44 or 46.

"Wanta bet?" Hemingway asked. He took the clerk's hand and punched himself in the stomach with it.

"Gee, he's got a hard tummy," the belt clerk said. He measured Hemingway's waistline. "Thirty-eight!" he reported. "Small waist for your size. What do you do—a lot of exercise?"

Hemingway hunched his shoulders, feinted, laughed, and looked happy for the first time since we'd left the hotel. He punched himself in the stomach with his own fist.

"Where you going—to Spain again?" the belt clerk asked.

"To Italy," Hemingway said, and punched himself in the stomach again. After Hemingway had decided on a brown calf belt, the clerk asked him whether he wanted a money belt. He said no—he kept his money in a checkbook.

Our next stop was the shoe department, and there Hemingway asked a clerk for some folding bedroom slippers.

"Pullman slippers," the clerk said. "What size?"

" 'Levens," Hemingway said bashfully. The slippers were produced, and he told the clerk he would take them. "I'll put them in my pocket," he said. "Just mark them, so they won't think I'm a shoplifter."

"You'd be surprised what's taken from the store," said the clerk, who was very small and very old. "Why, the other morning, someone on the first floor went off with a big roulette wheel. Just picked it up and—"

Hemingway was not listening. "Wolfie!" he shouted at a man who seemed almost seven feet tall and whose back was to us.

The man turned around. He had a big square red face, and at the sight of Hemingway it registered extreme joy. "Papa!" he shouted.

The big man and Hemingway embraced and pounded each other on the back for quite some time. It was Winston Guest. Mr. Guest told us he was going upstairs to pick up a gun and proposed that we come along. Hemingway asked what kind of gun, and Guest said a ten-gauge magnum.

"Beautiful gun," Hemingway said, taking his bedroom slippers from the clerk and stuffing them into his pocket.

In the elevator, Hemingway and Guest checked with each other on how much weight they had lost. Guest said he was now down to two hundred and thirty-five, after a good deal of galloping around on polo ponies. Hemingway said he was down to two hundred and eight, after shooting ducks in Cuba and working on his book.

"How's the book now, Papa?" Guest asked as we got out of the elevator.

Hemingway gave his fist-to-the-face laugh and said he was going to defend his title once more. "Wolfie, all of a sudden I found I could write wonderful again, instead of just biting on the nail," he said slowly. "I think it took a while for my head to get rebuilt inside. You should not, ideally, break a writer's head open or give him seven concussions in two years or break six ribs on him when he is forty-seven or push a rear-view-mirror support through the front of his skull opposite the pituitary gland or, really, shoot at him too much. On the other hand, Wolfie, leave the sons of bitches alone and they are liable to start crawling back into the womb or somewhere if you drop a porkpie hat." He exploded into laughter.

Guest's huge frame shook with almost uncontrollable laughter. "God, Papa!" he said. "I still have your shooting clothes out at the island. When are you coming out to shoot, Papa?"

Hemingway laughed again and pounded him on the back. "Wolfie, you're so damn big!" he said.

Guest arranged to have his gun delivered, and then we all got into the elevator, the two of them talking about a man who caught a black marlin last year that weighed a thousand and six pounds.

"How do you like it now, gentlemen?" Hemingway asked.

"God, Papa!" said Guest.

On the ground floor, Guest pointed to a mounted elephant head on the wall. "Pygmy elephant, Papa," he said.

"Miserable elephant," said Hemingway.

Their arms around each other, they went out to the street. I said that I had to leave, and Hemingway told me to be sure to come over to the hotel early the next morning so that I could go with him and Patrick to the Metropolitan Museum. As I walked off, I heard Guest say, "God, Papa, I'm not ashamed of anything I've ever done."

"Nor, oddly enough, am I," said Hemingway.

I looked around. They were punching each other in the stomach and laughing raucously.

The following morning, the door of the Hemingway suite was opened for me by Patrick, a shy young man of medium height, with large eyes and a sensitive face. He was wearing gray flannel slacks, a white shirt open at the collar, Argyle socks, and loafers. Mrs. Hemingway was writing a letter at the desk. As I came in, she looked up and said, "As soon as Papa has finished dressing, we're going to look at pictures." She went back to her letter.

Patrick told me that he'd just as soon spend the whole day looking at pictures, and that he had done a bit of painting himself. "Papa has to be back here for lunch with Mr. Scribner," he said, and added that he himself was going to stay in town until the next morning, when the Hemingways sailed. The telephone rang and he answered it. "Papa, I think it's Gigi calling you!" he shouted to the bedroom.

Hemingway emerged, in shirtsleeves, and went to the phone. "How are you, kid?" he said into it, then asked Gigi to come down to the Finca for his next vacation. "You're welcome down there, Gigi," he said. "You know that cat you liked? The one you named Smelly? We renamed him Ecstasy. Every one of our cats knows his own name." After hanging up, he told me that Gigi was a wonderful shot—that when he was eleven he had won second place in the shoot championship of Cuba. "Isn't that the true gen, Mouse?" he asked.

"That's right, Papa," said Patrick.

I wanted to know what "true gen" meant, and Hemingway explained that it was British slang for "information," from "intelligence." "It's divided into three classes—gen; the true gen, which is as true as you can state it; and the really true gen, which you can operate on," he said.

He looked at the green orchids. "My mother never sent *me* any flowers," he said. His mother was about eighty, he said, and lived in River Forest, Illinois. His father, who was a physician, had been dead for many years; he shot himself when Ernest was a boy. "Let's get going if we're going to see the pictures," he said. "I told Charlie Scribner to meet me here at one. Excuse me while I wash. In big city, I guess you wash your neck." He went back into the bedroom. While he was gone, Mrs. Hemingway told me that Ernest was the second of six children—Marcelline, then Ernest, Ursula, Madelaine, Carol, and the youngest, his only brother, Leicester. All the sisters were named after saints. Every one of the children was married; Leicester was living in Bogotà, Colombia, where he was attached to the United States Embassy.

Hemingway came out in a little while, wearing his new coat. Mrs. Hemingway and Patrick put on their coats, and we went downstairs. It was raining, and we hurried into a taxi. On the way to the Metropolitan, Hemingway said very little; he just hummed to himself and watched the street. Mrs. Hemingway told me that he was usually unhappy in taxis, because he could not sit in the front seat to watch the road ahead. He looked out the window and pointed to a flock of birds flying across the sky. "In this town, birds fly, but they're not serious about it," he said. "New York birds don't climb."

When we drew up at the Museum entrance, a line of school children was moving in slowly. Hemingway impatiently led us past them. In the lobby, he paused, pulled a silver flask from one of his coat pockets, unscrewed its top, and took a long drink. Putting the flask back in his pocket, he asked Mrs. Hemingway whether she wanted to see the Goyas first or the Breughels. She said the Breughels.

"I learned to write by looking at paintings in the Luxembourg Museum in Paris," he said. "I never went past high school. When you've got a hungry gut and the museum is free, you go to the museum. Look," he said, stopping before "Portrait of a Man," which has been attributed to both Titian and Giorgione. "They were old Venice boys, too."

"Here's what I like, Papa," Patrick said, and Hemingway joined his son in front of "Portrait of Federigo Gonzaga (1500-1540)," by Francesco Francia. It shows, against a landscape, a small boy with long hair and a cloak.

"This is what we try to do when we write, Mousie," Hemingway said, pointing to the trees in the background. "We always have this in when we write."

Mrs. Hemingway called to us. She was looking at "Portrait of the Artist," by Van Dyck. Hemingway looked at it, nodded approval, and said, "In Spain, we had a fighter pilot named Whitey Dahl, so Whitey came to me one time and said, 'Mr. Hemingway, is Van Dyck a good painter?' I said, 'Yes, he is.' He said, 'Well, I'm glad, because I have one in my room and I like it very much, and I'm glad he's a good painter because I like him.' The next day, Whitey was shot down."

We all walked over to Rubens' "The Triumph of Christ Over Sin and Death." Christ is shown surrounded by snakes and angels and is being watched by a figure in a cloud. Mrs. Hemingway and Patrick said they thought it didn't look like the usual Rubens.

"Yeah, he did that all right," Hemingway said authoritatively. "You can tell the real just as a bird dog can tell. Smell them. Or from having lived with very poor but very good painters."

That settled that, and we went on to the Breughel room. It was closed, we discovered. The door bore a sign that read, "NOW UNDERTAKING REPAIRS."

"They have our indulgence," Hemingway said, and took another drink from his flask. "I sure miss the good Breughel," he said as we moved along. "It's the great one, of the harvesters. It is a lot of people cutting grain, but he uses the grain geometrically, to make an emotion that is so strong for me that I can hardly take it." We came to El Greco's green "View of Toledo" and stood looking at it a long time. "This is the best picture in the Museum for me, and Christ knows there are some lovely ones," Hemingway said.

Patrick admired several paintings Hemingway didn't approve of. Every time this happened, Hemingway got into an involved, technical discussion with his son. Patrick would shake his head and laugh and say he respected Hemingway's opinions. He didn't argue much. "What the hell!" Hemingway said suddenly. "I don't want to be an art critic.

I just want to look at pictures and be happy with them and learn
from them. Now, this for me is a damn good picture." He stood back
and peered at a Reynolds entitled "Colonel George Coussmaker," which
shows the Colonel leaning against a tree and holding his horse's bridle.
"Now, this Colonel is a son of a bitch who was willing to pay money to
the best portrait painter of his day just to have himself painted,"
Hemingway said, and gave a short laugh. "Look at the man's arrogance
and the strength in the neck of the horse and the way the man's legs
hang. He's so arrogant he can afford to lean against a tree."

We separated for a while and looked at paintings individually, and
then Hemingway called us over and pointed to a picture labeled, in
large letters, "Catharine Lorillard Wolfe" and, in small ones, "By
Cabanel." "This is where I got confused as a kid, in Chicago," he said.
"My favorite painters for a long time were Bunte and Ryerson, two of
the biggest and wealthiest families in Chicago. I always thought the
names in big letters were the painters."

After we reached the Cézannes and Degas and the other Impressionists,
Hemingway became more and more excited, and discoursed on what
each artist could do and how and what he had learned from each.
Patrick listened respectfully and didn't seem to want to talk about
painting techniques any more. Hemingway spent several minutes looking
at Cézanne's "Rocks—Forest of Fontainbleau." "This is what we try
to do in writing, this and this, and the woods, and the rocks we have to
climb over," he said. "Cézanne is my painter, after the early painters.
Wonder, wonder painter. Degas was another wonder painter. I've never
seen a bad Degas. You know what he did with the bad Degas? He
burned them."

Hemingway took another long drink from his flask. We came to
Manet's pastel portrait of Mlle. Valtesse de la Bigne, a young woman
with blond hair coiled on the top of her head. Hemingway was silent
for a while, looking at it; finally he turned away. "Manet could show
the bloom people have when they're still innocent and before they've
been disillusioned," he said.

As we walked along, Hemingway said to me, "I can make a landscape
like Mr. Paul Cézanne. I learned how to make a landscape from Mr.
Paul Cézanne by walking through the Luxembourg Museum a thousand
times with an empty gut, and I am pretty sure that if Mr. Paul was
around, he would like the way I make them and be happy that I learned
it from him." He had learned a lot from Mr. Johann Sebastian Bach,
too. "In the first paragraphs of 'Farewell,' I used the word 'and' consciously over and over the way Mr. Johann Sebastian Bach used a note
in music when he was emitting counterpoint. I can almost write like
Mr. Johann sometimes—or, anyway, so he would like it. All such people
are easy to deal with, because we all know you have to learn."

"Papa, look at this," Patrick said. He was looking at "Meditation on the Passion," by Carpaccio. Patrick said it had a lot of strange animals in it for a religious painting.

"Huh!" Hemingway said. "Those painters always put the sacred scenes in the part of Italy they liked best or where they came from or where their girls came from. They made their girls the Madonnas. This is supposed to be Palestine, and Palestine is a long way off, he figures. So he puts in a red parrot, and he puts in deer and a leopard. And then he thinks, This is the Far East and it's far away. So he puts in the Moors, the traditional enemy of the Venetians." He paused and looked to see what else the painter had put in his picture. "Then he gets hungry, so he puts in rabbits," he said. "Goddam, Mouse, we saw a lot of good pictures. Mouse, don't you think two hours is a long time looking at pictures?"

Everybody agreed that two hours was a long time looking at pictures, so Hemingway said that we would skip the Goyas, and that we would all go to the Museum again when they returned from Europe.

It was still raining when we came out of the Museum. "Goddam, I hate to go out in the rain," Hemingway said. "Goddam, I hate to get wet."

Charles Scribner was waiting in the lobby of the hotel. "Ernest," he said, shaking Hemingway's hand. He was a dignified, solemn, slow-speaking gentleman with silvery hair.

"We've been looking at pictures, Charlie," Hemingway said as we went up in the elevator. "They have some pretty good pictures now, Charlie."

Scribner nodded and said, "Yuh, yuh."

"Was fun for country boy like me," Hemingway said.

"Yuh, yuh," said Scribner.

We went into the suite and took off our coats, and Hemingway said we would have lunch right there. He called room service and Mrs. Hemingway sat down at the desk to finish her letter. Hemingway sat down on the couch with Mr. Scribner and began telling him that he had been jamming, like a rider in a six-day bike race, and Patrick sat quietly in a corner and watched his father. The waiter came in and passed out menus. Scribner said he was going to order the most expensive item on the menu, because Hemingway was paying for it. He laughed tentatively, and Patrick laughed to keep him company. The waiter retired with our orders, and Scribner and Hemingway talked business for a while. Scribner wanted to know whether Hemingway had the letters he had written to him.

Hemingway said, "I carry them every place I go, Charlie, together with a copy of the poems of Robert Browning."

Scribner nodded, and from the inner pocket of his jacket took some papers—copies of the contract for the new book, he said. The contract provided for an advance of twenty-five thousand dollars against royalties, beginning at fifteen per cent.

Hemingway signed the contract, and got up from the couch. Then he said, "Never ran as no genius, but I'll defend the title again against all the good young new ones." He lowered his head, put his left foot forward, and jabbed at the air with a left and a right. "Never let them hit you solid," he said.

Scribner wanted to know where Hemingway could be reached in Europe. Care of the Guaranty Trust Company in Paris, Hemingway told him. "When we took Paris, I tried to take that bank and got smacked back," he said, and laughed a shy laugh. "I thought it would be awfully nice if I could take my own bank."

"Yuh, yuh," Scribner said. "What are you planning to do in Italy, Ernest?"

Hemingway said he would work part of each day and see his Italian friends and go duck-hunting in the mornings. "We shot three hundred and thirty-one ducks to six guns there one morning," he said. "Mary shot good, too."

Mrs. Hemingway looked up. "Any girl who marries Papa has to learn how to carry a gun," she said, and returned to her letter-writing.

"I went hunting once in Suffolk, England," Scribner said. Everyone waited politely for him to continue. "I remember they gave me goose eggs to eat for breakfast in Suffolk. Then we went out to shoot. I didn't know how to get my gun off safe."

"Hunting is sort of a good life," Hemingway said. "Better than Westport or Bronxville, I think."

"After I learned how to get my gun off safe, I couldn't hit anything," Scribner said.

"I'd like to make the big Monte Carlo shoot and the Championship of the World at San Remo," Hemingway said. "I'm in pretty good shape to shoot either one. It's not a spectator sport at all. But exciting to do and wonderful to manage. I used to handle Wolfie in big shoots. He is a great shot. It was like handling a great horse."

"I finally got one," Scribner said timidly.

"Got what?" asked Hemingway.

"A rabbit," Scribner said. "I shot this rabbit."

"They haven't held the big Monte Carlo shoot since 1939," Hemingway said. "Only two Americans ever won it in seventy-four years. Shooting gives me a good feeling. A lot of it is being together and friendly instead of feeling you are in some place where everybody hates you and wishes you ill. It is faster than baseball, and you are out on one strike."

The telephone rang, and Hemingway picked it up, listened, said a few words, and then turned to us and said that an outfit called Endorsements, Inc., had offered him four thousand dollars to pose as a Man of Distinction. "I told them I wouldn't drink the stuff for four thousand dollars," he said. "I told them I was a champagne man. Am trying to be a good guy, but it's a difficult trade. What you win in Boston, you lose in Chicago."

Nightmare and Ritual in Hemingway

by Malcolm Cowley

I

Going back to Hemingway's work after several years is like going back to a brook where you had often fished and finding the woods as deep and cool as they used to be. The trees are bigger, perhaps, but they are the same trees; the water comes down over the black stones as clear as always, with the same dull, steady roar where it plunges into the pool; and when the first trout takes hold of your line you can feel your heart beating against your fishing jacket. But something has changed, for this time there are shadows in the pool that you hadn't noticed before, and you have a sense that the woods are haunted. When Hemingway's stories first appeared, they seemed to be a transcription of the real world, new because they were accurate and because the world in those days was also new. With his insistence on "presenting things truly," he seemed to be a writer in the naturalistic tradition (for all his technical innovations); and the professors of American literature, when they got around to mentioning his books in their surveys, treated him as if he were a Dreiser of the lost generation, or perhaps the fruit of a mis-alliance between Dreiser and Jack London. Going back to his work in 1944, you perceive his kinship with a wholly different group of novelists, let us say with Poe and Hawthorne and Melville: the haunted and nocturnal writers, the men who dealt in images that were symbols of an inner world.

On the face of it, his method is not in the least like theirs. He doesn't lead us into castles ready to collapse with age, or into very old New England houses, or embark with us on the search for a whale that is also the white spirit of evil; instead he tells the stories he has lived or heard, against the background of countries he has seen. But, you reflect on reading his books again, these are curious stories that he has chosen from his wider experience, and these countries are presented in a strangely mortuary light. In no other writer of our time can you find such a profusion of corpses: dead women in the rain; dead soldiers bloated

"Nightmare and Ritual in Hemingway." The Introduction to *The Portable Hemingway*, edited by Malcolm Cowley (New York, 1945). Copyright © 1945 by The Viking Press, Inc. and reprinted with their permission.

in their uniforms and surrounded by torn papers; sunken liners full of bodies that float past the closed portholes. In no other writer can you find so many suffering animals: mules with their forelegs broken drowning in shallow water off the quay at Smyrna; gored horses in the bull ring; wounded hyenas first snapping at their own entrails and then eating them with relish. And morally wounded people who also devour themselves: punch-drunk boxers, soldiers with battle fatigue, veterans crazy with "the old rale," Lesbians, nymphomaniacs, bullfighters who have lost their nerve, men who lie awake all night while their brains get to racing "like a flywheel with the weight gone"—here are visions as terrifying as those of "The Pit and the Pendulum," even though most of them are copied from life; here are nightmares at noonday, accurately described, pictured without blur, but having the nature of obsessions or hypnagogic visions between sleep and waking.

And, going back to them, you find a waking-dreamlike quality even in the stories that deal with pleasant or commonplace aspects of the world. Take, for example, "Big Two-Hearted River," where the plot—or foreground of the plot—is simply a fishing trip in the northern peninsula of Michigan. Nick Adams, who is Hemingway's earliest and most personal hero, gets off the train at an abandoned sawmill town; he crosses burned-over land, makes camp, eats his supper, and goes to sleep; in the morning he looks for bait, finds grasshoppers under a log, hooks a big trout and loses it, catches two other trout, then sits in the shadow and eats his lunch very slowly while watching the stream; he decides to do no more fishing that day. There is nothing else in the story, apparently; nothing but a collection of sharp sensory details, so that you smell or hear or touch or see everything that exists near Big Two-Hearted River; and you even taste Nick Adams' supper of beans and spaghetti. "All good books are alike," Hemingway later said, "in that they are truer than if they had really happened and after you are finished reading one you will feel that all that happened to you and afterwards it all belongs to you: the good and the bad, the ecstasy, the remorse and sorrow, the people and the places and how the weather was." This story belongs to the reader, but apparently it is lacking in ecstasy, remorse, and sorrow; there are no people in it except Nick Adams; apparently there is nothing but "the places and how the weather was."

But Hemingway's stories are most of them continued, in the sense that he has a habit of returning to the same themes, each time making them a little clearer—to himself, I think, as well as to others. His work has an emotional consistency, as if all of it moved with the same current. A few years after "Big Two-Hearted River," he wrote another story that casts a retrospective light on his fishing trip (much as *A Farewell to Arms* helps to explain the background of Jake Barnes and Lady Brett, in *The Sun Also Rises*). The second story, "Now I Lay Me," deals with an American volunteer in the Italian army who isn't named but who

might easily be Nick Adams. He is afraid to sleep at night because, so
he says, "I had been living for a long time with the knowledge that if I
ever shut my eyes in the dark and let myself go, my soul would go out
of my body. I had been that way for a long time, ever since I had been
blown up at night and felt it go out of me and go off and then come
back." And the soldier continues:

> I had different ways of occupying myself while I lay awake. I would
> think of a trout stream I had fished along when I was a boy and fish its
> whole length very carefully in my mind; fishing very carefully under all
> the logs, all the turns of the bank, the deep holes and the clear shallow
> stretches, sometimes catching trout and sometimes losing them. I would
> stop fishing at noon to eat my lunch; sometimes on a log over the stream;
> sometimes on a high bank under a tree, and I always ate my lunch very
> slowly and watched the stream below me while I ate. . . . Some nights too
> I made up streams, and some of them were very exciting, and it was like
> being awake and dreaming. Some of those streams I still remember and
> think that I have fished in them, and they are confused with streams I
> really know.

After reading this passage, we have a somewhat different attitude toward the earlier story. The river described in it remains completely real
for us; but also—like those other streams the soldier invented during the
night—it has the quality of a waking dream. Although the events in the
foreground are described with superb accuracy and for their own sake,
we now perceive what we probably missed at a first reading: that there
are shadows in the background and that part of the story takes place
in an inner world. We notice that Nick Adams regards his fishing trip
as an escape, either from nightmare or from realities that have become
a nightmare. Sometimes his mind starts to work, even here in the wilderness; but "he knew he could choke it because he was tired enough," and
he can safely fall asleep. "Nick felt happy," the author says more than
once. "He felt he had left everything behind, the need for thinking, the
need to write, other needs. It was all back of him." He lives as if in an
enchanted country. There is a faint suggestion of old legends: all the
stories of boys with cruel stepmothers who wandered off into the forest
where the big trees sheltered them and the birds brought them food.
There is even a condition laid on Nick's happiness, just as in many
fairy tales where the hero must not wind a certain horn or open a certain
door. Nick must not follow the river down into the swamp. "In the
swamp the banks were bare, the big cedars came together overhead, the
sun did not come through, except in patches; in the fast deep water,
in the half light, the fishing would be tragic. In the swamp fishing was
a tragic adventure. Nick did not want it. He did not want to go down
the stream any further today."

But fishing is not the only activity of his heroes that Hemingway endows with a curious and almost supernatural value. They drink early and late; they consume enough beer, wine, anis, grappa, and Fundador to put them all into alcoholic wards, if they were ordinary mortals; but drinking seems to have the effect on them of a magic potion. Robert Jordan, in *For Whom the Bell Tolls*, is the soberest of Hemingway's heroes, the child, as it were, of middle age. Nevertheless he finds that a cup of absinthe "took the place of the evening papers, of all the old evenings in cafés, of all the chestnut trees that would be in bloom now in this month . . . of all the things he had enjoyed and forgotten and that came back to him when he tasted that opaque, bitter, tongue-numbing, brain-warming, stomach-warming, idea-changing liquid alchemy." There is much that he wants to remember, but also the fear of death that he wants to forget, and he personifies liquor as "the giant killer." On one occasion he reflects that writing about his fears might help him even more than drowning them in absinthe. He says to himself, after worrying about all the lives that have been lost as a result of his activities behind the Fascist lines: "But my guess is you will get rid of all that by writing about it. . . . Once you write it down it is all gone." Hemingway himself sometimes seems to regard writing as an exhausting ceremony of exorcism. And, as a young man after the First World War, he had painful memories of which he wanted to rid himself by setting them all down.

II

He was born on July 21, 1899, in Oak Park, Illinois, where his father was a physician. He went to school there, too, but what he regarded as his real home was a house in Michigan near the tip of the southern peninsula. The house was full of children all summer, for there were two boys and four girls in the family. In those days, the first-growth hemlock woods came down almost to the shore of the lake; and back in the woods was a settlement of Ojibways who lived by cutting the hemlocks for tanbark. Then one year all the woods were gone, "and there were only stumps, dried tree-tops, branches and fireweed where the woods had been." Ernest ran away from home when he was fifteen years old; that may have been the time he met the Battler beside the railway track near Mancelona. In 1917 he was graduated from Oak Park High School, where he had played football and had been chosen to write the class prophecy. He didn't go on to college, but instead got a job on the *Kansas City Star*; a few months later he went to Europe as a volunteer ambulance driver. He was badly wounded on the Italian front; he was given a silver medal (besides the Croce di Guerra); and after being patched together in a Milan hospital he served for a time in the Italian shock troops, the Arditi. One of the sights he could not forget was of the Austrian dead lying on their faces with their pockets turned out and each body surrounded by postcards and letters from home, a surprising quantity of paper. Another memory that became a nightmare was the evacuation of Smyrna by the Greeks, who left their baggage animals to drown. But that was something he saw four years later, when he was sent to the Middle East as a correspondent for the *Toronto Star.*

In Paris, which would be his home for many years after the war, he set about learning to become a writer. He had met Sherwood Anderson, who sent him to Gertrude Stein with a letter of introduction. He also became a good friend of Ezra Pound and he sometimes helped Ford Madox Ford to edit the *Transatlantic Review*, although his name did not appear on the masthead. These four—but especially Pound and Miss Stein—seem to have been his principal teachers; and what they gave him (or rather, what they confirmed in him) was an ideal of complete objectivity. When he sent his early manuscripts to Pound, they came back to him blue-penciled, with most of the adjectives gone. Miss Stein was content to make general comments, but they were usually followed. He afterwards said to John Peale Bishop, "Ezra was right half the time, and when he was wrong, he was so wrong you were never in any doubt about it. Gertrude was always right." As soon as he had saved a little money, Hemingway quit his job as a correspondent and devoted all his time to his stories. Once at a dinner in Paris with Dos Passos and the Lincoln Steffenses, he insisted that anybody could write. "You can," he said to Mrs. Steffens, making the gesture of giving her a left hook to the jaw; in those days he always gestured like a boxer. "It's hell. It takes it all out of you; it nearly kills you; but you can do it. Anybody can. Even you can, Stef. . . . I haven't done it yet, but I will." And Steffens adds, in his autobiography, "I think he thought that writing was a matter of honesty and labor."

"I was trying to write then," Hemingway tells us at the beginning of *Death in the Afternoon,*

> and I found the greatest difficulty, aside from knowing truly what you really felt, rather than what you were supposed to feel, and had been taught to feel, was to put down what really happened in action; what the actual things were which produced the emotion that you experienced. In writing for a newspaper you told what happened and, with one trick and another, you communicated the emotion aided by the element of timeliness which gives a certain emotion to any account of something that has happened on that day; but the real thing, the sequence of motion and fact which made the emotion and which would be as valid in a year or in ten years or, with luck and if you stated it purely enough, always, was beyond me and I was working very hard to try to get it.

In those days he seems to have regarded stories as, essentially, machines for arousing emotion. You didn't put the emotion itself into the story, any more than you would make a reaping machine out of wheat or a sewing machine out of cloth and thread; but you picked out the sharp details from life that had aroused your own emotion and, if you described them accurately, in their proper sequence and without closing your eyes to violence and horror, you had something that would continue to arouse the emotion of your readers. That was the method Hemingway followed in his early sketches and, within its self-imposed limitations, it was extremely successful. It was even successful beyond those limitations, for his pictures proved to have a vast power of suggestion. Take, for example, two of the "chapters," or interchapters, from *In Our Time*. Chapter III reads in full:

> We were in a garden in Mons. Young Buckley came in with his patrol from across the river. The first German I saw climbed up over the garden wall. We waited till he got one leg over and then potted him. He had so much equipment on and looked awfully surprised and fell down into the garden. Then three more came over further down the wall. We shot them. They all came just like that.

There is nothing more. There are no editorial reflections on the horrors of modern warfare. There is, in the story itself, no emotion whatever except the "awfully surprised" look of the first German who was shot. But the story has the power of arousing emotion in the reader, who tends to put himself either in the position of the English riflemen or, more likely, in that of the Germans climbing the wall to their deaths. And the wall itself is so vivid that, for the reader, it tends to become a sort of metaphor for all the impassable obstacles we see in nightmares: the swamps in which our feet are mired, the endless steps, the river that must, and cannot be crossed. Moreover, Hemingway returns to the same type of image in the following interchapter:

> It was a frightfully hot day. We'd jammed an absolutely perfect barricade across the bridge. It was simply priceless. A big old wrought-iron grating from the front of a house. Too heavy to lift and you could shoot through it and they would have to climb over it. It was absolutely topping. They tried to get over it, and we potted them from forty yards. They rushed it, and officers came out alone and worked on it. It was an absolutely perfect obstacle. Their officers were very fine. We were frightfully put out when we heard the flank had gone, and we had to fall back.

Here the sense of nightmare becomes more definite. The reader begins to feel that the "absolutely perfect obstacle" is a symbol for other obstacles recurring in Hemingway's novels: for the wound that divides Jake and Brett (in *The Sun Also Rises*); for the death in childbirth that separates Frederic from Catherine (in *A Farewell to Arms*); and even for the bridge that must be destroyed (in *For Whom the Bell Tolls*) at the cost of the hero's life. Moreover, the picture of a wall reappears in the two interchapters that follow. Chapter V begins: "They shot the six cabinet ministers at half-past six in the morning against the wall of a hospital." Chapter VI begins: "Nick sat against the wall of the church where they had dragged him to be clear of machine-gun fire in the street." In Hemingway's unconscious mind, all these walls may have been the images of death, though I doubt that he regarded them consciously as symbols. He was trying in those early days to state everything behavioristically, and it was not until later that he began to make a deliberate use of symbolism, together with other literary devices that he had avoided in the beginning, when he was teaching himself to write "commencing with the simplest things."

Later, in *A Farewell to Arms*, the rain becomes a conscious symbol of disaster. "Things went very badly," the hero tells us in the first chapter. "At the start of the winter came the permanent rain and with the rain came the cholera." Catherine Barkley is afraid of the rain because, she says, "sometimes I see me dead in it." Rain falls all during the retreat from Caporetto; it falls while Catherine is trying to have her baby in a Swiss hospital; and it is still falling when she dies and when Frederic pushes the nurses out of the room to be alone with her. "It wasn't any good," he says. "It was like saying goodbye to a statue. After a while I went out and left the hospital and walked back to the hotel in the rain." On the other hand, it is snow that is used as a symbol of death in "The Snows of Kilimanjaro" (along with other death symbols, like vultures, hyenas, and soaring in an imaginary airplane). And possibly snow has the same value in *For Whom the Bell Tolls*, where a spring snowfall adds to the danger of Robert Jordan's mission and indirectly causes his death.

Even in these later novels and stories, Hemingway almost never makes the error that weakens the effect of most symbolic fiction. Ordinarily we think of it as a type of writing in which the events in the foreground tend to become misty because the author has his eyes fixed on something else. Hawthorne, in *The Marble Faun*, was so preoccupied with inner meanings that he seemed to lose his sense of the real world; but that is almost never the case with Hemingway. It is true that Maria, in *For Whom the Bell Tolls*, is almost more of a dream than she is a woman. When Frederic Henry dives into the flooded Tagliamento, in *A Farewell to Arms*, he is performing a rite of baptism that prepares us for the new life he is about to lead as a deserter from the Italian army; his act is emotionally significant, but it is a little unconvincing on the plane of action. These are perhaps the only two cases in which Hemingway seems to loosen his grip on reality. Elsewhere his eyes are fixed on the foreground; but he gives us a sense of other shadowy meanings that contribute to the force and complexity of his writing.

By the early 1930's Hemingway's technique, apparently simple in the beginning, was becoming more elaborate. He had begun to talk about the possibility of writing what he called fourth-dimensional prose. "The reason everyone now tries to avoid it," he says in *Green Hills of Africa*, "to deny that it is important, to make it seem vain to try to do it, is because it is so difficult. Too many factors must combine to make it possible."

"What is this now?" asks Kandisky, the Austrian in leather breeches who likes to lead the life of the mind. And the author tells him:

> "The kind of writing that can be done. How far prose can be carried if anyone is serious enough and has luck. There is a fourth and fifth dimension that can be gotten."
>
> "You believe it?"
>
> "I know it."
>
> "And if a writer can get this?"
>
> "Then nothing else matters. It is more important than anything else he can do. The chances are, of course, that he will fail. But there is a chance that he succeeds."
>
> "But that is poetry you are talking about."
>
> "No. It is much more difficult than poetry. It is a prose that has never been written. But it can be written, without tricks and without cheating. With nothing that will go bad afterwards."

Now, I don't know exactly what Hemingway means by prose with "a fourth and fifth dimension." It would seem to me that any good prose has four dimensions, in the sense of being a solid object that moves through time, whereas the fifth dimension is here a mystical or meaningless figure of speech. But without understanding his choice of words, I do know that Hemingway's prose at its best gives a sense of depth and of moving forward on different levels that is lacking in even the best of his imitators, as it is in almost all the other novelists of our time. Moreover, I have at least a vague notion of how this quality in his work can be explained.

III

Considering his laborious apprenticeship and the masters with whom he chose to study; considering his theories of writing, which he has often discussed, and how they have developed with the years; considering their subtle and highly conscious application, as well as the very complicated personality they serve to express, it is a little surprising to find that Hemingway is almost always described as a primitive. Yet the word really applies to him, if it is used in what might be called its anthropological sense. The anthropologists tell us that many of the so-called primitive peoples have an extremely elaborate system of beliefs, calling for the almost continual performance of rites and ceremonies; even their drunken orgies are ruled by tradition. Some of the forest-dwelling tribes believe that every rock or tree or animal has its own indwelling spirit. When they kill an animal or chop down a tree, they must beg its forgiveness, repeating a formula of propitiation; otherwise its spirit would haunt them. Living briefly in a world of hostile forces, they preserve themselves—so they believe—only by the exercise of magic lore.

There is something of the same atmosphere in Hemingway's work. His heroes live in a world that is like a hostile forest, full of unseen dangers, not to mention the nightmares that haunt their sleep. Death spies on them from behind every tree. Their only chance of safety lies in the faithful observance of customs they invent for themselves. In an early story like "Big Two-Hearted River," you notice that Nick Adams does everything very slowly, not wishing "to rush his sensations any"; and he pays so much attention to the meaning and rightness of each gesture that his life in the wilderness becomes a series of little ceremonies

> Another hopper poked his face out of the bottle. His antennae wavered. Nick took him by the head and held him while he threaded the hook under his chin, down through his thorax and into the last segments of his abdomen. The grasshopper took hold of the hook with his front feet, spitting tobacco juice on it.

The grasshopper is playing its own part in a ritual; so too is the trout that swallows it, then bends the rod in jerks as it pumps against the current. The whole fishing trip, instead of being a mere escape, might be regarded as an incantation, a spell to banish evil spirits. And there are other rituals in Hemingway's work (besides drinking and writing, which I have mentioned already). Without too much difficulty we can recognize rites of animal sacrifice (as in *Death in the Afternoon*), of sexual union (in *For Whom the Bell Tolls*), of self-immolation (in "The Snows of Kilimanjaro"), of conversion (in *To Have and Have Not*), and of symbolic death and rebirth (in the Caporetto passage of *A Farewell to Arms*). When one of Hemingway's characters violates his own standards or the just laws of the tribe (as Ole Andreson has done in "The Killers"), he waits for death as stolidly as an Indian.

Memories of the Indians he knew in his boyhood play an important part in Hemingway's work; they reappear in *The Torrents of Spring* and in several of his shorter stories. Robert Jordan, in *For Whom the Bell Tolls*, compares his own exploits to Indian warfare, and he strengthens himself during his last moments by thinking about his grandfather, an old Indian fighter. *In Our Time*, Hemingway's first book of stories, starts by telling how Nick Adams' father is called to attend an Indian woman who has been in labor for two days. The woman lies screaming in a bunkhouse, while her husband, with a badly injured foot, lies in the bunk above her smoking his pipe. Dr. Adams performs a Caesarean section without anesthetic, then sews up the wound with fishing leaders.

When the operation is finished, he looks at the husband in the upper bunk and finds that he is dead; unable to bear his wife's pain, he has turned his face to the wall and cut his throat. A story Nick Adams later tells is of Trudy Gilby, the Indian girl with whom he used to go squirrel shooting and who, under the big hemlock trees, "did first what no one has ever done better." Most of Hemingway's heroines are in the image of Trudy; they have the obedience to their lovers and the sexual morals of Indian girls. His heroes suffer without complaining and, in one way or another, they destroy themselves like the Indian husband.

But Hemingway feels an even greater kinship with the Spaniards, because they retain a primitive dignity in giving and accepting death. Even when their dignity is transformed into a blind lust for killing, as sometimes happened during their civil war, they continue to hold his respect. Agustín, in *For Whom the Bell Tolls*, sees four of Franco's cavalrymen and breaks out into a sweat that is not the sweat of fear. "When I saw those four there," he says, "and thought that we might kill them I was like a mare in the corral waiting for the stallion." And Robert Jordan thinks to himself: "We do it coldly but they do not, nor ever have. It is their extra sacrament. Their old one that they had before the new religion came from the far end of the Mediterranean, the one they have never abandoned but only suppressed and hidden to bring it out again in wars and inquisitions." Hemingway himself seems to have a feeling for half-forgotten sacraments; his cast of mind is pre-Christian and prelogical.

Sometimes his stories come close to being adaptations of ancient myths. His first novel, for example, deals in different terms with the same legend that T. S. Eliot was not so much presenting as concealing in *The Waste Land*. When we turn to Eliot's explanatory notes, then read the book to which they refer as a principal source—*From Ritual to Romance*, by Jessie L. Weston—we learn that his poem is largely based on the legend of the Fisher King. The legend tells how the king was wounded in the loins and how he lay wasting in his bed while his whole kingdom became unfruitful; there was thunder but no rain; the rivers dried up, the flocks had no increase, and the women bore no children. *The Sun Also Rises* presents the same situation in terms of Paris after the First World War. It is a less despairing book than critics like to think; at times it is gay, friendly, even exuberant; but the hero has been wounded like the Fisher King, and he lives in a world that is absolutely sterile. I don't mean to imply that Hemingway owes a debt to *The Waste Land*. He had read the poem, which he liked at first, and the notes that followed it, which he didn't like at all; I doubt very much that he bothered to look at Jessie L. Weston's book. He said in 1924, when he was paying tribute to Joseph Conrad: "If I knew that by grinding Mr. Eliot into a fine dry powder and sprinkling that powder over Mr. Conrad's grave Mr. Conrad would shortly appear, looking very annoyed at the forced return, and commence writing, I would leave for London early tomorrow with a sausage grinder." And yet when he wrote his first novel, he dealt with the same legend that Eliot had discovered by scholarship; recovering it for himself, I think, by a sort of instinct for legendary situations.

And it is this instinct for legends, for sacraments, for rituals, for symbols appealing to buried hopes and fears, that helps to explain the power of Hemingway's work and his vast superiority over his imitators. The imitators have learned all his mannerisms as a writer, and in some cases they can tell a story even better than Hemingway himself; but they tell only the story; they communicate with the reader on only one level of experience. Hemingway does more than that. Most of us are also primitive in a sense, for all the machinery that surrounds our lives. We have our private rituals, our little superstitions, our symbols and fears and nightmares; and Hemingway reminds us unconsciously of the hidden worlds in which we live. Reading his best work, we are a little like Nick Adams looking down from the railroad bridge at the trout in Big Two-Hearted River:

> many trout in deep, fast-moving water, slightly distorted as he watched far down through the glassy convex surface of the pool, its surface pushing and swelling smooth against the resistance of the log-driven piles of the bridge. At the bottom of the pool were the big trout. Nick did not see them at first. Then he saw them at the bottom of the pool, big trout looking to hold themselves on the gravel bottom in a varying mist of gravel and sand.

During the last few years it has become the fashion to reprimand Hemingway and to point out how much better his work would be (with its undoubted power) if only he were a little more virtuous or reasonable or optimistic, or if he revealed the proper attitude toward progress and democracy. Critics like Maurice Coindreau (in French) and Bernard DeVoto have abused him without bothering to understand what he plainly says, much less what he suggests or implies. Even Maxwell Geismar, who is one of the few professors with a natural feeling for literary values, would like to make him completely over. "What a marvelous teacher Hemingway is," he exclaims,

> with all the restrictions of temperament and environment which so far define his work! What could he not show us of living as well as dying, of the positives in our being as well as the destroying forces, of 'grace under pressure' and the grace we need with no pressures, of ordinary life-giving actions along with those superb last gestures of doomed exiles!

Or, to put the matter more plainly, what a great writer Hemingway would be, in Geismar's opinion, if he combined his own work with equal parts of Trollope and Emerson.

And the critics have some justice on their side. It is true that Hemingway has seldom been an affirmative writer; it is true that most of his work is narrow and violent and generally preoccupied with death. But the critics, although they might conceivably change him for the worse, are quite unable to change him for the better. He is one of the novelists who write, not as they should or would, but as they must. Like Poe and Hawthorne and Melville, he listens to his personal demon, which might also be called his intuition or his sense of life. If he listened to the critics instead, he might indeed come to resemble Trollope or Emerson, but the resemblance would be only on the surface and, as he sometimes says of writing that tries hard to meet public requirements, it would all go bad afterwards. Some of his own writing has gone bad, but surprisingly little of it. By now he has earned the right to be taken for what he is, with his great faults and greater virtues; with his narrowness, his power, his always open eyes, his stubborn, chip-on-the-shoulder honesty, his nightmares, his rituals for escaping them, and his sense of an inner and an outer world that for twenty years were moving together toward the same disaster.

Hemingway's Ambiguity:
Symbolism and Irony

by E. M. Halliday

I

One of the curious things about *The Old Man and the Sea* was the sense of awe that it created in its author, its publisher, and (to judge by many of the reviewers) its readers. "Don't you think it is a strange damn story that it should affect all of us (me especially) the way it does?" [1] wrote Hemingway to one of *Life*'s editors. And Scribner's dust jacket responded like a good Greek chorus, "One cannot hope to explain why the reading of this book is so profound an experience." [2]

There has always been a certain mystery about Hemingway's effects in his best writing. From *In Our Time* (1925), with its puzzling "chapters" connecting (or separating) the stories, through *For Whom the Bell Tolls* (1940), with its oddly equivocal interpretation of the Spanish civil war, his best has evoked a somewhat doubtful sound from critics who nevertheless were at pains to recommend. Something, it was felt, was being missed; or if not missed, then sensed too vaguely for critical description. *A Farewell to Arms* (1929), declared Edward Hope in the New York *Herald Tribune*, was "one of those things—like the Grand Canyon— that one doesn't care to talk about." [3] Despite such reverent throwing up of hands by early critics many things were aptly observed; but the emphasis was heavily on Hemingway the realist, whose bright fidelity to the perceptible surfaces of life was accomplished through living dialogue and a prose finely engineered to the accurate rendering of sensuous experience. And the brilliance of his reflected surface together with the roughness of the things he preferred to write about—fishing, hunting, skiing, bullfighting, boxing, horse-racing, and war—perhaps made it

"Hemingway's Ambiguity: Symbolism and Irony." From *American Literature*, XXVIII (1956), 1-22. Copyright 1956 by the Duke University Press. Reprinted by permission of the Duke University Press.
[1] Quoted in *Time*, LX, No. 9 (Sept. 1, 1952), 48.
[2] *The Old Man and the Sea* (New York: Scribner, 1952).
[3] Quoted on the flyleaf of *A Farewell to Arms*, Bantam Edition (New York, 1954).

difficult to see one of the cardinal facts about Hemingway: that essentially he is a philosophical writer. His main interest, in representing human life through fictional forms, has consistently been to set man against the background of his world and universe, to examine the human situation from various points of view.

Not that he has a "system," for on the final questions Hemingway has always shown himself a skeptic. "It seemed like a fine philosophy," Jake Barnes says to himself at one bitter point in *The Sun Also Rises*. "In five years . . . it will seem just as silly as all the other fine philosophies I've had." [4] Like Jake, Hemingway has been "technically" a Roman Catholic, but the metaphysical doctrines of Christianity seem never to have taken a convincing hold. His most devout characters are only devoutly mystified by the universe: both Anselmo, the good old man of *For Whom the Bell Tolls*, and Santiago, of *The Old Man and the Sea*, disclaim their religiosity, and their Hail-Marys are uttered mechanically enough to evoke a chilly memory of the sleepless waiter in "A Clean, Well-Lighted Place," who prayed, "Hail nothing, full of nothing, nothing is with thee." [5] The parable of the doomed ants on the burning log, in *A Farewell to Arms*,[6] has been thought to represent Hemingway's *Weltanschauung* at its most pessimistic; but there is no reason, actually, to think that there has since been a fundamental change in his view of life. "Everything kills everything else in some way," [7] reflects the old Cuban fisherman of the latest book; and even the small bird that rests momentarily on his fishing line may fall to the hawks before reaching land, at best must take its chance "like any man or bird or fish." [8] The world, it seems, still breaks everyone, and only the earth and the Gulf Stream abide after the vortex of human vanities has subsided forever.

Given Hemingway's suspicion of ultimate doom and his passionate fondness for being alive, it is no surprise that his philosophical preoccupation is primarily ethical. Extinction may well be the end of all, as the writer of Ecclesiastes repeatedly remarked, but for Hemingway and his heroes this merely emphasizes the need to live each moment properly and skilfully, to sense judiciously the texture of every fleeting act and perception. The focus is conduct: "Maybe if you found out how to live in it you learned from that what it was all about," [9] says Jake Barnes. It is not accidental that the French existentialists have shown a strong feeling for Hemingway's work. Like them he has been poised in his hours of despair on the edge of nothingness, the abyss of nonmeaning

---

[4] *The Sun Also Rises* (New York: Scribner, 1926), p. 153.

[5] *The Short Stories of Ernest Hemingway* (New York: Scribner, 1938), p. 481.

[6] *A Farewell to Arms* (New York: Scribner, 1932), p. 350.

[7] *The Old Man and the Sea*, p. 117.

[8] *Ibid.*, p. 61.

[9] *The Sun Also Rises*, p. 153.

which confronts most of the characters in the stories of *Winner Take Nothing* (1933); and like them he has looked in his hours of hope to a salvation built out of individual human courage around a code, at once rational and intuitive, of strict, often ritualistic behavior. *"Nous sommes foutus . . . comme toujours,"* says Golz, the Loyalist general commanding the attack with which Jordan's mission is co-ordinated in *For Whom the Bell Tolls*. *". . . Bon. Nous ferons notre petit possible."* [10] As it was for Socrates and Jeremy Taylor, although for quite different reasons, dying well is for Hemingway the crucial corollary to living well. So Robert Jordan fights off an impulse to kill himself to end the anguish of a badly broken leg and avoid possible capture. "You can do nothing for yourself but perhaps you can do something for another," [11] he tells himself; yet we are to understand that he has died well not just because of his sacrifice, but because he has not abandoned the principle of fortitude. In the image of the crucifixion which has haunted Hemingway from "Today Is Friday" (1926) to *The Old Man and the Sea*, it is the unique courage of the forsaken and crucified man-God that takes his attention. "I'll tell you," says a Roman soldier in the earlier work, "he looked pretty good to me in there today." [12] We are part of a universe offering no assurance beyond the grave, and we are to make what we can of life by a pragmatic ethic spun bravely out of man himself in full and steady cognizance that the end is darkness.

II

Undoubtedly Hemingway's preoccupation with the human predicament and a moral code that might satisfactorily control it, in itself partly accounts for the sense of hidden significance which many have experienced in reading him. Obscured as this preoccupation has been by his choice of particular fictional materials and by his manner, which has always eschewed explication, it could nevertheless almost always be felt: it was impossible to avoid the impression that this writer was dealing with something of final importance to us all. Like the Elizabethans whom he evidently loves, he never lets us quite forget that death awaits every man at some turn perhaps not far along the way. And like nobody but Hemingway—that is, in his peculiar and distinguished manner as an artist—he continually reminds us that (as he expressed it once to Maxwell Perkins) it is our "performance en route" [13] that counts for good or bad.

But what is the essence of his peculiar manner? It is a manner of implication, clearly, as he himself has said in various notes of self-

[10] *For Whom the Bell Tolls* (New York: Scribner, 1940), pp. 428, 430.
[11] *Ibid.*, p. 466.
[12] *The Short Stories*, p. 457.
[13] Quoted by Perkins in *Scribner's Magazine*, LXXXI (March, 1927), .

criticism of which the figure in *Death in the Afternoon* is perhaps the most striking: "The dignity of movement of an ice-berg is due to only one-eighth of it being above water." [14] The question is what mode of narrative technique he exploits in order to make the ice-berg principle operative in his work. I do not remember seeing the word "symbolism" in critical writing about Hemingway before 1940, nor have I seen more than one review of *The Old Man and the Sea* that did not lean heavily on the word. The number of exegeses that explain Hemingway as a symbolist has increased geometrically since Malcolm Cowley suggested in 1944 that he should be grouped not among the realists, but "with Poe and Hawthorne and Melville: the haunted and nocturnal writers, the men who dealt in images that were symbols of an inner world." [15] It was a startling and pleasing suggestion. Mr. Cowley advanced it rather tentatively and did not press his discovery very far; but it was taken up with something like a hue and cry by other critics who, it seemed, had been testily waiting for the scent and were eager to get on with the hunt. Literary conversation soon began to reflect the new trend: I recall hearing it asserted on two proximate occasions that the sleeping bag in *For Whom the Bell Tolls* is an "obvious" symbol of the womb; and that a ketchup bottle in "The Killers" patently symbolizes blood. By 1949 it was no great surprise to open an issue of the *Sewanee Review* to an essay by Caroline Gordon called "Notes on Hemingway and Kafka." [16] It would have been surprising only if the analysis had not hinged on a comparison between the two writers as symbolists.

Is Hemingway genuinely a symbolist? I think he uses certain techniques of symbolism, but I think he does so in a very limited and closely controlled way, and that failure to recognize the controls leads—already has led—to distortions of his meaning and misappreciations of his narrative art. As a sample, Miss Gordon's essay is instructive on this point. Starting calmly, as her title suggests, with the assumption that Hemingway is a symbolist, she proceeds to compare him, not very favorably, with Kafka. And it turns out that Hemingway's trouble is simple—he is not *enough* of a symbolist: "this plane of action is for him a slippery sub-stratum glimpsed intermittently. It does not underlie the Naturalistic plane of action solidly, or over-arch it grandly, as Kafka's Symbolism does." [17]

But this is mistaking an artistic discipline for a fault. Hemingway has not attempted Kafka's kind of symbolism and fallen short: it is something foreign to Hemingway's art. The Kafka story used by Miss Gordon as the basis for her comparison is "The Hunter Gracchus," a carefully elaborated allegory revolving around the life of Christ—that

[14] *Death in the Afternoon* (New York: Scribner, 1932), p. 192.
[15] Introduction to *The Portable Hemingway* (New York: Viking, 1944), p. vii.
[16] *Sewanee Review*, LVII (Spring, 1949), 214-226.
[17] *Ibid.*, p. 226.

is to say, there are two distinct and parallel narrative lines, the primary, which operates within the confines of a more or less realistic world, and the secondary, which operates within the realm of religious myth and in this case is assumed by the author to be a prior possession on the part of the reader. Incidentally, Miss Gordon forces her comparison from both sides, claiming for Kafka, as something he shares with Hemingway, "a surface which is strictly Naturalistic in detail." [18] But this claim must rest on a curious understanding of the phrase "in detail" since the story on the "Naturalistic" level offers, among other attractions, a corpse that is mysteriously still alive, and a German-speaking dove the size of a rooster.

Hemingway, as far as I know, has never written an allegory—notwithstanding the bright interpretations of *The Old Man and the Sea* that illuminated cocktail parties a few years ago when it was published in *Life*—and for a very good reason. In successful allegory, the story on the primary level is dominated by the story on the secondary level, and if the allegorical meaning is to be kept clear, its naturalistic counterpart must pay for it by surrendering realistic probability in one way or another. A strain is imposed on the whole narrative mechanism, for mere connotative symbolism will not do to carry the allegory: there must be a denotative equation, part for part, between symbols and things symbolized in order to identify the actors and action on the allegorical level. The extreme difficulty of satisfactorily conducting the dual action throughout a prolonged narrative is classically illustrated by *The Faerie Queene* and by *The Pilgrim's Progress*. The allegorist who admires realism is constantly pulled in two directions at once, and is very lucky when he can prevent one or the other of his meanings from unbalancing him.

Still, Hemingway has used the symbolism of association to convey by implication his essential meaning from the time of his earliest American publication. It may well be that this was inevitable for a writer starting out with Hemingway's determination to communicate, as he put it (in *Death in the Afternoon*) "what really happened in action; what the actual things were which produced the emotion that you experienced." [19] Nothing could more clearly differentiate Hemingway's kind of realism from Zolaesque naturalistic description than this early statement of intent. Everything is to depend on judicious discrimination of objective details: *what really happened* is not by any means everything that happened; it is only "the actual things . . . which produced the emotion that you experienced." As a matter of fact "produced" is a little too strict, as Hemingway demonstrates again and again in *The Sun Also Rises* and *A Farewell to Arms*, where he depends heavily on the technique of objective epitome—a symbolist technique, if you like—to con-

[18] *Ibid.*, p. 222.
[19] *Death in the Afternoon*, p. 2.

vey the subjective conditions of his characters. The details selected are not so much those which *produce* the emotion as those which epitomize it; it is the action of the story which has produced the emotion. Thus at the crisis of *The Sun Also Rises*, when Jake Barnes presents Brett to Pedro Romero—a Pandarism for which he is obliged to hate himself—his agonized feelings are not discussed, but are nevertheless most poignantly suggested by the perceptions he reports:

> When I came back and looked in the café, twenty minutes later, Brett and Pedro Romero were gone. The coffee-glasses and our three empty cognac-glasses were on the table. A waiter came with a cloth and picked up the glasses and mopped off the table.[20]

In *A Farewell to Arms*, Frederic Henry goes dully out for breakfast from the Swiss maternity hospital where Catherine Barkley is fighting for life in ominously abnormal labor:

> Outside along the street were the refuse cans from the houses waiting for the collector. A dog was nosing at one of the cans.
> "What do you want?" I asked and looked in the can to see if there was anything I could pull out for him; there was nothing on top but coffee-grounds, dust and some dead flowers.
> "There isn't anything, dog," I said.[21]

There is, of course, a larger sense, germane to all good fiction, in which Hemingway may be said to be symbolic in his narrative method: the sense which indicates his typical creation of key characters who are representative on several levels. We thus find Jake Barnes's war-wound impotence a kind of metaphor for the whole atmosphere of sterility and frustration which is the *ambiance* of *The Sun Also Rises*; we find Catherine Barkley's naïve simplicity and warmth the right epitome for the idea and ideal of normal civilian home life to which Frederic Henry deserts; we find the old Cuban fisherman in some way representative of the whole human race in its natural struggle for survival. But the recent criticism of Hemingway as symbolist goes far beyond such palpable observations as these, and in considering the fundamental character of his narrative technique I wish to turn attention to more ingenious if not esoteric explications.

Professor Carlos Baker, in *Hemingway: The Writer as Artist* (1952), has established himself as the leading oracle of Hemingway's symbolism. His book is, I think, the most valuable piece of extended Hemingway criticism that we yet have, and to a large extent its contribution is one of new insights into the symbolist aspect of his subject's narrative method. He is sweeping:

[20] *The Sun Also Rises*, p. 194.
[21] *A Farewell to Arms*, p. 336.

From the first Hemingway has been dedicated as a writer to the rendering of *Wahrheit*, the precise and at least partly naturalistic rendering of things as they are and were. Yet under all his brilliant surfaces lies the controlling *Dichtung*, the symbolic underpainting which gives so remarkable a sense of depth and vitality to what otherwise might be flat two-dimensional portraiture.[22]

This may fairly be said to represent Mr. Baker's major thesis, and he develops and supports it with remarkable energy and skill. I do not wish to disparage his over-all effort—he is often very enlightening—but I do wish to argue that he has been rather carried away by his thesis, and that therein he eminently typifies the new symbolist criticism of Hemingway which in its enthusiasm slights or ignores other basic aspects of Hemingway's technique.

Mr. Baker's chapter on *A Farewell to Arms* is an original piece of criticism, and it solidly illustrates his approach. He finds that the essential meaning of this novel is conveyed by two master symbols, the Mountain and the Plain, which organize the *Dichtung* around "two poles":

> By a process of accrual and coagulation, the images tend to build round the opposed concepts of Home and Not-Home. . . . The Home-concept, for example, is associated with the mountains; with dry-cold weather; with peace and quiet; with love, dignity, health, happiness, and the good life; and with worship or at least the consciousness of God. The Not-Home concept is associated with low-lying plains; with rain and fog; with obscenity, indignity, disease, suffering, nervousness, war and death; and with irreligion.[23]

It is in terms of these antipodal concepts that Mr. Baker analyzes the semantic structure of *A Farewell to Arms*, a structure which he finds effective chiefly because of the adroit and subtle development of the correspondingly antipodal symbols, the Mountain and the Plain. He argues that from the first page of the story these are set up in their significant antithesis, that they are the key to the relationships among several of the leading characters, and that the central action—Frederic Henry's desertion from the Italian Army to join Catherine Barkley, the British nurse—can be fully appreciated only on this symbolic basis. "*A Farewell to Arms,*" he concludes, "is entirely and even exclusively acceptable as a naturalistic narrative of what happened. To read it only as such, however, is to miss the controlling symbolism: the deep central antithesis between the image of life and home (the mountain) and the image of war and death (the plain)." [24]

---

[22] Carlos Baker, *Hemingway: The Writer as Artist* (Princeton: Princeton University Press, 1952), p. 289.

[23] *Ibid.*, pp. 101, 102.

[24] *Ibid.*, pp. 108, 109.

Clearly there is some truth in this. The "deep central antithesis" cannot be denied, I would think, by anyone with an acceptable understanding of the book. The question at issue is one of technique; to what extent, and how precisely, is the central antithesis in fact engineered around the Mountain and the Plain as symbols?

One thing is noticeable immediately: as in virtually all of Hemingway, anything that can possibly be construed to operate symbolically does no violence whatsoever to the naturalism (or realism) of the story on the primary level. Nothing could be a more natural—or more traditional—symbol of purity, of escape from the commonplace, in short of elevation, than mountains. If thousands of people have read the passages in *A Farewell to Arms* which associate the mountains "with dry-cold weather; with peace and quiet; with love, dignity, health, happiness and the good life" without taking them to be "symbolic" it is presumably because these associations are almost second nature for all of us. Certainly this seems to be true of Frederic Henry: it is most doubtful that in the course of the novel he is ever to be imagined as consciously regarding the mountains as a symbol. This of course does not prove that Hemingway did not regard them as such, or that the full understanding of this novel as an art structure does not perhaps require the symbolic equation, *mountain* equals *life and home*. It does, however, point differentially to another type of symbolism, where the character in question is shown to be clearly aware of the trope, as when Catherine Barkley says she hates rain because "sometimes I see me dead in it," [25] or when Frederic Henry says of his plunge into the Tagliamento, "Anger was washed away in the river along with any obligation." [26]

But Mr. Baker has claimed a most exact and detailed use by Hemingway of the Mountain-Plain symbolism, and his ingenious interpretation deserves closer attention. Like many other critics he is an intense admirer of the novel's opening paragraph, which, he says, "does much more than start the book. It helps to establish the dominant mood (which is one of doom), plants a series of important images for future symbolic cultivation, and subtly compels the reader into the position of detached observer." [27] He proceeds to a close analysis of this paragraph:

> The second sentence, which draws attention from the mountainous background to the bed of the river in the middle distance, produces a sense of clearness, dryness, whiteness, and sunniness which is to grow very subtly under the artist's hands until it merges with one of the novel's two dominant symbols, the mountain-image. The other major symbol is the plain. Throughout the sub-structure of the book it is opposed to the mountain-image. Down this plain the river flows. Across it, on the dusty road among

[25] *A Farewell to Arms*, p. 135.
[26] *Ibid.*, p. 248.
[27] Baker, *op. cit.*, p. 94.

the trees, pass the men-at-war, faceless and voiceless and unidentified against the background of the spreading plain.[28]

This is highly specific, and we are entitled to examine it minutely. Mr. Baker says the river is "in the middle distance" in the direction of the mountains with the image of which, as he sees it, the symbolic images of the river are to merge into one great symbol. But is the river really in the middle distance? The narrator tells us he can see not only its boulders but its *pebbles,* "dry and white in the sun." The river must, of course, flow from the mountains, but in the perspective seen from the house occupied by Frederic Henry, it would appear to be very close at hand—closer than the plain, and quite in contrast to the distant mountains. And this raises the question of whether the clearness, dryness, whiteness, and sunniness offered by the river are in fact artfully intended to be associated with the mountain-image and what it is held to symbolize; or, disregarding the question of intent, whether they do in fact so operate in the artistic structure. Why must the river images be disassociated from the images of the plain across which the river, naturally, flows? Because the river images are of a kind which, if they work as symbols, are incongruent with what Mr. Baker has decided the Plain stands for; they must instead be allocated to the Mountain. This is so important to his thesis that the river shifts gracefully, but without textual support, into "the middle distance," closer to the mountains.

And what of the soldiers on the road? Since they must be firmly associated with the Plain ("war and death"), it is against that background that Mr. Baker sees them in Hemingway's opening paragraph— it would not do to see them against the background of the river, with its Mountain images. But let us look again at the paragraph.

> In the late summer of that year we lived in a house in a village that looked across the river and the plain to the mountains. In the bed of the river there were pebbles and boulders, dry and white in the sun, and the water was clear and swiftly moving and blue in the channels. Troops went by the house and down the road and the dust they raised powdered the leaves of the trees.

Mr. Baker says the road is across the river, as of course it would have to be if we are to see the figures of the soldiers against the background of the plain. Hemingway does not say the road is across the river. Indeed, everything indicates the opposite arrangement: a house on a road running along the near side of the river, across which the plain stretches out to the mountains. "Sometimes in the dark," begins the third paragraph of the novel, "we heard the troops marching under the window. . . ."

---

[28] *Ibid.,* pp. 94-95.

The truth is that a strong part of Mr. Baker's initially persuasive exegesis of the opening paragraph of *A Farewell to Arms* hangs on a reading that the written words will not support. This is not to deny that the paragraph establishes a mood of doom by its somber tone and the epitomic symbols of dust and falling leaves: what I am questioning is the over-all symbolic organization of the novel's structure in terms of the Mountain and the Plain, which Mr. Baker argues as a prime illustration of his unequivocal judgment of Hemingway as symbolist artist.

As a matter of fact, the plain presented in the opening pages of *A Farewell to Arms* is as troublesome as the river when it comes to supporting Mr. Baker's interpretation. There are plains in many countries that could well serve as symbols of emptiness, desolation, disaster, and death—we have some in the American West. But this does not appear to be that sort of plain: quite the contrary. "The plain," Frederic Henry narrates in the opening words of the second paragraph, "was rich with crops; there were many orchards of fruit trees. . . ." Mr. Baker tells us neither how these images of fertility and fruition are to fit in with "rain and fog; with obscenity, indignity, disease, suffering, nervousness, war and death," nor how we should symbolically interpret the conclusion of the sentence, ". . . and beyond the plain the mountains were brown and bare." One can easily grant that as the novel unfolds, the impression of war itself grows steadily more saturated with a sense of doomsday qualities: that was an essential part of Hemingway's theme. But to what degree is this impression heightened by the use of the Plain as symbol? The simple exigencies of history prevent exclusive association of the war with the plain as opposed to the mountains, as the narrator indicates on the first page: "There was fighting in the mountains and at night we could see flashes from the artillery." Yet if Mr. Baker is right we would expect to find, despite this difficulty, a salient artistic emphasis of the Plain in symbolic association with all those images which his interpretation sets against those coalescing around the Mountain symbol.

Mr. Baker makes much of the fact that Frederic Henry, during his leave, fails to take advantage of the offer of his friend the chaplain and go to the high mountain country of the Abruzzi, "where the roads were frozen and hard as iron, where it was clear cold and dry and the snow was dry and powdery. . . . I had gone to no such place but to the smoke of cafés and nights when the room whirled and you needed to look at the wall to make it stop, nights in bed, drunk, when you knew that that was all there was." [29] Here, Mr. Baker claims, "the mountain-image gets further backing from another lowland contrast." [30]

[29] *A Farewell to Arms*, p. 13.
[30] Baker, *op. cit.*, p. 102.

Granting the familiar association here of mountain-country with certain delectable and longed-for experiences, one would like to see, in support of the Mountain-Plain explication, a clearer identification of the contrasting, soldier-on-leave experiences, with the lowland or plain. And while wondering about this, one reads on in *A Farewell to Arms* and soon finds Frederic Henry and Catherine Barkley in Milan, where Henry is recuperating from his wound. They are having a wonderful time. They are in love, have frequent opportunities to be alone together in the hospital room, go often to the races,' dine at the town's best restaurants, and in general lead an existence that makes the most pleasant contrast imaginable to the dismal life at the front. "We had a lovely time that summer," [31] says the hero. What has happened here to the Mountain-Plain machinery? It does not seem to be operating; or perhaps it is operating in reverse, since Milan is definitely in the plain. Mr. Baker passes over these pages of the novel rather quickly, remarking that Catherine here "moves into association with ideas of home, love and happiness." [32] He seems to be aware of the difficulty, although he does not mention it as such: "She does not really [sic] reach the center of the mountain-image until, on the heels of Frederic's harrowing lowland experiences during the retreat from Caporetto, the lovers move to Switzerland. Catherine is the first to go, and Henry follows her there as if she were the genius of the mountains, beckoning him on." [33]

This is romantically pleasant, but inaccurate. Catherine does not go to Switzerland, but to the Italian resort village of Stresa, on Lake Maggiore. Stresa, moreover, although surrounded by mountains, is itself distinctly lowland: you can pedal a bicycle from Milan or Turin without leaving nearly flat country. Still, it can be allowed that the lovers are not free of the contaminating shadow of war until they have escaped up the lake to Switzerland and established themselves in their little chalet above Montreux. Here, again, the associations all of us are likely to make with high-mountain living assert themselves—clear, cold air; magnificent views; white snow; peace and quiet—and the hero and heroine are shown to be happily aware of these. The rain, however, which they have both come to regard as an omen of disaster, grants no immunity to the mountain; it refuses to preserve a unilateral symbolic association with the plain. Mr. Baker knows this, but does not discuss the extent to which it obscures his neat Mountain-Plain antithesis, making the point instead that "the March rains and the approaching need for a good lying-in hospital have driven the young couple down from their magic mountain" to "the lowlands" [34] of Lausanne. Here again

[31] *A Farewell to Arms*, p. 119.
[32] Baker, *op. cit.*, p. 104.
[33] *Ibid.*
[34] *Ibid.*, pp. 104, 108.

observation is fuzzy to the point of distortion: Lausanne happens to stand on a series of steep hills and is an extraordinarily poor specimen of a City of the Plain. This is clear, incidentally, without reference to an atlas, since there are several allusions to the hills and steep streets of Lausanne in the novel itself.[35] But Mr. Baker is caught up in his symbolic apparatus, and if one symbol of death (rain) has failed to stay where it belongs in his scheme (on the plain) he still is persuaded to see the topography of Switzerland in a light that will not darken his thesis.

What all this illustrates, it seems to me, is that Mr. Baker has allowed an excellent insight into Hemingway's imagery and acute sense of natural metonymy to turn into an interesting but greatly overelaborated critical gimmick. It is undeniable that in the midst of the darkling plain of struggle and flight which was the war in Italy, Frederic Henry thinks of the Swiss Alps as a neutral refuge of peace and happiness—surely millions must have lifted their eyes to those mountains with like thoughts during both World Wars. But in so far as this is symbolism it belongs to our race and culture; and if it is to be sophisticated into a precise scheme of artistic implication revolving around two distinct polar symbols, the signals transmitted from artist to reader must be more clearly semaphored than anything Mr. Baker has been able to point to accurately. I do not believe this is derogatory to Hemingway. Sensitive as always to those parts of experience that are suggestive and connotative, he used the mountain metaphor which is part of our figurative heritage to deepen the thematic contrast in *A Farewell to Arms*, between war and not-war. But nowhere did he violate realism for the sake of this metaphor; nor did he, as I read the novel, set up the artificially rigid and unrealistic contrast between the Mountain and the Plain which Mr. Baker's analysis requires.

Mr. Baker himself has summed up the sequel to his investigation of *A Farewell to Arms*. "Once the reader has become aware of what Hemingway is doing in those parts of his work which lie below the surface, he is likely to find symbols operating everywhere. . . ." [36] Mr. Baker does find them everywhere, and they not infrequently trip him into strangely vulnerable judgments. Finding an unprecedented display of symbolism in *Across the River and Into the Trees* (1950), for instance, he is willing to accord that disappointing novel a richly favorable verdict: "a prose poem, with a remarkably complex emotional structure, on the theme of the three ages of man. . . . If *A Farewell to Arms* was his *Romeo and Juliet* . . . this . . . could perhaps be called a lesser kind of *Winter's Tale* or *Tempest*." [37]

---

[35] See, for instance, pp. 328, 331, 334.
[36] Baker, *op. cit.*, p. 117.
[37] *Ibid.*, pp. 264, 287.

III

But we are not interested so much in the narrative technique of Hemingway's weakest work as we are in what happens in his best. To see symbolism as the master device of the earlier novels and short stories tends to obscure another and more characteristic type of ambiguity which makes his best work great fiction in the tacit mode. I mean Hemingway's irony. The extent to which the ironic method has packed his fiction with substrata of meaning has not yet, I think, been adequately appreciated in published criticism. And it needs to be appreciated; for irony as a literary device is singularly suited to the view of life which Hemingway has consistently dramatized now for a quarter of our century in such manner as to distinguish him as a writer.

If you look at Hemingway's earliest American publication in a medium of general circulation you are struck by this irony of view and method, just as it is strikingly there in *The Old Man and the Sea*. "Champs d'Honneur" was the title of one of six short poems printed in *Poetry* for January, 1923:

> Soldiers never do die well;
>   Crosses mark the places—
> Wooden crosses where they fell,
>   Stuck above their faces.
> Soldiers pitch and cough and twitch—
>   All the world roars red and black;
> Soldiers smother in a ditch,
>   Choking through the whole attack.[38]

One of the most interesting things about this is the strong ironic tension set up between the title and the verse itself; the harsh incongruity between the traditional notion of the soldier's heroic death and the grim reality. A tough irony of situation is also the keynote of *In Our Time* (1925), not only as clue to the individual meanings of most of the stories that make up the book, but as the very principle upon which it was composed. Many readers have tried to puzzle out a nice relationship between each story and the narrative fragment, numbered as a "chapter," which precedes it. But the principle in fact was irrelevance; what Hemingway did was to take the numbered sketches of *in our time* (Paris, 1924) and intersperse them with the longer stories to give a powerfully ironic effect of spurious order supporting the book's subject: modern civil disruption and violence seen against the timeless background of everyday human cross-purposes.

[38] *Poetry*, XXI (January, 1923), 195.

The ironic gap between expectation and fulfillment, pretense and fact, intention and action, the message sent and the message received, the way things are thought or ought to be and the way things are—this has been Hemingway's great theme from the beginning; and it has called for an ironic method to do it artistic justice. All of his work thus far published deserves study with special attention to this method.

I do not think, for example, that a reader must understand the symbolic pattern Mr. Baker claims for *A Farewell to Arms* in order to get the main point of the story; but unless he understands the irony of Catherine Barkley's death he surely has missed it completely. Long before this denouement, however, irony has drawn a chiaroscuro highlighting the meaning of the book. There is from the beginning the curious disproportion between Frederic Henry's lot in the army and his frame of mind. A noncombatant, he lives in comfortable houses, eats and drinks well, makes frequent visits to a brothel maintained exclusively for officers, and has extensive leaves urged on him by a sympathetic commanding officer. Despite such pleasures he is malcontent; and the more this fact emerges the more it becomes evident that his mood is a reflection not of his personal fortune, but of the whole dismal panorama of civilization disjointed by war. His manner of narration is already ironical: "At the start of the winter came the permanent rain and with the rain came the cholera. But it was checked and in the end only seven thousand died of it in the army." [39] Healthy in body, the hero is afflicted by a paralysis of the will, a torpor brought on by too many months of living close to the war; and this is the reason for his paradoxical failure to visit the home of his friend the chaplain while he is on leave: "I myself felt as badly as he did and could not understand why I had not gone. It was what I had wanted to do. . . ." [40] Even the one constructive effort he has been regularly capable of, the performance of his duty as an ambulance officer, has begun to seem absurdly inconsequential to him: when he returns from leave he finds that his absence apparently has made no difference whatever.

As the war wears on, its grotesqueries receive more attention; it begins to be felt, indeed, that they are perhaps after all indigenous to life itself, and only emphasized by war. Henry is given a protective St. Anthony by the heroine: "After I was wounded I never found him. Some one probably got it at one of the dressing stations." [41] The ambulance unit which he commands makes elaborate preparations to receive wounded soldiers during a forthcoming attack: while they are waiting—and eating cheese and spaghetti—in a dugout, an enemy shell lands squarely on top of them, thus making Lt. Henry himself part

---

[39] *A Farewell to Arms*, p. 4.
[40] *Ibid.*, p. 13.
[41] *Ibid.*, p. 47.

of the first load of wounded going to the rear. For this, he learns, he is to receive a bronze medal; his friend Rinaldi hopes it may be silver.

The episode in Milan, so recalcitrant to Mr. Baker's symbolist scheme, has an integral function in the ironic structure of the narrative. Recuperating far behind the lines, the hero becomes part of the incongruously pleasant civilian scene which always—to the incredulous and bitter astonishment of most combat soldiers—goes on while men die at the front. Yet to add a further ironic twist to this, there is Hemingway's satirical portrait of Ettore, the American-Italian who is a "legitimate hero" in the Italian Army. Not only does he see the social life of wartime Milan as perfectly normal, but it is clear that his view of the war as a whole is the reverse of Henry's: "Believe me, they're fine to have," he says, exhibiting his wound stripes. "I'd rather have them than medals. Believe me, boy, when you get three you've got something." [42]

Back at the front for only two days, Henry finds himself mixed up in the nightmarish retreat from Caporetto. Hemingway's famous description of this debacle is a stringent comment on the bewildering stupidity and chaos of war, but he takes the occasion to inject again a shot of special irony. With one ambulance mired to the hubs on a rainsoaked back road, Lt. Henry shoots a sergeant who, in his anxiety to keep up with the retreat, tries to get away on foot instead of staying to cut brush for the spinning wheels. The sergeant is only wounded, but he is quickly dispatched, with Henry's acquiescence, by Bonello, one of the ambulance drivers. "All my life I've wanted to kill a sergeant," [43] Bonello says proudly; but a few hours later he too deserts, to let himself be captured by the enemy. The climax of this grim comedy is of course Frederic Henry's own desertion. Threatened with military justice akin to that he so summarily had dealt the sergeant, he dives into the Tagliamento River; and his sarcastic remarks on his would-be executioners ring with hyperironic overtones against the baffle of the earlier incident:

> I saw how their minds worked; if they had minds and if they worked. They were all young men and they were saving their country. . . . The questioners had that beautiful detachment and devotion to stern justice of men dealing in death without being in any danger of it.[44]

There are many other ironic strokes in *A Farewell to Arms*, but it is this series, identifying the activities of war with all that is brutal and meaningless in human life, that gives the novel its predominantly ironic texture. The catastrophe, Catherine Barkley's shocking death, has the ambivalent effect of partly canceling this identification while at **the**

[42] *Ibid.*, p. 130.
[43] *Ibid.*, p. 222.
[44] *Ibid.*, pp. 240, 241.

same time violently reinforcing the total effect of irony. It is as if the author had said, "Do not imagine that the kind of cruelty and disruption I have shown you are confined to war: they are the conditions of life itself." It is thus only at the end that the full ironic ambiguity of the title springs into view.

The title of Hemingway's other great war novel is likewise an index of its strongly ironic theme. It was strange how many reviewers and critics underweighed the epigraph from Donne and the meaningful paradox of the whole sentence furnishing the title: "And therefore never send to know for whom the bell tolls: it tolls for thee." Appraisals from both Right and Left accused Hemingway of having gone over to the other side, while certain critics less politically biased found that his theme was confused or that it had backfired. "At the center of *For Whom the Bell Tolls*," wrote Maxwell Geismar, "there is a basic confusion of Hemingway's intention. The novel attempts to be a constructive statement on human life. Yet Hemingway's underlying sense of destruction often contradicts this." [45]

But Hemingway was not confused. As always, he wanted to show something true about human life (not necessarily something "constructive"); and he had come to take a more complex view of humanity at war than he projected in *A Farewell to Arms*. "A plague on both your houses"—the prevailing mood of Frederic Henry—has been replaced by Robert Jordan's unillusioned sense of the community of the human predicament. No man is an island, it turns out; but the storms that sweep the human continent are of such force, and the quakes that rack its surface so disruptive, that none of us can depend on better fortune than that of Jordan, who died making his own small and paradoxical effort to maintain its integrity. His affiliation with the Loyalists is no simple partisan allegiance; and to extend and support the hero's explicit awareness of the inevitable contradictions of his position, Hemingway poses a series of situations pregnant with irony.

Outstanding is Pilar's account of the start of "the movement" in Pablo's home town, with its unflinching report of the steadily mounting sadism which infused the execution of the local Fascists. There is a remarkable tone to this report, as if Pilar were at confession, anxious to tell the whole truth and omitting not even the most shameful details, yet seeking at the same time to make it understood how these grisly acts could have occurred among normally decent Spanish peasants. She tells how, at first, many of the peasants were sickened by Pablo's plan to flail the Fascists down between a double line of men leading to the edge of a steep cliff. But within the ironic frame of the entire episode, in relation to the book, there are lesser ironies: for it is the cowardly behavior of the Fascists themselves that brings these peasants to a pitch of mob hatred and violence equal to Pablo's inveterate cruelty.

[45] *Writers in Crisis* (Boston: Houghton, 1942), p. 81.

Throughout all this the reader is never allowed to forget that it is the Loyalists who are committing the atrocities described, and that the leaders of the massacre are the very people with whom Jordan is now allied. Robert Penn Warren cites the irony of this, but he suggests that *For Whom the Bell Tolls* is not Hemingway's best novel "primarily because . . . Hemingway does not accept the limitations of his premises . . . the irony . . . runs counter to the ostensible surface direction of the story."[46] So it does—but this is the nature of irony; and this is why it is so valuable to Hemingway in his intense effort to dramatize fully the implications of Donne's epigraph in relation to the ironical self-destruction which is civilized warfare. It is a mistake to think of *For Whom the Bell Tolls* as a document of social optimism in its intent, as opposed to the dark pessimism of Hemingway's earlier books. The darkness is relieved, deliberately, only by a faint existentialist glimmer: the general human enterprise seems very likely to end in failure, but each of us must do what he can—*"Nous ferons notre petit possible."*

It is to this end that the irony of the Loyalist massacre of the Fascists, which early in the book sets the theme of human sacrifice in a highly critical perspective, is complemented by the irony of the denouement. For the central action—the blowing of the bridge—which is responsible for the death of El Sordo, Anselmo, Fernando, and, indeed, Robert Jordan, is rendered a strategic failure by the loose tongues of their comrades behind the lines.

To these two fundamental veins of irony many scenes provide tributary support: three may be cited as exemplary. There is the one in which Jordan reads the letters found in the pockets of a Fascist cavalryman he has just shot, and discovers he is from a Spanish town that Jordan knows well:

> How many is that you have killed? he asked himself. I don't know. Do you think you have a right to kill any one? No. But I have to. . . . But you like the people of Navarra better than those of any other part of Spain. Yes. And you kill them. Yes. . . . Don't you know it is wrong to kill? Yes. But you do it? Yes. And you still believe absolutely that your cause is right? Yes.[47]

This irony of Jordan's self-conscious ambivalence is heightened by juxtapositions of which he knows nothing. In the midst of El Sordo's great last fight, we are suddenly given a decidedly sympathetic portrait of Lt. Berrendo, second in command of the Fascist cavalry. Julian, his best friend, has just been killed by Sordo, and Captain Mora, the blustering officer in command, is shouting blasphemies at the hilltop in

[46] Introduction to *A Farewell to Arms* (New York: Scribner, 1949), p. xxv.
[47] *For Whom the Bell Tolls*, pp. 303-304.

an effort (which carries its own small irony, in view of his imminent death) to prove that no one is left alive up there. Later, after Mora has become El Sordo's "Comrade Voyager," Berrendo reluctantly has his troopers decapitate the dead guerrillas for "proof and identification," and the Fascists start back towards their headquarters:

> Then he thought of Julian, dead on the hill, dead now, tied across a horse there in the first troop, and as he rode down into the dark pine forest, leaving the sunlight behind him on the hill, riding now in the quiet dark of the forest, he started to say a prayer for him again.[48]

At this point Anselmo, watching from a hillside, sees them ride past; and on his way back to the guerrilla cave he crosses El Sordo's hilltop where he finds the headless bodies of his comrades: "As he walked he prayed for the souls of Sordo and of all his band. It was the first time he had prayed since the start of the movement." [49] The episode thus ends in ironic equilibrium, with both sides petitioning Heaven. But we have not yet seen our last of Lt. Berrendo. It is he who looms in the sights of Robert Jordan's machine gun in the last paragraph of the story, lending the finale an ironic depth that protects it from false heroics. For these two young soldiers, preponderant as our sympathy may be for one rather than the other, the same bell tolls. The novel is Hemingway's fullest work so far in scope and artistic realization, and to its fulfillment the ambiguity of irony contributes an essential part.

IV

It would be foolish to argue that the work of any first-rate writer owes its success exclusively or even predominantly to any one narrative artifice. Hemingway has used techniques of symbolism and techniques of irony and used them well; what we want in criticism is an even view of his use of these and other artistic resources that does not exaggerate one at the expense of others. A point deserving great attention and emphasis about this writer is his devotion to the implict rather than the explicit mode: and both symbolism and irony truly serve this artistic purpose. Hemingway, in fact, stirs thought as to the interrelationship of these two kinds of ambiguity. It is remarkable how often they operate together in his stories: an ironic fact, perception, or event on the primary level may epitomize an irony in a broader context, and thus doubly deserve selection and accurate report by the narrator. As an illustration of his early effort to communicate "what really happened in action," Hemingway tells in *Death in the Afternoon* how he worked on the problem of accurately depicting a certain bullfight incident:

[48] *Ibid.,* p. 326.

[49] *Ibid.,* p. 327.

Waking in the night I tried to remember what it was that seemed just out
of my remembering and that was the thing that I had really seen and,
finally, remembering all around it, I got it. When he stood up, his face white
and dirty and the silk of his breeches opened from waist to knee, it was the
dirtiness of the rented breeches, the dirtiness of his slit underwear and the
clean, clean, unbearably clean whiteness of the thighbone that I had seen,
and it was that which was important.[50]

Clearly, it was the startling irony of the contrast that struck Hemingway
here as "important"; but certainly (if not so clearly) there is also the
symbolic suggestion of another contrast going far beyond the physical—
the ironically pathetic gap, perhaps, between the matador's professional
failure and his untouched inner pride which is the subject of "The
Undefeated."

In a fictional narrative the double operation, ironic and symbolic,
can often be seen more sharply: take *The Old Man and the Sea*, where
in effect the same subject is dramatized. The old fisherman's physical
triumph in catching the great fish is ironically cut down—or transmuted
—into spiritual triumph by the marauding sharks who leave him with
only the skeleton of the largest marlin ever seen in Cuba. Without
working out the metaphor in precise terms it can be said that the irony
of the event itself would hardly be so effective without the broadening
and deepening of its implication through symbolic suggestion.

It may be true that all perceptions are reducible finally to perceptions of likeness or perceptions of difference. Perhaps this offers a
clue to the effectiveness of both symbolism and irony for a writer who,
like Hemingway, makes it his life's business to tell a truth, as he once
put it, "truer . . . than anything factual can be." [51] With all his
famous skill in writing with his eye upon the object, he understood
from the beginning that it was only the object in relationship to other
objects and to the observer that really counted: significance is, in short,
a matter of likeness and difference. This is to speak broadly; and to
apply the generalization to symbolism and irony requires a good deal
of qualification. Yet symbolism does depend essentially on likeness, and
irony on difference; and as artistic tools both are means of interpreting
imaginatively, and with the flexibility of implication, a complex reality.
Symbolism signifies through a harmony, irony through a discord; symbolism consolidates, irony complicates; symbolism synthesizes, irony analyzes.

For all of this, I would not like to see Hemingway go down in
new literary histories as either "a symbolist" or (less likely, if somewhat more appropriately) "an ironist." Taken at face value the de-
nomination "symbolist" has meanings in the common language of

[50] *Death in the Afternoon*, p. 20.
[51] Introduction to *Men at War* (New York, 1952), p. xi.

criticism that are quite inapplicable to him. But beyond this, Hemingway uses symbolism, as I have tried to show, with a severe restraint that in his good work always staunchly protects his realism. So likewise does he use irony. It is the ambiguity of life itself that Hemingway has sought to render, and if irony has served him peculiarly well it is because he sees life as inescapably ironic. But if we must classify him let us do him justice: with all his skilful use of artistic ambiguity, he remains the great *realist* of twentieth-century American fiction.

Observations on the Style of
Ernest Hemingway

by Harry Levin

I

Hemingway's hatred for the profession of letters stems quite obviously
from a lover's quarrel. When Richard Gordon is reviled by his dissatisfied wife in *To Have and Have Not*, her most embittered epithet
is "you writer." Yet Hemingway's writing abounds in salutes to various
fellow writers, from the waitress' anecdote about Henry James in *The
Torrents of Spring* to Colonel Cantwell's spiritual affinity with D'Annun-
zio. And from Nick Adams, who takes Meredith and Chesterton along
on fishing trips, to Hemingway himself, who arranges to be interviewed
on American literature in *Green Hills of Africa*, his heroes do not shy
away from critical discussion. His titles, so often quoted from books by
earlier writers, have been so apt that they have all but established a
convention. He shows an almost academic fondness, as well as a remarkable flair, for epigraphs: the Colonel dies with a quotation on
his lips. Like all of us, Hemingway has been influenced by T. S. Eliot's
taste for Elizabethan drama and metaphysical poetry. Thus Hemingway's
title, "In Another Country," is borrowed from a passage he elsewhere
cites, which he might have found in Marlowe's *Jew of Malta* or possibly
in Eliot's "Portrait of a Lady." *A Farewell to Arms*, which echoes Love-
lace's title, quotes in passing from Marvell's "To His Coy Mistress,"
echoed more recently by Robert Penn Warren, which is parodied in
Death in the Afternoon. Hemingway is no exception to the rule that
makes parody the starting point for realistic fiction. Just as Fielding
took off' from Richardson, so Hemingway takes off from Sherwood
Anderson—indeed his first novel, *The Torrents of Spring*, which parodies
Anderson's *Dark Laughter*, is explicit in its acknowledgments to *Joseph
Andrews*. It has passages, however, which read today like a *pastiche* of
the later Hemingway:

"Observations on the Style of Ernest Hemingway" (abridged). From *Contexts
of Criticism* by Harry Levin (Cambridge: Harvard University Press, 1957). Copyright
1957 by The President and Fellows of Harvard College. Reprinted by permission of
the author and Harvard University Press.

Yogi was worried. There was something on his mind. It was spring, there was no doubt of that now, and he did not want a woman. He had worried about it a lot lately. There was no question about it. He did not want a woman. He couldn't explain it to himself. He had gone to the Public Library and asked for a book the night before. He looked at the librarian. He did not want her. Somehow she meant nothing to him.

A recoil from bookishness, after a preliminary immersion in it, provided Fielding's master, Cervantes, with the original impetus for the novel. In "A Banal Story" Hemingway provides us with his own variation on the theme of *Don Quixote*, where a writer sits reading about romance in a magazine advertisement, while in far-off Madrid a bullfighter dies and is buried. The ironic contrast—romantic preconception exploded by contact with harsh reality—is basic with Hemingway, as it has been with all novelists who have written effectively about war. The realism of his generation reacted, not only against Wilsonian idealism, but against Wilsonian rhetoric. Hence the famous paragraph from the Caporetto episode describing Frederic Henry's embarrassment before such abstract words as "glory" and "honor," which seem to him obscene beside the concrete names of places and numbers of roads. For a Spaniard, Hemingway notes in *Death in the Afternoon*, the abstraction may still have concreteness: honor may be "as real a thing as water, wine, or olive oil." It is not so for us: "All our words from loose using have lost their edge." And "The Gambler, the Nun, and the Radio" brings forward a clinching example: "Liberty, what we believed in, now the name of a Macfadden publication." That same story trails off in a litany which reduces a Marxist slogan to meaninglessness: "the opium of the people" is everything and nothing. Even more desolating, in "A Clean, Well-Lighted Place," is the reduction of the Lord's prayer to nothingness: "Our nada who art in nada . . ." Since words have become inflated and devalued, Hemingway is willing to recognize no values save those which can be immediately felt and directly pointed out. It is his verbal skepticism which leads toward what some critics have called his moral nihilism. Anything serious had better be said with a smile, stranger. The classic echo, "irony and pity," jingles through *The Sun Also Rises* like a singing commercial.

There is something in common between this attitude and the familiar British habit of understatement. "No pleasure in anything if you mouth it too much," says Wilson, the guide in "The Short, Happy Life of Francis Macomber." Yet Jake, the narrator of *The Sun Also Rises*, protests—in the name of American garrulity—that the English use fewer words than the Eskimos. Spanish, the language of Hemingway's preference, is at once emotive and highly formal. His Spanish, to judge from *Death in the Afternoon*, is just as ungrammatical as his English. In "The Undefeated" his Spanish bullfighters are made to speak the slang of American prizefighters. Americanisms and Hispanisms, archaic and polyglot elements are so intermingled in *For Whom the Bell Tolls* that it calls to mind what Ben Jonson said of *The Faerie Queene*: "Spenser writ no language." Hemingway offers a succinct example by translating *"Eras mucho caballo"* as "Thou wert plenty of horse." It is somewhat paradoxical that a writer, having severely cut down his English vocabulary, should augment it by continual importation from other languages, including the Swahili. But this is a facet of the larger paradox that a writer so essentially American should set the bulk of his work against foreign backgrounds. His characters, expatriates for the most part, wander through the ruins of Babel, smattering many tongues and speaking a demotic version of their own. Obscenity presents another linguistic problem, for which Hemingway is not responsible; but his coy ways of circumventing the taboos of censorship are more of a distraction than the conventional blanks. When he does permit himself an expression not usually considered printable, in *Death in the Afternoon*, the context is significant. His interlocutor, the Old Lady, requests a definition and he politely responds: "Madam, we apply the term now to describe unsoundness in abstract conversation or, indeed, any overmetaphysical tendency in speech."

For language, as for literature, his feeling is strongly ambivalent. Perhaps it could be summed up by Pascal's maxim: "True eloquence makes fun of eloquence." Like the notorious General Cambronne, Hemingway feels that one short spontaneous vulgarism is more honest than all those grandiloquent slogans which rhetoricians dream up long after the battle. The disparity between rhetoric and experience, which became so evident during the First World War, prompted the Twenties to repudiate the genteel stylistic tradition and to accept the American vernacular as our norm of literary discourse. "Literary" is a contradiction in terms, for the resultant style is basically oral; and when the semiliterate speaker takes pen in hand, as Hemingway demonstrates in "One Reader Writes"—as H. L. Mencken demonstrated in "A Short View of Gamalielese"—the result is even more artificial than if it had been written by a writer. A page is always flat, and we need perspective to make it convey the illusion of life in the round. Yet the very fact that words mean so much less to us than the things they represent in our lives is a stimulus to our imaginations. In "Fathers and Sons" young Nick Adams reads that Caruso has been arrested for "mashing," and asks his father the meaning of that expression.

"It is one of the most heinous of crimes," his father answered. Nick's imagination pictured the great tenor doing something strange, bizarre, and heinous with a potato masher to a beautiful lady who looked like the pictures of Anna Held on the inside of cigar boxes. He resolved, with considerable horror, that when he was old enough he would try mashing at least once.

The tone of this passage is not altogether typical of Hemingway. Rather, as the point of view detaches itself affectionately and ironically from the youth, it approximates the early Joyce. This may help to explain why it suggests a more optimistic approach to language than the presumption that, since phrases can be snares and delusions, their scope should be limited to straight denotation. The powers of connotation, the possibilities of oblique suggestion and semantic association, are actually grasped by Hemingway as well as any writer of our time. Thus he can retrospectively endow a cheap and faded term like "mashing" with all the promise and poetry of awakening manhood. When Nick grows up, foreign terms will hold out the same allure to him; like Frederic Henry, he will seek the actuality that resides behind the names of places; and Robert Jordan will first be attracted to Spain as a professional philologist. But none of them will find an equivalence between the word and the thing; and Hemingway, at the end of *Death in the Afternoon*, laments that no book is big enough to do final justice to its living subject. "There was so much to write," the dying writer realizes in "The Snows of Kilimanjaro," and his last thoughts are moving and memorable recollections of some of the many things that will now go unwritten. Walt Whitman stated this challenge and this dilemma, for all good writers, when he spoke of expressing the inexpressible.

II

The inevitable compromise, for Hemingway, is best expressed by his account of Romero's bullfighting style: "the holding of his purity of line through the maximum of exposure." The maximum of exposure —this throws much light upon the restlessness of Hemingway's career, but here we are primarily concerned with the holding of his purity of line. It had to be the simplest and most flexible of lines in order to accommodate itself to his desperate pursuit of material. His purgation of language has aptly been compared, by Robert Penn Warren, to the revival of diction that Wordsworth accomplished with *Lyrical Ballads*. Indeed the question that Coleridge afterward raised might once again be asked: why should the speech of some men be more real than that of others? Today that question restates itself in ideological terms: whether respect for the common man necessitates the adoption of a commonplace standard. Everyone who writes faces the same old problems, and the original writers—like Wordsworth or Hemingway—are those who develop new ways of meeting them. The case of Wordsworth would show us, if that of Hemingway did not, that those who break down conventions tend to substitute conventions of their own. Hemingway's prose is not without precedents; it is interesting to recall that his

76   *Harry Levin*

maiden effort, published by *The Double Dealer* in 1922, parodied the
King James Bible. He has his forerunners in American fiction, from
Cooper to Jack London, whose conspicuous lack was a style as dynamic
as their subject matter. The ring-tailed roarers of the frontier, such as
Davy Crockett, were Colonel Cantwell's brothers under the skin; but
as contrasted with the latter's tragic conception of himself, they were
mock-heroic and serio-comic figures, who recommend themselves to the
reader's condescension. Mark Twain has been the most genuine influence,
and Hemingway has acknowledged this by declaring—with sweeping
generosity—that *Huckleberry Finn* is the source of all modern American
literature.

But Mark Twain was conducting a monologue, a virtual *tour de force*
of impersonation, and he ordinarily kept a certain distance between
his narrative role and his characters. And among Hemingway's elder
contemporaries, Ring Lardner was a kind of ventriloquist, who made
devastating use of the vernacular to satirize the vulgarity and stupidity of
his dummies. It remained for Hemingway—along with Anderson—to
identify himself wholly with the lives he wrote about, not so much
entering into them as allowing them to take possession of him, and
accepting—along with their sensibilities and perceptions—the limitations
of their point of view and the limits of their range of expression. We
need make no word-count to be sure that his literary vocabulary, with
foreign and technical exceptions, consists of relatively few and short
words. The corollary, of course, is that every word sees a good deal of
hard use. Furthermore, his syntax is informal to the point of fluidity,
simplifying as far as possible the already simple system of English
inflections. Thus "who" is normally substituted for "whom," presumably
to avoid schoolmarmish correctness; and "that," doing duty for "which,"
seems somehow less prophetic of complexity. Personal pronouns frequently get involved in what is stigmatized, by teachers of freshman
composition, as faulty reference; there are sentences in which it is
hard to tell the hunter from his quarry or the bullfighter from the bull.
"When his father died he was only a kid and his manager buried him
perpetually." So begins, rather confusingly, "The Mother of a Queen."
Sometimes it seems as if Hemingway were taking pains to be ungrammatical, as do many educated people out of a twisted sense of *noblesse
oblige*. Yet when he comes closest to pronouncing a moral, the last
words of Harry Morgan—the analphabetic hero of *To Have and Have
Not*—seem to be half-consciously fumbling toward some grammatical
resolution: "A man . . . ain't got no hasn't got any can't really isn't
any way out . . ."

The effectiveness of Hemingway's method depends very largely upon
his keen ear for speech. His conversations are vivid, often dramatic,
although he comes to depend too heavily upon them and to scant the

other obligations of the novelist. Many of his wisecracks are quotable out of context, but as Gertrude Stein warned him: "Remarks are not literature." He can get his story told, and still be as conversational as he pleases, by telling it in the first person. "Brother, that was some storm," says the narrator, and the reader hears the very tone of his voice. In one of Hemingway's critical digressions, he declares that he has always sought "the real thing, the sequence of motion and fact which [*sic*] made the emotion . . ." This seems to imply the clear-cut mechanism of verbal stimulus and psychological response that Eliot formulates in his theory of the objective correlative. In practice, however, Hemingway is no more of a behaviorist than Eliot, and the sharp distinction between motion and emotion is soon blurred. Consider his restricted choice of adjectives, and the heavy load of subjective implication carried by such uncertain monosyllables as "fine" and "nice." From examples on nearly every page, we are struck by one which helps to set the scene for *A Farewell to Arms*: "The town was very nice and our house was very fine." Such descriptions—if we may consider them descriptions— are obviously not designed for pictorial effect. When the Colonel is tempted to call some fishing-boats picturesque, he corrects himself: "The hell with picturesque. They are just dammed beautiful." Where "picturesque" might sound arty and hence artificial, "beautiful"—with "damned" to take off the curse—is permissible because Hemingway has packed it with his own emotional charge. He even uses it in *For Whom the Bell Tolls* to express his aesthetic appreciation of gunfire. Like "fine" and "nice," or "good" and "lovely," it does not describe; it evaluates. It is not a stimulus but a projected response, a projection of the narrator's euphoria in a given situation. Hemingway, in effect, is saying to the reader: *Having wonderful time. Wish you were here.*

In short, he is communicating excitement; and if this communication is received, it establishes a uniquely personal relationship; but when it goes astray, the diction goes flat and vague. Hemingway manages to sustain his reputation for concreteness by an exploring eye for the incidental detail. The one typescript of his that I have seen, his carbon copy of "The Killers" now in the Harvard College Library, would indicate that the arc-light and the tipped-back derby hat were later observations than the rest. Precision at times becomes so arithmetical that, in "The Light of the World," it lines up his characters like a drill-sergeant: "Down at the station there were five whores waiting for the train to come in, and six white men and four Indians." Numbers enlarge the irony that concludes the opening chapter of *A Farewell to Arms* when, after a far from epic invocation, a casual introduction to the landscape, and a dusty record of troops falling back through the autumn, rain brings the cholera which kills "only seven thousand." A trick of multiplication, which Hemingway may have picked up from

Gertrude Stein, is to generalize the specific episode: "They always picked
the finest places to have the quarrels." When he offers this general
view of a restaurant—"It was full of smoke and drinking and singing"—
he is an impressionist if not an abstractionist. Thence to expressionism
is an easy step: ". . . the room whirled." It happens that, under pressure
from his first American publishers, the author was compelled to modify
the phrasing of "Mr. and Mrs. Elliott." In the original version, sub-
sequently restored, the title characters "try to have a baby." In the
modified version they "think of having a baby." It could be argued that,
in characterizing this rather tepid couple, the later verb is more expressive
and no more euphemistic than the earlier one; that "think," at any
rate, is not less precise or effectual than "try." But, whereas the sense of
effort came naturally, the cerebration was an afterthought.

If we regard the adjective as a luxury, decorative more often than
functional, we can well understand why Hemingway doesn't cultivate it.
But, assuming that the sentence derives its energy from the verb, we
are in for a shock if we expect his verbs to be numerous or varied or
emphatic. His usage supports C. K. Ogden's argument that verb-forms
are disappearing from English grammar. Without much self-deprivation,
Hemingway could get along on the so-called "operators" of Basic
English, the sixteen monosyllabic verbs that stem from movements of
the body. The substantive verb *to be* is predominant, characteristically
introduced by an expletive. Thus the first story of *In Our Time* begins,
and the last one ends, with the story-teller's gambit: "there was," "there
were." In the first two pages of *A Farewell to Arms* nearly every other
sentence is of this type, and the third page employs the awkward construction "there being." There is—I find the habit contagious—a tendency to immobilize verbs by transposing them into gerunds. Instead of
writing *they fought* or *we did not feel*, Hemingway writes "there was
fighting" and "there was not the feeling of a storm coming." The
subject does little more than point impersonally at its predicate: an
object, a situation, an emotion. Yet the idiom, like the French *il y a,*
is ambiguous; inversion can turn the gesture of pointing into a physical
act; and the indefinite adverb can indicate, if not specify, a definite
place. Contrast, with the opening of *A Farewell to Arms*, that of "In
Another Country": "In the fall the war was always there, but we did
not go to it any more." The negative is even more striking, when
Frederic Henry has registered the sensations of his wound, and dares to
look at it for the first time, and notes: "My knee wasn't there." The
adverb is *there* rather than *here,* the verb is *was* rather than *is,* because
we—the readers—are separated from the event in space and time. But
the narrator has lived through it, like the Ancient Mariner, and now
he chooses his words to grip and transfix us. *Lo!* he says. *Look! I was
there.*

III

Granted, then, that Hemingway's diction is thin; that, in the technical sense, his syntax is weak; and that he would rather be caught dead than seeking the *mot juste* or the balanced phrase. Granted that his adjectives are not colorful and his verbs not particularly energetic. Granted that he commits as many literary offenses as Mark Twain brought to book with Fenimore Cooper. What is behind his indubitable punch, the unexampled dynamics of Hemingway's style? How does he manage, as he does, to animate this characteristic sentence from "After the Storm"?

> I said "Who killed him?" and he said "I don't know who killed him but he's dead all right," and it was dark and there was water standing in the street and no light and windows broke and boats all up in the town and trees blown down and everything all blown and I got a skiff and went out and found my boat where I had her inside of Mango Key and she was all right only she was full of water.

Here is a good example of Hemingway's "sequence of motion and fact." It starts from dialogue and leads into first-person action; but the central description is a single clause, where the expletive takes the place of the observer and his observations are registered one by one. Hence, for the reader, it lives up to Robert Jordan's intention: "You . . . feel that all that happened to you." Hemingway puts his emphasis on nouns because, among parts of speech, they come closest to things. Stringing them along by means of conjunctions, he approximates the actual flow of experience. For him, as for Marion Tweedy Bloom, the key word is *and,* with its renewable promise of continuity, occasionally varied by *then* and *so.* The rhetorical scheme is *polysyndeton*—a large name for the childishly simple habit of linking sentences together. The subject, when it is not taken for granted, merely puts us in touch with the predicate: the series of objects that Hemingway wants to point out. Even a preposition can turn this trick, as "with" does in this account of El Sordo waiting to see the whites of his enemy's eyes:

> Come on, Comrade Voyager . . . Keep on coming with your eyes forward . . . Look. With a red face and blond hair and blue eyes. With no cap on and his moustache is yellow. With blue eyes. With pale blue eyes. With pale blue eyes with something wrong with them. With pale blue eyes that don't focus. Close enough. Too close. Yes, Comrade Voyager. Take it, Comrade Voyager.

Prose gets as near as it can to physical conflict here. The figure enlarges as it advances, the quickening impression grows clear and sharp and almost unbearable, whereupon it is blackened out by El Sordo's rifle. Each clipped sentence, each prepositional phrase, is like a new frame in a strip of film; indeed the whole passage, like so many others, might have been filmed by the camera and projected on the screen. The course of Harry Morgan's launch speeding through the Gulf Stream, or of Frederic Henry's fantasy ascending the elevator with Catherine Barkley, is given this cinematographic presentation. *Green Hills of Africa* voices the long-range ambition of obtaining a fourth and fifth dimension in prose. Yet if the subordinate clause and the complex sentence are the usual ways for writers to obtain a third dimension, Hemingway keeps his writing on a linear plane. He holds the purity of his line by moving in one direction, ignoring sidetracks and avoiding structural compli- cations. By presenting a succession of images, each of which has its brief moment when it commands the reader's undivided attention, he achieves his special vividness and fluidity. For what he lacks in structure he makes up in sequence, carefully ordering visual impressions as he sets them down and ironically juxtaposing the various items on his lists and inventories. "A Way You'll Never Be" opens with a close-up showing the debris on a battlefield, variously specifying munitions, medicaments, and left-overs from a field kitchen, then closing in on the scattered papers with this striking montage-effect: "group postcards showing the machine-gun unit standing in ranked and ruddy cheefulness as in a football picture for a college annual; now they were humped and swollen in the grass. . . ." It is not surprising that Hemingway's verse, published by *Poetry* in 1923, is recognizably imagistic in character—and perhaps his later heroics are foreshadowed by the subject of one of those poems, Theodore Roosevelt.

In her observant book, *L'Age du roman américain*, Claude-Monde Magny stresses Hemingway's "exaltation of the instant." We can note how this emphasis is reflected in his timing, which—after his placing has bridged the distance from *there* to *here*—strives to close the gap between *then* and *now*. Where Baudelaire's clock said "remember" in many lan- guages, Robert Jordan's memory says: "Now, *ahora, maintenant, heute*." When death interrupts a dream, in "The Snows of Kilimanjaro," the ultimate reality is heralded by a rising insistence upon the word "now." It is not for nothing that Hemingway is the younger contemporary of Proust and Joyce. Though his time is neither *le temps perdu* nor the past nostagically recaptured, he spends it gathering roses while he can, to the ever accelerating rhythm of headlines and telegrams and loud- speakers. The act, no sooner done than said, becomes simultaneous with the word, no sooner said than felt. Hemingway goes so far, in "Fathers and Sons," as to render a sexual embrace by an onomatopoetic sequence of adverbs. But unlike Damon Runyon and Dickens, he seldom narrates in the present tense, except in such sporting events as "Fifty Grand." Rather, his timeliness expresses itself in continuous forms of the verb and in his fondness for all kinds of participial constructions. These, compounded and multiplied, create an ambiance of overwhelming activity, and the epithets shift from El Sordo's harassed feelings to the impact of the reiterated bullets, as Hemingway recounts "the last lung-aching, leg-dead, mouth-dry, bullet-spatting, bullet-cracking, bullet-singing run up the final slope of the hill." More often the meaning takes the opposite turn, and moves from the external plane into the range of a character's senses, proceeding serially from the visual to the tactile, as it does when the "Wine of Wyoming" is sampled: "It was very light and clear and good and still tasted of the grapes."

When Nick Adams goes fishing, the temperature is very tangibly indicated: "It was getting hot, the sun hot on the back of his neck." The remark about the weather is thereby extended in two directions, toward the distant source of the heat and toward its immediate perception. Again in "Big Two-Hearted River," Nick's fatigue is measured by the weight of his pack: ". . . it was heavy. It was much too heavy." As in the movies, the illusion of movement is produced by repeating the same shot with further modification every time. Whenever a new clause takes more than one step ahead, a subsequent clause repeats it in order to catch up. Repetition, as in "Up in Michigan," brings the advancing narrative back to an initial point of reference. "Liz liked Jim very much. She liked it the way he walked over from the shop and often went to the kitchen door to watch him start down the road. She liked it about his moustache. She liked it about how white his teeth were when he smiled." The opaque verb "like," made increasingly transparent, is utilized five more times in this paragraph; and the fumbling preposition "about" may be an acknowledgment of Hemingway's early debt to Gertrude Stein. The situation is located somewhere between a subjective Liz and and objective Jim. The theme of love is always a test of Hemingway's objectivity. When Frederic kisses Catherine, her responses are not less moving because they are presented through his reflexes; but it is her sentimental conversation which leaves him free to ask himself: "What the hell?" At first glance, in a behavioristic formula which elsewhere recurs, Colonel Cantwell seems so hard-boiled that motions are his only emotions: "He saw that his hand was trembling." But his vision is blurred by conventionally romantic tenderness when he contemplates a heroine whose profile "could break your . . . or anyone else's heart." Hemingway's heroines, when they aren't bitches, are fantasies—or rather, the masculine reader is invited to supply his own, as with the weather in Mark Twain's *American Claimant*. They are pin-up girls.

If beauty lies in the eye of the beholder, Hemingway's purpose is to make his readers beholders. This is easily done when the narration is conducted in the first person; we can sit down and drink, with Jake Barnes, and watch Paris walk by. The interpolated chapters of *In Our Time*, most of them reminiscences from the army, employ the collective *we*; but, except for "My Old Man," the stories themselves are told in the third person. Sometimes, to strengthen the sense of identification, they make direct appeal to the second person; the protagonist of "Soldier's Home" is "you" as well as "he"—and, more generally, "a fellow." With the exception of Jake's confessions, that is to say *The Sun Also Rises*, all of Hemingway's novels are written in the *style indirect libre*—indirect discourse which more or less closely follows the consciousness of a central character.[1] An increasing tendency for the author to intrude, commenting in his own person, is one of the weaknesses of *Across the River*. He derives his strength from a power to visualize episodes through the eyes of those most directly involved; for a page, in "The Short, Happy Life of Francis Macomber," the hunt is actually seen from the beast's point of view. Hemingway's use of interior monologue is effective when sensations from the outer world are entering the stream of a character's consciousness, as they do with such a rush at El Sordo's last stand. But introspection is not Hemingway's genre, and the night-thoughts of *To Have and Have Not* are among his least successful episodes. His best are events, which are never far to seek; things are constantly happening in his world; his leg-man, Nick Adams, happens to be the eye-witness of "The Killers." The state of mind that Hemingway communicates to us is the thrill that Nick got from skiing in "Cross Country Snow," which "plucked Nick's mind out and left him only the wonderful, flying, dropping sensation in his body."

IV

If psychological theories could be proved by works of fiction, Hemingway would lend his authority to the long contested formula of William James, which equates emotion with bodily sensation. Most other serious writers, however, would bear witness to deeper ranges of sensibility and more complex processes of motivation than those he sees fit to describe. Some of them have accused Hemingway of aggressive anti-intellectualism: I am thinking particularly of Aldous Huxley. But Huxley's own work is so pure an example of all that Hemingway has recoiled from, so intellectual in the airiest sense, and so unsupported by felt experience, that the argument has played into Hemingway's hands. We have seen enough of the latter to know that he doesn't really hate books—himself having written a dozen, several of which are, and will remain, the best of their kind. As for his refusal to behave like a man of letters, he reminds us of Hotspur, who professes to be a laconic Philistine and turns out—with no little grandiloquence—to be the most poetic character in Shakespeare's play. Furthermore, it is not Hemingway, but the slogan-mongers of our epoch, who have debased the language;

---

[1] *A Farewell to Arms* is also narrated in the first person.—R.P.W.

he has been attempting to restore some decent degree of correspondence between words and things; and the task of verification is a heavy one, which throws the individual back on his personal resources of awareness. That he has succeeded within limits, and with considerable strain, is less important than that he has succeeded, that a few more aspects of life have been captured for literature. Meanwhile the word continues to dematerialize, and has to be made flesh all over again; the firsthand perception, once it gets written down, becomes the second-hand notation; and the writer, who attains his individuality by repudiating literary affectation, ends by finding that he has struck a new pose and founded another school.

It is understandable why no critique of Hemingway, including this one, can speak for long of the style without speaking of the man. Improving on Buffon, Mark Schorer recently wrote: "[Hemingway's] style is not only his subject, it is his view of life." It could also be called his way of life, his *Lebensstil*. It has led him to live his books, to brave the maximum of exposure, to tour the world in an endless search for wars and their moral equivalents. It has cast him in the special role of our agent, our plenipotentiary, our roving correspondent on whom we depend for news from the fighting fronts of modern consciousness. Here he is, the man who was there. His writing seems so intent upon the actual, so impersonal in its surfaces, that it momentarily prompts us to overlook the personality behind them. That would be a serious mistake; for the point of view, though brilliantly intense, is narrowly focused and obliquely angled. We must ask: who is this guide to whom we have entrusted ourselves on intimate terms in dangerous places? Where are his limitations? What are his values? We may well discover that they differ from our assumptions, when he shows us a photograph of a bullfighter close to a bull, and comments: "If there is no blood on his belly afterwards you ought to get your money back." We may be ungrateful to question such curiosity, when we are indebted to it for many enlargements of our vicarious knowledge; and it may well spring from the callowness of the tourist rather than the morbidity of the *voyeur*, from the American zest of the fan who pays his money to reckon the carnage. When Spain's great poet, García Lorca, celebrated the very same theme, averting his gaze from the spilling of the blood, his refrain was "*Que no quiero verla!*" ("I do not want to see it!").

Yet Hemingway wants to see everything—or possibly he wants to be in a position to tell us that he has seen everything. While the boy Nick, his seeing eye, eagerly watches a Caesarian childbirth in "Indian Camp," the far from impassive husband turns away; and it is later discovered that he has killed himself. "He couldn't stand things"—so runs the diagnosis of Nick's father, the doctor. This, for Nick, is an initiation to suffering and death; but with the sunrise, shortly afterward, youth and well-being reassert themselves; and the end of the story reaffirms the generalization that Hazlitt once drew: "No young man ever thinks he shall die." It is easy enough for such a young man to stand things, for he is not yet painfully involved in them; he is not a sufferer but a wide-eyed onlooker, to whom the word "mashing" holds out mysterious enticements. Hemingway's projection of this attitude has given his best work perennial youthfulness; it has also armed his critics with the accusation that, like his Robert Cohn, he is "a case of arrested development." If this be so, his plight is generalized by the Englishman Wilson, who observes that "Americans stay little boys . . . all their lives." And the object of Wilson's observation, Francis Macomber, would furnish a classic case history for Adler, if not for Freud—the masculine sense of inferiority which seeks to overcome itself by acts of prowess, both sanguinary and sexual. Despite these two sources of excitement, the story is a plaintive modulation of two rather dissonant themes: *None but the brave deserves the fair* and *The female of the species is more deadly than the male*. After Francis Macomber has demonstrated his manhood, the next step is death. The world that remains most alive to Hemingway is that stretch between puberty and maturity which is strictly governed by the ephebic code: a world of mixed apprehension and bravado before the rite of passage, the baptism of fire, the introduction to sex.

Afterward comes the boasting along with such surviving ideals as Hemingway subsumes in the word *cojones*—the English equivalent sounds more skeptical. But for Jake Barnes, all passion spent in the First World War, or for Colonel Cantwell, tired and disgruntled by the Second, the aftermath can only be elegiac. The weather-beaten hero of *Across the River*, which appears in 1950, is fifty years old and uneasily conscious of that fact; whereas "the childish, drunken heroics" of *The Sun Also Rises* took place just about twenty-five years ago. From his spectacular arrival in the Twenties, Hemingway's course has paralleled that of our century; and now, at its midpoint, he balks like the rest of us before the responsibilities of middle age. When, if ever, does the *enfant du siècle,* that *enfant terrible,* grow up? (Not necessarily when he grows a beard and calls himself "Mr. Papa.") Frederic Henry plunges into the Po much as Huck Finn dived into the Mississippi, but emerges to remind us even more pointedly of Fabrice del Dongo in Stendhal's *Chartreuse de Parme,* and of our great contemporary shift from transatlantic innocence to old-world experience. Certain intimations of later years are present in Hemingway's earier stories, typically Ad Francis, the slap-happy ex-champ in "The Battler." Even in "Fifty Grand," his most contrived tale, the beat-up prizefighter suffers more than he acts and wins by losing—a situation which has its corollary in the title of Hemingway's third collection, *Winner Take Nothing*. The ultimate article of his credo, which he shares with Malraux and Sartre, is the good fight for the lost cause. And the ultimate protagonist is Jesus in "Today is Friday," whose crucifixion is treated like an athletic feat, and whose capacity for taking punishment rouses a fellow feeling in the Roman soldiers. The stoic or masochistic determination to take it brings us back from Hemingway to his medium, which—although it eschews the passive voice—is essentially a receiving instrument, especially sensitized for recording a series of violent shocks.

The paradox of toughness and sensitivity is resolved, and the qualities and defects of his writing are reconciled, if we merely remember that he was—and still is—a poet. That he is not a novelist by vocation, if it were not revealed by his books, could be inferred from his well-known retort to F. Scott Fitzgerald. For Fitzgerald the rich were different—not quantitatively, because they had more money, but qualitatively, because he had a novelistic interest in manners and morals. Again, when we read André Gide's reports from the Congo, we realize what *Green Hills of Africa* lacks in the way of social or psychological insight. As W. M. Frohock has perceived, Hemingway is less concerned with human relations than with his own relationship to the universe—a concern which might have spontaneously flowered into poetry. His talents come out most fully in the texture of his work, whereas the structure tends to be episodic and uncontrived to the point of formlessness. *For Whom the Bell Tolls*, the only one of his six novels that has been carefully constructed, is in some respects an over-expanded short story. Editors rejected his earliest stories on the grounds that they were nothing but sketches and anecdotes, thereby paying incidental tribute to his sense of reality. Fragments of truth, after all, are the best that a writer can offer; and, as Hemingway has said, "Any part you make will represent the whole if it's made truly." In periods as confusing as the present, when broader and maturer representations are likely to falsify, we are fortunate if we can find authenticity in the lyric cry, the adolescent mood, the tangible feeling, the trigger response. If we think of Hemingway's temperamental kinship with E. E. Cummings, and of Cummings' "Buffalo Bill" or "Olaf glad and big," it is easy to think of Hemingway as a poet. After the attractions and distractions of timeliness have been outdated, together with categorical distinctions between the rich and the poor, perhaps he will be remembered for a poetic vision which renews our interrupted contact with the timeless elements of man's existence: bread, wine, bed, music, and just a few more of the concrete universals. When El Sordo raises his glance from the battlefield, he looks up at the identical patch of the blue sky that Henry Fleming saw in *The Red Badge of Courage* and that looked down on Prince Andrey in *War and Peace*.

Men Without Women

by Leslie Fiedler

For Fitzgerald, "love" was essentially yearning and frustration; and there is consequently little consummated genital love in his novels, though he identified himself with that sexual revolution which the Twenties thought of as their special subject. The adolescent's "kiss" is the only climax his imagination can really encompass; and despite his occasionally telling us that one or another of his characters has "taken" a woman, it is the only climax he ever realizes in a scene. In his insufferable early books, the American institution of *coitus interruptus,* from bundling to necking, a favorite national pastime, finds at last a laureate; and even in his more mature works, his women move from the kiss to the kill with only the barest suggestion of copulation between. Hemingway, on the other hand, is much addicted to describing the sex act. It is the symbolic center of his work: a scene to which he recurs when nostalgically evoking his boyhood as in "Up in Michigan"; illustrating the virtues of the sturdy poor as in *To Have and To Have Not*; reflecting on civil strife and heroism as in *For Whom the Bell Tolls*; or projecting the fantasies of a man facing old age as in *Across the River and Into the Trees*. There are, however, no *women* in his books! In his earlier fictions, Hemingway's descriptions of the sexual encounter are intentionally brutal, in his later ones unintentionally comic; for in no case, can he quite succeed in making his females human, and coitus performed with an animal, a thing, or a wet dream is either horrible or ridiculous. If in *For Whom the Bell Tolls* Hemingway has written the most absurd love scene in the history of the American novel, this is not because he lost momentarily his skill and authority; it is a give-away—a moment which illuminates the whole erotic content of his fiction.

Hemingway is only really comfortable in dealing with "men without women." The relations of father to son, of battle-companions, friends on a fishing trip, fellow inmates in a hospital, a couple of waiters preparing to close up shop, a bullfighter and his manager, a boy and a

"Men Without Women." From *Love and Death in the American Novel* by Leslie A. Fiedler (New York, 1959). Copyright © 1959 by Criterion Books, Inc. Reprinted by permission of the publishers.

gangster: these move him to simplicity and truth. Perhaps he is best of all with men who stand alone—in night-time scenes when the solitary individual sweats in his bed on the verge of nightmare, or arises to confront himself in the glass; though he is at home, too, with the Rip Van Winkle archetype, with men in flight from women. Certainly, he returns again and again to the fishing trip and the journey to the war—those two traditional evasions of domesticity and civil life. Yet he feels an obligation to introduce women into his more ambitious fictions, though he does not know what to do with them beyond taking them to bed. All his life, he has been haunted by a sense of how simple it all was once, when he could take his Indian girl into the clean-smelling woods, stretch out beside her on the pine-needles (her brother standing guard), and rise to no obligations at all. In a story called "Fathers and Sons," he writes a tribute to that prototypical, mindless, undemanding, scarcely human girl: "Could you say she did first what no one has ever done better and mention plump brown legs, flat belly, hard little breasts, well holding arms, quick searching tongue, the flat eyes, the good taste of mouth . . . and hemlock needles stuck against your belly. . . . Long time ago good. Now no good."

In Hemingway the rejection of the sentimental happy ending of marriage involves the acceptance of the sentimental happy beginning of innocent and inconsequential sex, camouflages the rejection of maturity and of fatherhood itself. The only story in which he portrays a major protagonist as having a child is the one in which he remembers with nostalgia his little Trudy of the "well holding arms, quick searching tongue," and looks forward to the time when his son will have a gun and they can pop off to the forest like two boys together. More typically he aspires to be not Father but "Papa," the Old Man of the girl-child with whom he is temporarily sleeping; and surely there is no writer to whom childbirth more customarily presents itself as the essential catastrophe. At best he portrays it as a plaguey sort of accident which forces a man to leave his buddies behind at the moment of greatest pleasure as in "Cross Country Snow"; at worst, it becomes in his fiction that horror which drives the tender-hearted husband of "Indian Camp" to suicide, or which takes Catherine away from Lieutenant Henry in *A Farewell to Arms*. Poor things, all they wanted was innocent orgasm after orgasm on an island of peace in a world at war, love-making without end in a scarcely real country to which neither owed life or allegiance.

But such a relationship can, of course, never last, as Hemingway-Nick Adams-Lieutenant Henry has always known: "They all ended the same. Long time ago good. Now no good." Only the dead woman becomes neither a bore nor a mother; and before Catherine can quite become either she must die, killed not by Hemingway, of course, but by childbirth! It is all quite sad and lovely at the end: the last kiss bestowed on what was a woman and is now a statue, the walk home through the rain. Poe himself could not have done better, though he was haunted not by the memory of a plump little Indian on the hemlock needles but a fantasy of a high-born maiden "loved with a love that was more than love" and carried away by death. In an odd way Hemingway's Trudy and Poe's Annabel Lee are sisters under the skin, projections both of a refusal to surrender the innocence of childhood—to leave seashore or woodland Eden where child loves child: projections both of the desire for death!

Had Catherine lived, she could only have turned into a bitch; for this is the fate in Hemingway's imagination of all Anglo-Saxon women. In him, the cliché of Dark Lady and Fair survives, but stood on its head, exactly reversed. The Dark Lady, who is neither wife nor mother, blends with the image of Fayaway, the exotic servant-consort reconstructed by Melville in *Typee* out of memories of an eight-year-old Polynesian girl-child. In Hemingway, such women are mindless, soft, subservient; painless devices for extracting seed without human engagement. The Fair Lady, on the other hand, who gets pregnant and wants a wedding, or uses her sexual allure to assert her power, is seen as a threat and a destroyer of men. But the seed-extractors are Indians or Latins, black-eyed and dusky in hue, while the castrators are at least Anglo-Saxon if not symbolically blond. Neither are permitted to be virgins; indeed, both are imagined as having been often possessed, though in the case of the Fair Woman promiscuity is used as a device for humiliating and unmanning the male foolish enough to have entered into a marriage with her. Through the Dark anti-virgin, on the other hand, a new lover enters into a blameless communion with the other uncommitted males who have possessed her and departed, as well as with those yet to come. It is a kind of homosexuality once-removed, the appeal of the whorehouse (Eden of the world of men without women) embodied in a single figure.

When Hemingway's bitches are Americans, they are hopeless and un-mitigated bitches; symbols of Home and Mother as remembered by the boy who could never forgive Mama for having wantonly destroyed Papa's Indian collection! Mrs. MacComber, who, in "The Short Happy Life of Francis MacComber," kills her husband for having alienated the affections of the guide with whom she is having one of her spiteful little affairs, is a prime example of the type. And "the woman," in "The Snows of Kilimanjaro" another, who with her wealth has weaned her husband from all that sustained his virility, betrayed him to aimlessness and humiliation. Like Fitzgerald's betrayed men, he can choose only to die, swoon to the death he desires at the climax of a dream of escape. But even his escape is a defeat, for in his fantasy, the plane in which he has fled lands finally at the top of Mount Kilimanjaro "wide as all the world, great, high, and unbelievably white. . . ." It is the whiteness from which the American author tries so vainly to flee, the blank whiteness of the irrational taboo in Melville, the antarctic whiteness of polar disaster in Poe, the whiteness of the White Goddess herself—who having been denied as giver of life and source of love, must be recognized as dealer of death!

The British bitch is for Hemingway only a demi-bitch, however, as the English are only, as it were, demi-Americans. Catherine is delivered from her doom by death; Brett Ashley in *The Sun Also Rises* (1926) is permitted, once at least, the gesture of herself rejecting her mythical role. But it is quite a feat at that, and Brett cannot leave off congratulating herself: "You know it makes one feel rather good deciding not to be a bitch." Yet Brett never becomes a woman really; she is mythicized rather than redeemed. And if she is the most satisfactory female character in all of Hemingway, this is because for once she is presented not as an animal or as a nightmare but quite audaciously as a goddess, the bitch-goddess with boyish bob (Hemingway is rather fond of women who seem as much boy as girl), the Lilith of the Twenties. No man embraces her without being in some sense castrated, except for Jake Barnes who is unmanned to begin with; no man approaches her without *wanting* to be castrated, except for Romero, who thinks naively that she is—or can easily become—a woman. Indeed, when Brett leaves that nineteen-year-old bullfighter, one suspects that, though she avows it is because she will not be "one of those bitches who ruins children," she is really running away because she thinks he might *make* her a woman. Certainly, Romero's insistence that she let her hair grow out has something to do with it: "He wanted me to grow my hair out. Me, with long hair. I'd look so like hell. . . . He said it would make me more womanly. I'd look a fright."

To yield up her cropped head would be to yield up her emancipation from female servitude, to become feminine rather than phallic; and this Brett cannot do. She cannot become a woman, that is to say, no matter how hard she tries, for Hemingway has imagined her—and for once he has imagined a character who convincingly wills the role he has imposed upon her. She thinks of herself as a flapper, though the word perhaps would not have occurred to her, as a member of the "Lost Generation"; but the Spaniards know her immediately as a terrible goddess, the avatar of an ancient archetype. She tries in vain to enter into the circle of Christian communion, but is always turned aside at the door; she changes her mind, she has forgotten her hat—the apparent reason never matters; she belongs to a world alien and prior to that of the Christian churches in which Jake finds a kind of peace. In Pamplona, Brett is surrounded by a group of *riau-riau* dancers, who desert a religious procession to follow her, set her up as a rival to Saint Fermin: "Some dancers formed a circle around Brett and started to dance. They wore big wreaths of white garlic around their necks. . . . They were all chanting. Brett wanted to dance but they did not want her to. They wanted her as an image to dance around." Incapable of love except as a moment in bed, Brett can bestow on her worshipers nothing more than the brief joy of a drunken ecstasy—followed by suffering and deprivation and regret. In the end, not only are her physical lovers unmanned and degraded, but even Jake, who is her priest and is protected by his terrible wound, is humiliated. For her service is a betrayal not only of his Catholic faith but of his pure passion for bullfighting and trout-fishing; and the priest of the bitch-goddess is, on the purely human level, a pimp!

.   .   .

In America, the earthly paradise for men only is associated, for obvious historical reasons, with the "West"; and it is possible to regard the classic works which we have been discussing, in this sense, as "Westerns." Despite certain superficial differences, they are, indeed, all closely related to the pulp stories, the comic books, movies, and TV shows, in which the cowhand and his side-kick ride in silent communion through a wilderness of sagebrush, rocks, and tumbleweed. The Western, understood in this way, does not even require an American setting, being reborn, for instance, in Hemingway's *The Sun Also Rises* in the improbable environs of Paris and Burguete. One must not be confused by the exotica of expatriation: bullfights, French whores, and *thés dansants*. Like the American East, Paris in Hemingway's book stands for the world of women and work, for "civilization" with all its moral complexity, and it is presided over quite properly by the bitch-goddess Brett Ashley. The mountains of Spain, on the other hand, represent the West: a world of male companions and sport, an anti-civilization, simple and joyous, whose presiding genius is that scarcely articulate arch-buddy, "good, old Bill."

For Hemingway there are many Wests, from Switzerland to Africa; but the mountains of Spain are inextricably associated in his mind with the authentic American West, with Montana whose very name is the Spanish word for the mountains that make of both isolated fast-nesses holy places. It is in the Hotel Montana that Lady Ashley ends up after her abortive romance with the bullfighter Romero; and it is from the University of Montana that Robert Jordan, hero of *For Whom the Bell Tolls*, takes off to Spanish Civil War. But it is not only a pun that binds together for Hemingway his two paradisal retreats; it is also the sacred sport of fishing. Though the monastery of Roncesvalles stands on a peak high above Jake's place of refuge, it serves only to remind Hemingway's characters of a religion now lapsed for them. "It's a remarkable place," one of them says of the monastery; but Bill, the good companion, observes mournfully, "It isn't the same as fishing, though, is it?"

It is in the trout stream of Burguete that Jake and Bill immerse themselves and are made whole again and clean; for that stream links back to the rivers of Hemingway's youth, the rivers of upper Michigan, whose mythical source is the Mississippi of Tom Sawyer and Huck Finn. "We stayed five days at Burguete and had good fishing. The nights were cold and the days were hot. . . . It was hot enough so that it felt good to wade in a cold stream, and the sun dried you when you came out. . . ." They are boys again, back on Jackson's Island, which is to say, safe in the Neverland of men without women. Jake is, in his quest for the Great Good Place, at one with almost all the other heroes of Hemingway; and somehow it is he who has managed to find again the magical stream of which the wounded, half-mad *tenente* in "Now I Lay Me" can only dream: "I would think of a trout stream I had fished along when I was a boy and fish its whole length carefully in my mind. . . . But some nights I could not fish, and on those nights I was cold-awake and said my prayers over and over. . . ." Like Jake in life, the *tenente* in his fantasy is tempted away from the pure ritual of fishing to impure thoughts of sex, reflections on "all the girls I had ever known and what kind of wives they would make." Such blasphemies bring with them their own punishment, "killed off trout-fishing and interfered with my prayers." And so he repents, "went back to trout-fishing, because I found I could remember all the streams and there was always something new about them, while the girls . . . blurred and all became the same. . . ."

In the double-barreled story, "Big Two-Hearted River," it is impossible to tell whether the hero (called Nick this time) is moving throught reality or fantasy. We can know only that he has returned, or dreams he has returned, once more to the River that is always different and always the same; and that this time he fishes it inch by inch to the edge of the tragic swamp which he will not enter. This time there is no question of choosing between fishing and praying; fishing has become clearly a prayer, or at least a ritual, in the midst of which a disguised prayer is uttered in the guise of a childish epithet. "Chrise," Nick says at one point, when he knows he is at last really *there*, "Geezus Chrise," and Hemingway tells us he says it "happily." In the dreams of the River both in "Now I Lay Me" and "Big Two-Hearted River," however, the Hemingway hero imagines himself alone; in *The Sun Also Rises*, a second self is with him, a companion to share the inarticulate sentimentality that becomes finally too embarrassing to bear, bursting with pure masculine love. " 'Old Bill' I said. 'You bum!' " And when the time for parting comes, when the bluff, immaculate honeymoon is over, when the telegram arrives to announce that the outsiders are coming, Brett and Cohn, woman and Jew, it is a third fisherman, an Englishman called

Harris, who blurts out in his drunkenness what neither Jake nor Bill can quite confess: "I've not had so much fun since the war. . . . We *have* had a good time."

What Hemingway's emphasis on the ritual murder of fish conceals is that it is not so much the sport as the occasion for immersion which is essential to the holy marriage of males. Water is the symbol of the barrier between the Great Good Place and the busy world of women.

In Our Time: A Review

by D. H. Lawrence

In Our Time calls itself a book of stories, but it isn't that. It is a series of successive sketches from a man's life, and makes a fragmentary novel. The first scenes, by one of the big lakes in America—probably Superior—are the best; when Nick is a boy. Then come fragments of war—on the Italian front. Then a soldier back home, very late, in the little town way west in Oklahoma. Then a young American and wife in postwar Europe; a long sketch about an American jockey in Milan and Paris; then Nick is back again in the Lake Superior region, getting off the train at a burnt-out town, and tramping across the empty country to camp by a trout stream. Trout is the one passion life has left him —and this won't last long.

It is a short book: and it does not pretend to be about one man. But it is. It is as much as we need know of the man's life. The sketches are short, sharp, vivid, and most of them excellent. (The "mottoes" in front seem a little affected.) And these few sketches are enough to create the man and all his history: we need know no more.

Nick is a type one meets in the more wild and woolly regions of the United States. He is the remains of the lone trapper and cowboy. Nowadays he is educated, and through with everything. It is a state of *conscious,* accepted indifference to everything except freedom from work and the moment's interest. Mr. Hemingway does it extremely well. Nothing matters. Everything happens. One wants to keep oneself loose. Avoid one thing only: getting connected up. Don't get connected up. If you get held by anything, break it. Don't be held. Break it, and get away. Don't get away with the idea of getting somewhere else. Just get away, for the sake of getting away. Beat it! "Well, boy, I guess I'll beat it." Ah, the pleasure in saying that!

Mr. Hemingway's sketches, for this reason, are excellent: so short, like striking a match, lighting a brief sensational cigarette, and it's over. His young love affair ends as one throws a cigarette end away. "It isn't fun any more."—"Everything's gone to hell inside me."

It is really honest. And it explains a great deal of sentimentality. When a thing has gone to hell inside you, your sentimentalism tries to pretend it hasn't. But Mr. Hemingway is through with the sentimentalism. "It isn't fun any more. I guess I'll beat it."

And he beats it, to somewhere else. In the end he'll be a sort of tramp, endlessly moving on for the sake of moving away from where he is. This is a negative goal, and Mr. Hemingway is really good, because he's perfectly straight about it. He is like Krebs, in that devastating Oklahoma sketch: he doesn't love anybody, and it nauseates him to have to pretend he does. He doesn't even *want* to love anybody; he doesn't want to go anywhere, he doesn't want to do anything. He wants just to lounge around and maintain a healthy state of nothingness inside himself, and an attitude of negation to everything outside himself. And why shouldn't he, since that is exactly and sincerely what he feels? If he really *doesn't* care, then why should he care? Anyhow, he doesn't.

Adventures of Nick Adams

by Philip Young

Maria: "You were too young. . . . You were too young for such
things."
Pilar: "Don't speak of such things. It is unhealthy."

For Whom the Bell Tolls

On the Place Contrescarpe at the summit of the rue Cardinal Le-
moine, Harry remembered, there was a room at the top of a tall hotel,
and it was in this room that he had written "the start of all he was to
do." Harry, dying of gangrene in a story called "The Snows of Kilimanjaro," can easily be connected with Ernest Hemingway, who wrote the
story, and Hemingway has in mind some prose which finally went into
his first significant book. This posed as a book of short stories, and was
published in New York in 1925 with the title *In Our Time.* After Hor-
ace Liveright had bowdlerized one story (an amusing but rather nasty
piece called "Mr. and Mrs. Elliot") and had cut out another completely
("Up in Michigan"), it consisted of thirteen short stories and several interchapter sketches. And it was as germinal a book for Hemingway as
ever a book for a writer. It was truly the start of everything he was ever
going to do.

The title *In Our Time* may simply have been meant to indicate, as is
commonly thought, that the material was contemporary, and to some extent representative of early twentieth-century experience. But Hemingway delights in irony and in titles that are quotations; it is almost certain that he intended here a sardonic allusion to that phrase from the
Book of Common Prayer which Neville Chamberlain was later to make
notorious: "Give peace in our time, O Lord," for the stories are mainly
of violence or evil in one form or another. It is that there is no peace in
them.

These stories alternate in the book with sixteen short "sketches," which
are of contemporary scenes and for the most part are of sickening vio-

lence. These are arranged at least roughly according to the order in which their author experienced them. With one very notable exception, however, they have no other real relation to the stories. Moreover, half of the stories are unrelated to the main interest of the book, which is the spotty but careful development of an important but little-understood character named Nick Adams.

The stories about Nick are subtly, even obscurely, organized and presented. It is not always apparent that Nick is any more than an observer of the events they relate, and his age is never mentioned. But the book cannot really be understood at all without the clear perception that the stories are arranged in the chronological order of his boyhood and young manhood, and that the volume is in large part devoted to a scrupu-lously planned account of his character, and the reasons for it. The well-known "Big Two-Hearted River," for example, cannot possibly be read with comprehension unless one understands the earlier stories. One would think it no more than it pretends to be—a story about a man fishing—and it would be, as readers have often complained, quite point-less. So the unrelated sketches and the stories not about Nick are to be more or less put aside for the moment in order that an obscure but meaningful pattern may emerge.

In Our Time opens with an "Introduction by the Author"—"Intro-duction" in the sense that it sets the tone for the whole collection; "by the Author" in that the events are particularly significant for him. This piece describes Turks and Greeks at a quai at Smyrna, where there are women who will not give up their dead babies, and soldiers who dispose of their baggage mules by breaking their legs and dumping them into the shallow water of the port to drown. And there is the harbor itself with "plenty of nice things floating around in it." "I got so I dreamed about things," says the "I" of the sketch in an apparently unimportant remark which actually looks very far ahead.

The first of the seven Nick stories, and a "typical" one, is "Indian Camp." A typical Nick Adams story is of an initiation, is the telling of an event which is violent or evil, or both, or at the very least is the de-scription of an incident which brings the boy into contact with some-thing that is perplexing and unpleasant. One of the reasons that these stories have not been generally understood is that it is not at first appar-ent that the stories are about Nick at all; they seem to be about other people, and it simply seems to happen that Nick is around. "Indian Camp," for example, tells about a doctor, Nick's father, who has to de-liver an Indian woman of a baby by Caesarean section, with a jack knife, and without anesthetic. The woman's invalid husband lies in a bunk above his screaming wife, Nick—a young boy—holds a basin for his father, and a man and three women hold the mother down until the child is successfully born. When it is over the doctor looks in the bunk above and discovers that the husband, who has been through two days of screaming, had found the operation on his wife more than he could take, and had cut his head nearly off with a razor.

"Take Nick out of the shanty, George," the doctor said.
There was no need of that. Nick, standing in the door of the kitchen, had a good view of the upper bunk when his father, the lamp in one hand, tipped the Indian's head back.

This is Nick's initiation to pain, and to the violence of birth and death. The story ends (with Nick and his father rowing off from the camp) so "objectively," so completely without comment, that it is easy to understand why readers have not seen that Nick is the central character in a book of short stories that is nearly a novel about him, so closely related are the seven stories in which he appears. Here as elsewhere Nick is not recognized as protagonist unless one perceives that the last page of the five-page piece would be irrelevant if the story were about Indians or the doctor, and also unless one looks back later to see that Hemingway has begun with this first story a pattern of contacts with violence and evil for Nick that he develops in the rest of the stories until he has built what is actually a plot. Like the later and more famous "Killers," "Indian Camp" is Nick's story, with Indians and gangsters only devices for offering him some direct experience of peace in our time.

The next two stories of the collection are called "The Doctor and the Doctor's Wife" and "The End of Something," and they give the boy's first contacts with things that are not violent, but which complicate his young life considerably because they deeply perplex. They are prefaced with two very short examples of contemporary serenity. One is of a military evacuation with a girl holding a blanket over the head of an otherwise unattended woman who is having a baby; the other is about shooting Austrians to death, one after another. The two Nick stories which follow are somewhat more placid, but they are in the nature of early lessons which can be just as unsettling to a boy as violence. "The Doctor and the Doctor's Wife" teaches Nick something about the solidarity of the male sex; more precisely, it presents him with the conclusion that he is completely dissatisfied with his mother. A workman tries to pick a fight with Doctor Adams so that he can more easily avoid paying a large bill he owes for treatment of his wife. The doctor refuses to fight, and Nick's mother, who is a Christian Scientist and will not believe that a man would do what the workman has just done, quotes Scripture. When the doctor tells Nick that his mother wants him, and Nick wants to go hunting with his father instead, the doctor says, "All right. Come on, then," and they go squirrel shooting, leaving the doctor's wife to wonder where Nick is. Nick is still a small boy, apparently (he calls his father "Daddy"), but even so it is clear that he cannot stomach his mother's naïve refusal to admit evil.

"The End of Something" is the end of a sort of love affair that an adolescent Nick has had with a girl named Marjorie. For some reason, possibly because he feels he has an unpleasant task to perform, Nick is "out of sorts." He takes the girl trolling for trout, demonstrates some knowledge of fish and fishing, and finally gets the girl to leave, perhaps for good. These two stories make up the beginning of a somewhat peculiar attitude toward women which the Hemingway hero is going to have when he is grown—grown, for example, into Robert Jordan of *For Whom the Bell Tolls.* "The End of Something" is also one of the stories of which people complain that it has no "point." This is partly because what point it does have is subtle and slight. The "Old Lady" of *Death in the Afternoon* was not alone when she complained to Hemingway, after he told her another story that ended rather mysteriously:

> And is that all of the story? Is there not to be what we called in my youth a wow at the end?
> Ah, Madame, it is years since I added the wow to the end of a story.

When the old lady insists, however, on hearing the "point," and the author gives it to her, she complains:

> This seems to me a very feeble wow.
> Madame, the whole subject is feeble and too hearty a wow would overbalance it.

The end of "The End of Something," too, is rather less of a bang than a whimper: things can suddenly go all wrong with the pleasantest of love affairs. But the real difficulty in finding the meaning of this story of *In Our Time* is the same difficulty that has been encountered with "Indian Camp": the story is like a chapter of a novel (the book has Roman numeral chapter headings in addition to the usual story titles); it is like a chapter of a novel in that it by no means has all of its meaning when taken in isolation.

The next story, which follows a peaceful one-paragraph sketch describing more shooting of soldiers who are this time coming over a "simply priceless" barricade, is called "The Three-Day Blow," and relates, among other things, how "The End of Something" felt to Nick: the end of his affair with Marjorie felt like the autumnal three-day wind storm that is blowing: "All of a sudden everything was over. . . . Just like when the three-day blows come and rip all the leaves off the trees." The story extends the pattern of the previous ones and reveals the lesson Nick learned from the preceding episode. The lesson was not pleasant at the time, and it was also disturbing. Nick accomplished his purpose in "The End of Something," and got rid of the girl, but he was not at all happy about it. It is Nick's friend Bill who reveals the lesson, remarking that after all Nick might get back into the affair again. This thought is surprising to Nick: the end "had seemed so absolute. . . . He felt happy now. There was not anything that was irrevocable." And that is about all the "point" there is to this story; Nick is learning things. And now *we* learn—learn why it was that Nick forced that break with Marjorie: she was of the "wrong" class for a doctor's son. It is again Bill who brings this out. You just can't mix oil and water, he says; it's just like it was with Bill and "Ida that works for Strattons." Here is more perplexity for Nick, and the whole business makes him extremely uncomfortable. He did it, but he doesn't want to talk about it, as he says, and it is not until this point that we can really understand why he was "out of sorts" in "The End of Something."

"The Three-Day Blow"—a many-sided story—is also a kind of tour de force, a skillful representation of the conversation of adolescent boys. Nick and Bill discuss sports, drinking, women, and literature while with affected nonchalance they get drunk on Bill's father's whisky. Thus the story also effectively documents Nick's introduction to drunkenness, a condition which is to become important for the Hemingway protagonist and is therefore worth recording.

But these are not the primary issues of the book, and with the next one-paragraph sketch called Chapter V we are abruptly taken back from the experiences which perplex to the pattern of violence, pain, and evil which began with the introduction to the book and the first story in it. This sketch describes the execution by firing squad of six cabinet ministers, and commences a crescendo which continues through the story that follows and then is climaxed by the next sketch to come, in which Nick is wounded in the war. After that event, the going is all downhill.

The center of attraction in the Chapter V sketch is a cabinet minister who is sick with typhoid. He presents a difficulty to his captors because he is too weak to support himself against the wall where he is to be executed. Finally he has to be shot separately, sitting in a puddle of water before the wall with his head on his knees.

This scene serves to introduce the story of Chapter V, called "The Battler." People who complain about the sordid nature of many of Hemingway's stories seldom if ever cite this one, perhaps because the unpleasantness is more in the undertones and in things not said than in the outer events, which, though not happy, are not entirely extraordinary in our time. But if the subtleties are drawn out and examined, "The Battler" is as unpleasant as anything its author ever wrote.

It opens with an adolescent Nick who has left home and is out on his own for the first time. He has been "riding the rods" and has just been knocked off a moving freight by a brakeman. He is limping up the tracks, heading for the next town on foot, when in crossing a bridge he sees below him in the darkness a campfire with a man sitting beside it. Nick, in answer to the man's question, reveals that he got his black eye from the brakeman:

"It must have made him feel good to bust you," the man said seriously.

In the firelight Nick makes out the stranger's face, which was queerly formed and mutilated. "It was like putty in color. Dead looking in the firelight." The man notices how the boy is staring and obligingly exhibits one cauliflower ear and a stump where the other ear should have been. This makes the boy "a little sick." The small man reveals then that he is Ad Francis, an ex-prizefighter Nick has heard of, and that he is "not quite right" in the head, is "crazy." He also demonstrates that his heart thumps only forty times a minute. A Negro named Bugs then appears with some ham and eggs, which he fries in the fire. This is a very large Negro who is extremely soft-spoken and polite to his punch-drunk companion, and to Nick, whom he addresses with oppressive deference as "Mister Adams." He makes sandwiches:

"Just close that sandwich, will you, please, and give it to Mister Francis."
Ad took the sandwich and started eating.
"Watch out how that egg runs," the negro warned. "This is for you, Mister Adams. The remainder for myself. . . . May I offer you a slice of bread dipped right in the hot ham fat?" Bugs said.

The men and the boy are eating when suddenly the situation, which has been growing somewhat uneasy, becomes extremely uncomfortable. Ad, who has been sitting in complete silence for some time, starts without provocation to pick a fight with Nick.

"You're a hot sketch. Who the hell asked you to butt in here?"
"Nobody."
"You're damn right nobody did. Nobody asked you to stay either. You come in here and act snotty about my face and smoke my cigars and drink my liquor. . . . You're going to get your can knocked off. Do you get that?"

The battler approaches the boy and the situation all of a sudden is saved by the Negro, who creeps up behind Ad, sets himself, and taps him across the base of the skull with a cloth-wrapped blackjack. Bugs then tenderly treats the unconscious man with water until his eyes close; while he lies there still unconscious the boy and the Negro talk by the fire. This, Bugs explains smiling, is the way he has to "change" Ad from time to time—"he won't remember nothing of it." As they drink coffee the Negro sketches in Ad's past, the unpalatable decline of his career and intellect, and reveals that the two men met in jail, and have been together ever since, "seeing the country."

"Right away I liked him and when I got out I looked him up. . . . I like to be with him. . . ."

After this conversation the story draws to a close. Bugs says that he should wake Ad now, and with a graceful apology he tells Nick that he'd better move along so that it won't be necessary to tap Ad again. He gives the boy directions and another sandwich to take along—"all this in a low, smooth, polite nigger voice." Nick walks out of the firelight and back to the tracks where he stops to listen:

The low soft voice of the negro was talking. Nick could not hear the words. Then he heard the little man say, "I got an awful headache, Bugs."
"You'll feel better, Mister Francis," the negro's voice soothed. "Just you drink a cup of this hot coffee."

The story ends with Nick starting away up the tracks. For the first time in the book we get an obvious word about what the *effect* of what he has seen, done, and heard has had on him: Nick has been so stunned by this twosome that he walked quite a distance before he "found he had a ham sandwich in his hand and put it in his pocket."

Clearly, like "Indian Camp," this is a story of a boy coming in contact with violence and evil, and here for a moment the force of the impression has been registered. The story is also, however, among the most suggestive of Hemingway's; there is more that is sinister and unpleasant about this gentle, large, courteous, and thoughtful blackjacking colored man than may at first meet the eye, and it can have only one very probable interpretation. The tender, motherly, male-nursing Bugs is too comfortable in the relationship with the little, demented ex-fighter. The companionship which started as a prison friendship and which is self-sufficient financially (the couple is sent money by Ad's ex-manager and wife) seems self-sufficient in other ways. Although Nick understands no more than that something is very wrong here, the reader may get the never-stated but potently suggested notion that it is not only Ad who is "queer." This theme, which crops up in five other stories and in all but one of the novels, is normally used by Hemingway as it is used here—a kind of ultimate in evil. When this atmosphere is added to the violence of getting punched off a moving train at night, and nearly being beaten by an ex-champion, and meeting a highly polished Negro hobo who habitually blackjacks his companion in sweet good humor and then nurses him back to consciousness with a love that was present even in the blow, it is not difficult to see that here is another nice thing that the Author, as in his Introduction, may get to dream about.

The sketch, Chapter VI, which immediately follows "The Battler" is the only place in the book where the interchapter material meets with the stories, and this crossing heavily marks the climax of *In Our Time*. A short paragraph reveals that Nick is in the war, tells us that he has been hit in the spine, and that he has made a "separate peace" with the enemy, is no longer fighting the war for democracy. It would be quite impossible to exaggerate the importance of this short scene, which is to be duplicated by a new protagonist named Frederic Henry in *A Farewell to Arms*, and to serve as climax for all of Hemingway's heroes for at least the next twenty-five years.

This event, Nick's serious injury, does two things for *In Our Time* and for the development of the character of the Hemingway hero. First, the wound culminates, climaxes and epitomizes the wounds he has been getting as a growing boy. Life—as we have already partly seen—was really like this up in Michigan, where Nick was already well on the way to becoming a casualty. The effect of the wounds Nick Adams has been suffering (and will suffer more of when Hemingway later goes back, with more Nick stories, to fill in) is just beginning to be hinted at: this shell that has caught Nick in the spine is of a piece with the blows he took when he saw the jack-knife Caesarean, the nearly decapitated Indian, the battler, and the blackjacking Negro, when he felt himself forced to repudiate his mother and his girlfriend, when he hit the cinders after a blow in the face on a freight train. This wound, which is to be the same wound which emasculates Jake in *The Sun Also Rises* and is to hospitalize Lt. Henry in *A Farewell to Arms*, and whose scar Col. Cantwill bears more than thirty years later in *Across the River and Into the Trees*, is significant even beyond these facts.

From here on in, the Hemingway hero is to be a wounded man, wounded not only physically but—as soon becomes clear—psychically as well. The pattern of Nick Adams' development, which exists so far only in sketchiest outline, is of a boy who, while with his father up in Michigan, and without him on his own as a hobo or with friends, has been learning some lessons about life. These lessons have more often than not proved to be the sort of experiences which could very well cripple an impressionable and sensitive boy. This is the kind of boy Nick is, as the author was shortly to make clear, and his experiences have indeed crippled him, as Hemingway was also to show, as surely as his initiation to shrapnel has done. This culminating blow in the spine is symbol and climax for a process that has been going on since we first met Nick; it is an outward and visible sign of an inward and spiritual dis-grace.

If there were no more to the event than this, it would be crucial for the development of the Hemingway protagonist, who will show the effects of his physical and psychical injuries right up to his most recent appearance. But in addition the injury has an immediate result that is as important as the wound itself. Nick's first reaction, as he waits in the hot sun for a stretcher, is to turn to his friend Rinaldi who is also hit and say: "You and me we've made a separate peace. . . . Not patriots." Of course this could be taken to mean only that for these two the war is over. But the remark "not patriots" implies much more than that. When Lt. Henry in *A Farewell to Arms* (whose friend is also named Rinaldi) is wounded and has recovered, he is unpatriotic to the point of deserting the army and society as a whole. This sketch sharply adumbrates the novel. A "good soldier" would still be fighting the war in spirit if no longer in body, but Nick has decided to hell with it. He is *not* a patriot, and at this precise point begins the long break with society that is to take the Hemingway protagonist into his expatriation in *The Sun Also Rises*, is to be repeated in *A Farewell to Arms*, is to take Hemingway himself big game hunting in the *Green Hills of Africa* and to the bullfights in *Death in the Afternoon*, and is to help him make Harry Morgan in *To Have and Have Not* an outlaw up until the moment of his death, when he mends the break and decides that he was wrong. The wound itself the hero will never lose, either as an outward or an inward scar, as long as he lives.

All of this, of course, remained to be shown. It took Hemingway several books and many years to deal with the implications of this short paragraph, and—to make the pattern clearer—he also had to fill in many of the gaps in the sketchy outline we have of Nick. Even before he patched up Nick's biographical framework, however, he added one more important story dealing with Nick's adventures to *In Our Time*, and before that a less significant and transitional one called "Cross-Country Snow."

This latter story is prefaced with a paragraph, Chapter XII, which describes a fatally struck bull who is looking straight at his conqueror in the bullfight, "roaring blood . . . and his legs caving." The story itself finds Nick recuperated from his injury, except that he cannot "telemark." The war is over, and Nick and a friend are skiing in Switzerland. Skiing (like fishing and hunting and bullfighting and drinking) is one of the things that becomes a very important personal indulgence for the Hemingway protagonist now that he is outside society. The trouble here is that by now he is also married. What is more, his wife Helen is pregnant, and they have to return to America. Nick doesn't particularly want to go, although he approves the idea of the baby. He says, somewhat hysterically, that if you can't ski, life "isn't worth while." However, he must go back, and the opposition between the fellowship and freedom of the slopes, and the mixed blessings of the United States and parenthood, are about all the meaning the story has.

But "Big Two-Hearted River" gets us back to the main show. This is a long, two-part tale which finds Nick back up in Michigan fishing. It is extraordinary for the often-remarked brilliance of the description of the fishing trip, which Nick takes alone, but there is a lot more to it than that. Yet of all the critics who have struggled with it, only Malcolm Cowley has written perceptively, and no one seems to have really understood it. Cowley sees that some of Hemingway's stories are "nightmares at noonday." "Big Two-Hearted River" is apparently a collection of sharp sensory details, he says, but if it is read closely one realizes that actually it is a kind of "waking dream." There are shadows in the story that one does not see at first; the thing goes on several levels. The fishing is an escape "from a nightmare or from realities that have become a nightmare"; it is for Nick a kind of rite, an incantation, "a spell to banish evil spirits."

Edmund Wilson, who is usually a perceptive critic, too, and who wrote an introduction for an edition of *In Our Time*, refers to the Nick we see in this story as a "boy." This slip is only apparently trivial, for to fail to see that the boy Nick is by now a man is to fail to see the development that has been taking place in his character, and how the stories are related to each other; it is to miss seeing what *kind* of man he is, and therefore, of course, what made him that way, and thus it is to read the whole piece wrongly. In order to read it rightly, one must place it firmly in the evolution of the hero Hemingway has been tracing, and see how it is the unhappy result of the quiet and sketchy but meaningful pattern the author has been building up. The story is crucial for all of Hemingway because here and for the first time we get a sustained look at the remarkable effects of what has happened to the boy who innocently accompanied his father into the Indian camp so many years ago.

At the outset of the story we are told that Nick has returned to country that had been burned out a year ago, though he hadn't known about it. He is excited over the trip because "it was a long time since Nick had looked into a stream and seen trout." Later he remembers that he and a friend of his, who is very wealthy and owns a yacht, were once going to cruise the northern shore of Lake Superior, but "that was a long time ago. . . ." Obviously, Nick is a grown man now, who has been away. He has been abroad, as we have seen, and in a war.

The opening page of the fishing trip establishes the atmosphere of shadows and tensions Cowley is conscious of. When Nick first sees the river he is going to work he sees trout "keeping themselves steady in the current with wavering fins" and others "in deep, fast moving water, slightly distorted," and at the bottom of the pool he finally can make out the big ones. The whole trip is seen as these first fish are seen. Nick goes about his business exactly as if he were a trout keeping himself steady in the current, the whole affair is seen sharply but is slightly distorted, and there are now several deep pools in Nick's personality—where in the shadows lurk the "big ones." Nick is clearly in escape from something: as he walked along he "felt happy. He felt that he had left everything behind. . . . It was all back of him." He walks to where he is going to camp, pausing to catch grasshoppers for bait along the way, and then he finds a level piece of ground and pitches his tent. Each step of the process—smoothing the ground, arranging the blankets, cutting the tent pegs and raising the canvas—is related in a regular and monotonous sequence unrelieved by even a phrase of comment or a break in the rhythm. The action goes along against a backdrop of something only dimly seen; Nick goes through the motions now in a dead-pan, one-two-three-four routine which is rather new to him, and which suggests much less that he is the mindless primitive the Hemingway hero is so often thought to be than that he is desperately protecting his mind against whatever it is that he is escaping. Finally he gets the tent up, and crawls in to test it:

Nick was happy as he crawled inside the tent. He had not been unhappy all day. This was different though. Now things were done. There had been this to do. Now it was done.

Then why it is that he is happy becomes a little clearer:

He was settled. Nothing could touch him. It was a good place to camp. He was there, in the good place.

Next Nick came out of the tent and, with the same deliberateness with which he made camp, he cooked supper. He ate, and everything was going well until suddenly "his mind was starting to work." This was all right, however, for here was a night when he could stop it (later on there will be nights when he cannot): "He knew he could choke it because he was tired enough." He falls asleep at once, and Part I of the story ends.

Part II opens on the following morning and takes Nick through a day of fishing. This fishing (and the breakfast he eats before it and the lunch he puts up for himself) is again described in terms of chronologically ordered, mechanical, deliberate movements which begin to wear on one's nervous system. But here at least there can be, with proper understanding, no objection to the pulsing monotony of the sentence-cadence: He did this. And then he did that. And then he did that, and this—and so on, paragraphs together. There can be no objection because the tense, exasperating effect of this rhythm on the reader is extraordinarily appropriate to the state of Nick's nerves, which is above all what Hemingway is trying to convey. A terrible panic is just barely under control, and the style—this is the "Hemingway style" at its most extreme—is the perfect expression of the content of the story. Nick's mechanical movements—of

cooking, casting, baiting his hook, and the rest—are the mindless movements of, say, a woman who all alone busies herself with a thorough
housecleaning on the morning after the sudden death of her husband, or
the movements of the hands of a badly shell-shocked veteran, who, while
he can control himself, is performing simple jobs over and over in a fac-
tory: this, and then that. And then that and this. When there is the
extreme excitement of a big strike from a trout the style changes
abruptly. The pressure is off the man, he is nowhere but right there
playing the fish, and then the sentences lengthen greatly and become
appropriately graceful:

> With the core of the reel showing, his heart feeling stopped with the ex-
> citement, leaning back against the current that mounted icily his thighs,
> Nick thumbed the reel hard with his left hand.

He loses this large one, and the excitement has been so great that he
feels sick and has to sit down. He does not dare "to rush his sensations
any." He tries to smoke, and when a baby trout strikes at the match he
throws into the current he laughs. This tells him that everything is all
right, he can sit there a while: "He would finish the cigarette."

Nick fishes all day, and in the course of following him around we see
that he is very frightened by the something that is lurking in the back
of his mind and that he is escaping. Also we get a picture of a man who
has a great deal in the way of outdoor "know-how" and who is superstitious as well. He knows precisely how to disengage and throw back a
small trout so it will not suffer from the experience, and he spits on his
bait for luck. Nothing much ever really happens. We learn that there is
a place where "the river narrowed and went into a swamp," and that he
doesn't want to go downstream into it today (this region has some connotation for him that is unpleasant but enigmatic, for the time being),
and the story ends with him returning to his camp encouraged, but
thinking that he has gone as far with himself as is best for one day—
"there were plenty of days coming when he could fish the swamp."

Clearly, "Big Two-Hearted River" presents a picture of a sick man, and
of a man who is in escape from whatever it is that made him sick. And
Nick apparently knows what is the matter and what he must do about it,
and must not do. He must keep physically occupied, keep his hands busy;
he must not think or he will be unable to sleep, he must not get too
excited or he will get sick, and he must not go into the swamp, which
unlike the tent, "the good place," is the bad place for him. It is as though
he were on a doctor's prescription, and indeed he is on the strictest sort of
emotional diet, but is his own nutritionist.

By now the causes of this condition should be equally clear. Fragmentary as the outline is so far it can already be seen that the causes of

the difficulties which "Big Two-Hearted River" gives symptoms of are the experiences, already partly related, of the man's past: the blows which he has suffered—physical, psychical, moral, spiritual and emotional —have damaged him. He has been complicated and wounded by what he has seen, done, and been through. This is the whole "point" of an otherwise pointless story and with it Hemingway brings his book to a close. When one extracts from the book as we have done the stories in which Nick appears one sees that actually Hemingway has plotted out a story which covers perhaps as much as twenty years in the life of Nick Adams, first leading actor in a coherent drama which he has been steadily writing ever since 1923.

To fill in some of the gaps in Nick's development Hemingway included two more stories about him in his collection *Men without Women* (1927) and three more in *Winner Take Nothing* (1933). The first four of these are relevant here; the fifth fits in more properly later. The two stories which appeared in the 1927 volume, "Ten Indians" and "The Killers," take us first to Nick's early boyhood up in Michigan, and second to the trip, very likely, he was on in "The Battler."

In the Indian story we find "Nickie"—as he is now addressed—a young boy who is being kidded about having an Indian girlfriend named Prudence Mitchell. He is pleased about this until his father, who had walked that afternoon up to the Indian camp of the story of that name, tells the boy that he saw Prudie and Frank Washburn "threshing around" in the woods. When the father comes back in the room we learn that Nick has been crying, and he tells himself, "If I feel this way my heart must be broken." He goes to bed, and in the morning he is awake a long time before he remembers this tragic fact; he has learned another lesson.

"The Killers" is more significant for the pattern developed here. The scene is laid in a lunchroom where the boy—a guess would be that he is in his teens—watches and listens to two gangsters who are waiting for an ex-prizefighter, whom they are going to kill. Nick and a colored cook are bound and gagged in the kitchen, but when the victim does not appear the "killers" release them and leave. Nick knows where the fighter, Ole Andreson, lives, and he goes to warn him. He finds that the man is aware that he is going to be murdered and will do nothing to escape his fate. He is "an awfully nice man" who thanks Nick for his interest, and declines again to do anything to protect himself; Nick leaves. Back at the lunchroom we get the "point" of the story, which clearly consists of the boy's reaction to this somewhat sickening situation. Hemingway delineates three distinct responses: the cook (who, being colored and a short-order cook to boot, presumably has trouble enough of his own) wants nothing whatsoever to do with it—" 'I don't even listen to it,' he said and shut the door." George, the counterman in the diner, is more affected: "It's a hell of a thing." But it is of course the effect the incident has had on Nick that Hemingway is interested in:

> "I'm going to get out of this town," Nick said. . . . "I can't stand to think about him waiting in the room and knowing he's going to get it. It's too damned awful."

George then gives him the advice which Nick is later to give himself: "Well . . . you better not think about it."

It is obvious here that Nick, far from being callous, is an extremely sensitive, even an abnormally sensitive, human being. Of the three reactions here it is George's which is probably most "average": Nick's is roughly as excessive as the cook's is deficient. Nick cannot "stand to think about him waiting in the room and knowing he's going to get it," and he has got to clear the town completely. If the Hemingway hero were the "bovine," "dull-witted," "wooden-headed," "heavy-footed," "village idiot" that Wyndham Lewis to much applause once made him out, then such a story as this one would be unthinkable. The contact Nick has made here with threatened violence and with evil has made its mark on him, and in "The Killers" the whole pattern of Hemingway's method of dealing with his boy is suggested in the space of a few sentences.

"The Light of the World" fills in more of this period "on the bum," and although the thing is not violent it does, like the two other incidents recording the trip Nick made, indicate that life up in Michigan might provide a boy with no better training for a proper middle-class existence in America than a war in Europe, especially if he got off on his own and saw some of it. Nick and an older friend called Tom, whom he is now traveling with, come into a small town in the evening, experience a little difficulty with a man in a bar who says that as "punks" they "stink," and go down to hang around the railroad station. The story is mainly taken up with the conversation in the waiting room, where there are five very fat prostitutes, six white men (of whom one is homosexual) and four silent Indians. This talk is fairly tough; two of the whores get into an argument ("you dried up old hot-water bottle," "you big mountain of pus"); the homosexual tries to pick up the boys; Nick is considering a woman of 250 pounds when the older Tom gets him to leave and the story ends. Nothing much has happened, except that Nick has been in close contact with things a young boy who had stayed at home would normally not meet—with things that the conventions governing the average boyhood do not define or present answers for, and that raise problems which the Scripture-quoting Mrs. Adams would not even admit, let alone deal with. In the course of the piece the boy has been in on a discussion of adultery, fornication, homosexual and heterosexual "perversions," has conversed somewhat professionally with a mammoth prostitute and has been attracted to her, and has successfully escaped the advances of what one of the men calls a "sister." One gets the idea that this little vacation spent riding freights from town to town is bringing him into contact with more than may be "good for him."

And that the experience of the war was not good for him is made patent by "A Way You'll Never Be" (in *Winner Take Nothing*, 1933). This can be placed, in time of action, between the Chapter VI sketch in which Nick was wounded in a visible way, and "Cross Country Snow," where he was about to return to the United States after the war. In this story one learns a good deal more about what made Nick the sick man that he was when, back in America, he fished the Big Two-Hearted. One also finds that the Chapter VI paragraph telescoped the relation of the wounding to quitting the war and society somewhat: after Nick was hurt he did return to a very peculiar kind of action for a time, before he finally walked out. This development also fits the experience of Lt. Henry in *A Farewell to Arms*.

"A Way You'll Never Be" (one depends on it) finds Nick in a simulated American uniform making his way by bicycle through the Austrian dead to an Italian infantry battalion, where he seeks out a captain who was a friend of his before Nick got hit. It seems that it is his job (or at least he believes this is so) to be seen in this uniform, the hope being that it will help the Italian troops to feel that the Yanks are coming. Before Paravicini, the captain, discovers something is wrong with Nick, they talk about various things, including drinking; Nick reveals that during attacks he used to get drunk on a mixture of Grappa and ether. Para says:

> "You're much braver in an attack than I am."
> "No," Nick said. "I know how I am and I prefer to get stinking. . . ."

But Nick doesn't want to talk about this. Paravicini asks him if he is really all right and Nick says that he is, except that he cannot sleep without a light in the room. And then, suddenly:

> "What's the matter? I don't seem crazy to you, do I?"
> "You seem in top-hole shape."
> "It's a hell of a nuisance once they've had you certified as nutty," Nick said.

He finally agrees to lie down for a while, his trouble starts, and now we learn what it was that he was so closely guarding himself against on the fishing trip. Para has gone, and Nick pictures a night when he was in Para's outfit; a bombardment before an attack is taking place, and Para has him lead a hysterical platoon two at a time out into the shelling to show them that it can be done. Nick has his chin strap bound tight across his mouth. Then, in a crazy way, he sees himself becoming a casualty, and then his mind goes completely:

And there was Gaby Delys, oddly enough, with feathers on; you called me
baby doll a year ago tadada you said that I was rather nice to know tadada
with feathers on, with feathers off, the great Gaby . . .

He comes out of this after a time, and is ashamed to see that various
soldiers at the Command Post have been watching him. He begins to
talk to them, explains that he is now "reformed out of the war" and is
simply "demonstrating an American uniform." But then he begins to
deliver a disquisition on grasshoppers and locusts, about which he is
very erudite. An adjutant sends for the captain and Nick goes on with
his speech. He jabbers along, a second runner goes to get Paravicini and
finally the captain comes. Nick improves somewhat, though he complains
of his helmet, the like of which he has seen "full of brains too many
times," and then he must lie down again.

He sees in his mind a bad place—a house and a long stable and a
river, which imagery is customary for him during these spells, and so
meaningful to him that almost twenty years later under the name now of
Dick Cantwell he will make a personal pilgrimage to this very place in
reality. "Every night" he had this vision, in "A Way You'll Never Be,"
and "what frightened him so that he could not get rid of it was that long
yellow house and the different width of the river." Nearly two decades
were to elapse before Hemingway was to reveal, in *Across the River and
Into the Trees,* that this scenery comes to Nick because this is the place
where he was wounded. Furthermore, nearly one decade had already
elapsed since he had described another bad place, an entrance to a
swamp which Nick feared unaccountably on the Big Two-Hearted River.
And now Hemingway gives a clue to that mystery. In the story of his
actual insanity, where in terror he relives the event of being badly shot
up, it is something about "the different width of the river" which ter-
rifies him. Later, when he is fishing the Big Two-Hearted, he dreads and
is unable to go past the spot where "the river narrowed" and went into
the swamp: the geography of the place where he was blown up is
naturally, and deeply, associated in his mind with the blow itself; it was,
as we guessed at the time, the re-experience of shrapnel that he avoided
by fishing. A change in the width of the river was what made the swamp
horrible: it is in such a way that Hemingway's work extends backward
and forward, is enigmatic and then clearer, and is integrated, and bound
tight about a core of shock.

"A Way You'll Never Be" is a discomforting as well as a revealing
story. One never knows what is going on—why the half-crazy soldier is
allowed to go about on the loose, or if he really is permitted to, or
whether or not he is actually supposed to be demonstrating this bogus
uniform, or what. But one thing is obvious: there are many things Nick
Adams cannot stand to think about at all.

And this is the end, for the moment, of the stories about him. To assemble them all chronologically and look at them very briefly makes the pattern Hemingway has been building up for his protagonist clear; the nature of Nick's character can also be made out. Here is a boy, and after that a man, who both in his early environment and later out on his own has been coming in contact with "life" in our time. Each of these contacts has been in some way violent, evil, or unsettling in that no ready answers are available. The effect of these episodes is equally apparent. They have complicated and damaged the man, who, when an ex-infantryman, is a very unwell soldier. He cannot sleep at night; when he can sleep he has nightmares. He has seen a great deal of unpleasantness, not only in the war but up in Michigan as well; and he has been wounded by these experiences in a physical way, and—since the spine blow is both fact and symbol—also in a psychical way. What has happened to Nick, in short, has made him sick.

This pattern is climaxed by rebellion, by two desertions which can already be dimly seen. One is of the respectable home Nick has left, and later—when the damage begun at Indian Camp is epitomized with a shell fragment—he deserts the whole of organized society.

Nick's character, too, has emerged. Here is a sensitive, humorless, honest, rather passive male. He is the outdoor man, who revels in the life of the senses, loves to hunt and fish and takes pride in his knowledge of how to do such things. He is virile even as an adolescent, and very conscious of his nerve; maturity has forced a reckoning with his nerves as well. Once grown, he is a man who knows his way around, but he is superstitious, too, and is developing a complex ritual whereby thinking can be stopped, the evil spirits placated and warded off.

This pattern, this process and this figure, with whatever distortions seen, were going to be known half the world over, for the relationship of this Nick to what is called the "Hemingway hero" is intimate, to put it mildly: Nick *is* the Hemingway hero, the first one. The drawing of him is very sketchy as yet, but it is true and Hemingway never takes it back to cancel half a line: the experiences of childhood, adolescence, and young manhood which shape Nick Adams have shaped as well Lt. Henry, Jake Barnes, Col. Cantwell, and several other heroes. They all have had Nick's childhood, Nick's adolescence, Nick's young manhood. It is obvious that this man is not the simple primitive he is mistaken for, and it is equally clear that a good deal of what there is of the primitive in him is a defense, which trembles and cracks, against a terror which he cannot face head on. The "escapes" are escapes from horror; the Hemingway hero, the big, tough, outdoor man, is also the wounded man, and descriptions of certain scenes in the life of Nick Adams have explained how he got that way. The man will die a thousand times before his death, but from his wounds he will never completely recover as long as Hemingway lives and records his adventures.

"A Clean, Well-Lighted Place"

by Sean O'Faolain

Here is a story, if there ever was one, with what are called "unsuspected depths." A reader might, in a tired moment, go through it casually, unaffected, or at any rate not much affected, and if asked afterwards what it was all about have some trouble in giving a meaningful answer. No reader whose sensibilities were awake could fail to be aware that he was being unusually stirred, yet even he also might have difficulty in saying what it is all about. It is something of a joke, in view of the common belief that Hemingway is a tough, laconic writer, that the reason for the difficulty is that this story by an acknowledged "realist" is as near, in its quality and its effect, to a poem as prose can be without ceasing to be honest prose. I put the word "realist" in quotation marks because these stock terms prove to be inadequate whenever we apply to literature the primal test, not what it is meaning, or saying, but of what it is doing *to us*—what kind of emotional satisfaction, or pleasure, it is giving us, of what quality, at what level. That *is* the primal test; afterward it is our secondary pleasure to "see how well he did it."

Our feelings here are, surely, mainly of pity and awe. We spend a bit of a night—by inference, many, many nights, by extension a whole life—in the company of three Spaniards, one very old, one middle-aged, one still young. The camera is angled, at a distance, on a café-front; it closes in on an old man, who says only two words; it passes from him to the two waiters; it ends with the middle-aged waiter, and it rests longest on him. With him it becomes a ray entering into his soul. Age, death, despair, love, the boredom of life, two elderly men seeking sleep and forgetfulness, and one still young enough to feel passion, cast into an hour and a place whose silence and emptiness, soon to become more silent and more empty still—it all creates in us, at first, a sad mood in which patience and futility feebly strive with one another, involve us, mesmerize us. Grimness is in the offing. Hemingway's kindness and tenderness save us from that. For Hemingway, deep down, is one of the kindest and most

tender of writers. If our final feelings here are of pity and awe it is he
who communicates them to us. I believe that Hemingway's "realism" is
merely the carapace or shell that protects, grips, holds from overspilling
a nature fundamentally emotional and tender.

I hear all through this almost-silent movie romantic horns faintly
blowing. The dew on the dust; the deaf old man; the shimmering leaves,
lit by the electric lamp among them, casting their light shadows; the girl
and the soldier, in the brass number of whose collar the whole night
glows; the silent night-guards around the corner; the youth telling the
old man, who cannot hear, that he should have died long ago; the old
man's dead wife; the young man's wife waiting for him in her hot bed;
the older waiter's empty room that he fears because it will bring more of
those thoughts of death and nothingness put into his head as he looks
across the terrace at old age drinking itself away; the gleam of fear, and
perhaps of memory, in "He had a wife once too," and in the joke about
lust (the soldier) and about unfaithfulness ("You have no fear of going
home before your usual hour?")—all concentrated in the confession, "I'm
with all those who like to stay late at the café . . . With all those who
need a *light* at night." At this point the meaning of the title becomes
clear, and in the following references to light, as one of the defenses of
man's sad soul against the Baudelaireian horror of Nothingness. As it
becomes clear, the romantic notes darken. We realize that such notes as
love, youth, the lighted leaves, the dew all carry dark shadows, that the
silence is ominous and the night inimical. Youth implies age, love is an
apple that must fall from its tree, the dew will dry, the light will go out.
How unblatantly Hemingway does it! How subdued the irony of his title
and his theme! And yet there is also a firm line and intention in it all.
He has a strength that need never be confused with violence. He is a
delicate sculptor of great muscle.

As for the craft by which Hemingway produces effects on us, transfers
a somber yet soothing mood to us, this is so artfully contrived that the
popular idea of the man is that he has no art at all—than which no art
can be more successful. Yet his art is, in fact, a very clean, well-lighted
place, practical, cool, sharp, colorless like an Italian café before the
Italian decorators moved in, entirely functional and unobtrusive. His
style is one of the most self-conscious, original, and personal styles ever
invented, based on a proper respect for words such as a man might
develop from the habit of sending cablegrams from battlefields at a high
price per word. It is hard to describe an effect of simplicity originating
in the silences and suppressions of a man of such deep feeling.

The Discovery of Evil:
An Analysis of "The Killers"

by Cleanth Brooks and Robert Penn Warren

There are certain fairly obvious points to be made about the technique of this story. It breaks up into one long scene and three short scenes. Indeed, the method is so thoroughly scenic that not over three or four sentences are required to make the transitions. The focus of narration is objective throughout, practically all information being conveyed in simple realistic dialogue. In the first scene the revelation of the mission of the gangsters is accomplished through a few significant details—the fact that the gangsters eat with gloves (to avoid leaving fingerprints), the fact that they keep their eyes on the mirror behind the bar, the fact that, after Nick and the cook have been tied up, the gangster who has the shotgun at the service window stations his friend and George out front "like a photographer arranging for a group picture"—all of this before the specific nature of their mission is made clear.

Other observations concerning the technique of the story could be made—the cleverness of composition, the subtlety with which the suspense is maintained in the first scene by the banter of the gangsters, and then is transferred to another level in the second scene. But such observations, though they are worth making, do not answer the first question which, to the reader, usually presents itself, or should be allowed to present itself. That question is: what is the story about?

The importance of giving an early answer to this question is indicated by the fact that a certain kind of reader, upon first acquaintance with the story, is inclined to feel that the story is exhausted in the first scene, and in fact that the first scene itself does not come to focus—does not have a "point." Another kind of reader sees that the first scene, with its lack of resolution, is really being used to "charge" the second scene. He finds his point in Ole Andreson's decision not to try to escape the gangsters—to stop "all that running around." This reader feels that the story should end here. He sees no relevance in the last several pages of the story, and wonders why the author has flattened out his effect. The first reader we may say, feels that "The Killers" is the gangsters' story—a story of action which does not come off. The second and more sophisticated reader interprets it as Andreson's story, though perhaps with some wonder that Andreson's story has been approached so indirectly and is allowed to trail off so irrelevantly. In other words, the reader is inclined to transpose the question, What is the story? into the question, Whose story is it? When he states the question in this way, he confronts the fact that Hemingway has left the story focused not on the gangsters, nor on Andreson, but on the boys at the lunchroom. Consider the last sentences of the story:

> "I'm going to get out of this town," Nick said.
> "Yes," said George. "That's a good thing to do."
> "I can't stand to think about him waiting in the room and knowing he's going to get it. It's too damned awful."
> "Well," said George, "you better not think about it."

So, of the two boys, it is obviously Nick on whom the impression has been made. George has managed to come to terms with the situation. By this line of reasoning, it is Nick's story. And the story is about the discovery of evil. The theme, in a sense, is the Hamlet theme, or the theme of Sherwood Anderson's "I Want to Know Why."

This definition of the theme of the story, even if it appears acceptable, must, of course, be tested against the detailed structure. In evaluating the story, as well as in understanding it, the skill with which the theme has been assimilated must be taken into account. For instance, to put a concrete question: does the last paragraph of the story illuminate for the reader certain details which had, at their first appearance, seemed to be merely casual, realistic items? If we take the theme to be the boy's discovery of evil, several such details do find their fulfillment and meaning. Nick had been bound and gagged by the gangsters, and has been released by George. To quote: "Nick stood up. He had never had a towel in his mouth before. 'Say,' he said. 'What the hell?' He was trying to swagger it off." Being gagged was something you read about in a thriller and not something which happened to you; and the first effect is one of excitement, almost pleasurable, certainly an excuse for a manly pose. (It may be worth noting in this connection that Hemingway uses the specific word *towel* and not the general word *gag*. It is true that the word *towel* has a certain sensory advantage over the word *gag*—because it suggests the coarseness of the fabric and the unpleasant drying effect on the membranes of the mouth. But this advantage in immediacy is probably overshadowed by another: the towel is sanctified in the thriller as the gag, and here that cliché of the thriller has come true.) The way the whole incident is given—"He had *never* had a towel in his mouth *before*"—charges the apparently realistic detail as a pointer to the final discovery.

Another pointer appears in the gangster's wisecrack about the movies: "You ought to go to the movies more. The movies are fine for a bright boy like you." In one sense, of course, the iterated remarks about the movies, coming just after the gangsters have made their arrangements in the lunchroom, serve as a kind of indirect exposition: the reader knows the standard reason and procedure for gang killings. But at another level, these remarks emphasize the discovery that the unreal clichés of horror have a reality.

The boy to whom the gangster speaks understands the allusion to the movies, for he immediately asks: "What are you going to kill Ole Andreson for? What did he ever do to you?"

"He never had a chance to do anything to us. He never even seen us," the gangster replies. The gangster accepts, and even glories a little in, the terms by which he lives—terms which transcend the small-town world. He lives, as it were, by a code, which lifts him above questions of personal likes or personal animosities. This unreal code—unreal because it denies the ordinary personal elements of life—has, like the gag, suddenly been discovered as real. This unreal and theatrical quality is reflected in the description of the gangsters as, after leaving the lunchroom, they go out under the arc light and cross the street: "In their tight overcoats and derby hats they looked like a vaudeville team." It even permeates their dialogue. The dialogue itself has the sleazy quality of mechanized gag and wisecrack, a kind of inflexible and stereotyped banter that is always a priori to the situation and overrides the situation. On this level the comparison to the vaudeville team is a kind of explicit summary of details which have been presented more indirectly and dramatically. On another level, the weary and artificial quality of their wit has a grimmer implication. It is an index to the professional casualness with which they accept a situation which to the boys is shocking. They are contemptuous and even bored, with the contempt and boredom of the initiated when confronted by callow lay observers. This code, which has suddenly been transferred from the artificial world of the thriller and movie into reality, is shocking enough, but even more shocking to Nick is the fact that Ole Andreson, the hunted man, accepts the code, too. Confronted by the news which Nick brings, he rejects all the responses which the boy would have considered normal: he will not call the police; he will not regard the thing as a mere bluff; he will not leave town. "Couldn't you fix it up some way?" the boy asks. "No. I got in wrong."

As we observed earlier, for a certain type of reader this is the high point of the story, and the story should end here. If one is to convince such a reader that the author is right in proceeding, one is obligated to answer his question: What is the significance of the rather tame, and apparently irrelevant, little incident which follows, the conversation with Mrs. Bell? It is sometimes said that Mrs. Bell serves to give a bit of delayed exposition or even to point the story by gaining sympathy for Andreson, who is, to her, "an awfully nice man," not at all like her idea of a pugilist. But this is not enough to satisfy the keen reader, and he is right in refusing to be satisfied with this. Mrs. Bell is, really, the Porter at Hell Gate in *Macbeth*. She is the world of normality, which is shocking now from the very fact that it continues to flow on in its usual course. To her, Ole Andreson is just a nice man, despite the fact that he has been in the ring; he ought to go out and take his walk on such a nice day. She points to his ordinary individuality, which is in contrast to the demands of the mechanical code. Even if the unreal horror of the movie thriller has become real, even if the hunted man lies upstairs on his bed trying to make up his mind to go out, Mrs. Bell is still Mrs. Bell. She is not Mrs. Hirsch. Mrs. Hirsch owns the place, she just looks after it for Mrs. Hirsch. She is Mrs. Bell.

At the door of the rooming house Nick has met Mrs. Bell—normality unconscious of the ironical contrast it presents. Back at the lunchroom, Nick returns to the normal scene, but the normal scene conscious of the impingement of horror. It is the same old lunchroom, with George and the cook going about their business. But they, unlike Mrs. Bell, know what has happened. Yet even they are scarcely deflected from their ordinary routine. George and the cook represent two different levels of response to the situation. The cook, from the first, has wanted no part of it. When he hears Nick's voice, on his return, he says, "I don't even listen to it." And he shuts the door. But George had originally suggested that Nick go see Andreson, telling him, however, "Don't go if you don't want to." After Nick has told his story, George can comment, "It's a hell of a thing," but George, in one sense at least, has accepted the code, too. When Nick says: "I wonder what he did?" George replies, with an echo of the killers' own casualness: "Double-crossed somebody. That's what they kill them for." In other words, the situation is shocking to the cook only in so far as it involves his own safety. George is aware of other implications but can dismiss them. For neither of them, does the situation mean the discovery of evil. But for Nick, it is the discovery, for he has not yet learned to take George's adult advice: "Well, you better not think about it."

The Two African Stories

by Carlos Baker

Dangerous Game

In the two stories which grew out of his African adventure, Hemingway abandoned his experimental attempt to see whether an "absolutely
true book" like *Green Hills of Africa* could compete on terms of equality
with a work of the imagination. In "The Short Happy Life of Francis
Macomber" and "The Snows of Kilimanjaro" he was still determined
to tell "the truth"; but now he was ready to invent the characters, and
to imagine the circumstances in which they were to be entangled. The
circumstances in these two stories differ markedly. At the same time they
share certain inward thematic stresses. Both deal, for example, though
in varying ways, with the achievement and loss of moral manhood. Both
look further into the now familiar men-without-women theme. The
focal point in each is the corrupt power of women and money, two of
the forces aggressively mentioned in *Green Hills of Africa* as impediments
to American writing men.

Francis Macomber does not write. He is a wealthy American sportsman
hunting the Tanganyika plains with his wife. But he must nevertheless
wrestle with problems relating to women, money, and moral manhood.
Easily the most unscrupulous of Hemingway's fictional females, Margot
Macomber covets her husband's money but values even more her power
over him. To Wilson, the Macombers' paid white hunter, who is drawn
very reluctantly into the emotional mess of a wrecked marriage, Margot
exemplifies most of the American wives he has met in the course of his
professional life. Although his perspectives are limited to the international sporting set, the indictment is severe. These women, he reflects,
are "the hardest in the world; the hardest, the cruelest, the most predatory, and the most attractive, and their men have softened or gone to
pieces nervously as they have hardened." [1] With Margot in mind, this
story might well have carried the title which Hemingway attached to
one of his despatches from Tanganyika to *Esquire*: "Notes on Dangerous

[1] *First Forty-Nine Stories* (Scribner, 1938), p. 107.

Game." The lion and the buffalo are vanquishable in a way that Margot is not.

Too much money and a woman also underlie the predicament of Harry, the dying author in "The Snows of Kilimanjaro." Having given up to a luxurious way of life by marrying wealth and then growing into complete dependence on it, he has died artistically long before his physical death. What harrows him more than the knowledge of approaching dissolution is the consciousness of all the literary riches, none of them committed to paper, which will go with him underground. Worst of all are the sharply etched memories of his former life—Liberty, Integrity, Opportunity—qualities which were all once joyously owned and now are all irrecoverably lost.

So both stories are moral tragedies tipped with irony. Macomber dies at the very moment he is commencing to live. Harry's death by gangrene symbolizes all spiritual suicides among American writers. "We destroy them in many ways," said Hemingway sardonically in *Green Hills of Africa*. "First, economically. They make money . . . increase their standard of living and . . . are caught. They have to write to keep up their establishment, their wives, and so on, and they write slop . . . not on purpose, but because it is hurried. . . . Then, once they have betrayed themselves, they justify it and you get more slop." [2] Whether through women or the desire for money, self-betrayal is what kills a man before he has lived out his time. Women and money are nothing but instruments and agents: they exist, sometimes passively, sometimes aggressively, to help the individual writer in his moral self-destruction. If he surrenders, the fault is his own. The emphasis on the value of integrity in these short stories suggests that they may be thought of as two more chapters in the history of Hemingway's artistic obsessions.

The happy life of Francis Macomber begins on the plains of East Africa and lasts about thirty minutes. The tall young man has previously disgraced himself before his wife, his British white hunter, and his gunbearers, by ignominious flight from a wounded and charging lion. Besides the loss of his own self-respect, such as it was, the extreme mental tortures of the experience include the barbed and vicious scorn of his wife, the lifted eyebrows and unspoken insults of the white hunter Wilson, and the visible disapproval of the native boys in his entourage. After a night of torment, during which he is obliged to watch his wife sleepily returning from the Englishman's tent, the party goes after buffalo. Since the wife knows her husband for a coward, she seems to have him where she wants him, which is under her thumb.

Suddenly, in the midst of the second day's shooting and with the white hunter as an aid, Macomber loses his fear. His wife at once senses and hates this change because it undermines her power. But Wilson

² *Green Hills of Africa* (Scribner, 1935), p. 23.

silently welcomes Macomber into manhood, and together they enter the tall grass after one of the wounded buffalo, leaving the wife behind them in the open car.

Almost immediately the buffalo charges. Fearless and happy in its path stands Macomber, a coward no longer, reveling in his new-found self-trust, firing repeatedly until the buffalo is practically upon him. Then a bullet from his wife's Mannlicher plows through his skull from back to front and the short happy life is over.

The great technical virtue of this story—and it is one of Hemingway's favorites possibly for this reason—is the development of an emotional intensity to a degree seldom approached in modern literature. The ragged feelings generated by the lion-incident and verbalized in a kind of noonday nightmare during the conversations in the dining-tent, are just short of unendurable to any who have entered into the spirit of the situation. Yet the tension actually mounts when, during the next day's shooting, we watch the Macombers in their contest for the possession of a soul.

Hemingway silently points up this contest by the varying positions of the central trio in their boxlike open car. On the way to the lion, Macomber sits in front, with Margot and Wilson in the back. After that day's débâcle, Macomber slumps in the back seat beside his frozen wife, Wilson staring straight ahead in the front. When Macomber has proved himself with the three buffalo, it is Margot who retreats into the far corner of the back seat, while the two men happily converse vis-à-vis before her. And finally, as Macomber kneels in the path of the buffalo, it is his wife from her commanding position in the back seat of the car who closes the contest.

Of equal interest is the skill with which Hemingway balances off the two days of hunting against each other. Part of the balance is achieved by the repetition of first effect: the buffalo, like the lion of the preceding day, is wounded, takes cover, and charges without warning. This time, however, the charge moves into a reversed moral situation. Between times, by various devices, the reader has been fully awakened to the degree of physical courage needed in facing wounded and dangerous animals. But where the lion was an instrument for the establishment and build-up of emotional tension, the oncoming horns of the buffalo are the pronged forceps for Macomber's moral birth. Two different worlds fill the two adjacent days.

The yardstick figure, Wilson, a fine characterization, is the man free of woman and of fear. He is the standard of manhood towards which Macomber rises, the cynical referee in the nasty war of man and wife, and the judge who presides, after the murder, over the further fortunes of Margot Macomber. His dominance over the lady is apparent from the moment she sees him blast the lion from which Macomber ran. But he accepts that dominance only because it is thrust upon him. The kind of dominance he really believes in, and would gladly transfer to the suffering husband, is well summarized in a passage from Shakespeare's *Henry IV* which he quotes as a kind of tribute to Macomber's own loss of fear on the second day: "By my troth, I care not; a man can die but once; we owe God a death . . . and let it go which way it will, he that dies this year is quit for the next. . . ." [3] Having brought out, almost by accident, this attitude he has lived by, Wilson is much embarrassed. "But he had seen men come of age before and it always moved him. It was not a matter of their twenty-first birthday."

Those who object that true manhood is not necessarily proved by one's ability to face a charging beast may be doing Hemingway an injustice. Dramatically speaking, physical courage is often a convenient and economical way of symbolizing moral courage. We are glad, for example, at Hamlet's skill and bravery with the foils. In this African story Hemingway is obviously dealing with both kinds of courage, though, as the situation naturally requires, it is the physical aspect which is stressed.

It would be possible to argue that Francis and Margot Macomber are more nearly caricatures than people. The probability is that the line-drawing in their portraits is the natural consequence of an approach to material chosen for its intrinsic emotional intensity rather than to provide opportunity for depth of characterization. One rightly concludes that they are as fully developed as they need to be for the purposes of the narrative. Further development might well impede the quick march of the short, happy life.

Still it is true that Hemingway's satirical steam, never far below the surface, tends to erupt whenever he deals with leisure-class wastrels. The tendency is visible, for example, in the accounts of Cohn and Campbell in *The Sun Also Rises*. In *Death in the Afternoon*, the author scornfully watches the bored, sport-shod, ex-collegians who leave the *corrida* early. The same reaction appears in his sketches of the wealthy yachtsmen in Key West harbor in *To Have and Have Not*, part of which was written at the same time as the Francis Macomber story. It is almost as if, throughout the Depression, Hemingway had resolutely set himself to oppose F. Scott Fitzgerald's temperamental conviction that the rich are glamorous. As Hemingway's scorn rises, the satirical steam-pressure rises with it, and the result is often close to caricature.

If the story of the Macombers is judged, as it probably should be judged, in terms of an experiment in the development of emotional intensity, it is hard to match. As an instance of tragic irony, exemplified in overt action, it has its faults. But dullness is not one of them, and formally speaking the story is very nearly perfect.[4]

[3] *First Forty-Nine Stories*, p. 131. The speech is made by one of the country soldiers, Feeble, in *II Henry IV*, III, ii, 253-258.

[4] This story was Hemingway's choice for *This Is My Best*, ed. Whit Burnett (New York: Dial Press, 1942). He so wrote Mr. Burnett 5/12/42.

Lesson from the Master

"The Snows of Kilimanjaro" is a tragedy of a different order.[5] Its setting is the final afternoon and evening in the second life of a writer named Harry, dying of gangrene in a camp near the edge of the Tanganyika plains country. "Francis Macomber" proceeds through and by action; "The Snows of Kilimanjaro" is an experiment in the psychology of a dying man. Like *Across the River and Into the Trees,* it contains almost no overt physical activity, though much is implied. Judged in terms of its intention, it is a triumphant piece of writing.

Hemingway's own experiences on safari help to account for the origin of the story. The undeveloped germ of "Francis Macomber" may have been the occasion when Hemingway and M'Cola entered a bush-covered area in pursuit of a lion they heard but never saw. The general outline of "The Snows" was almost certainly suggested by Hemingway's own grave illness, the flight out of the plains country, and the distant view of the enormous, snow-capped mountain of Kilimanjaro. During the flight east, and no doubt also during the period of treatment in Nairobi —his head aching and his ears ringing from the effects of emetine[6]— Hemingway had ample time to reflect on a topic which would naturally occur to him in such a situation: the death of a writer before his work is done. As in "Francis Macomber," however, most of the other circumstances of the story were invented.

Like Hemingway, the writer Harry in the story has been "obsessed" for years with curiosity about the idea of death. Now that it is close he has lost all curiosity about it, feeling only a "great tiredness and anger" over its inexorable approach. "The hardest thing," Hemingway had written in *Green Hills of Africa,* is for the writer "to survive and get his work done." [7] This is mainly because the time available is so short and the temptations not to work are so strong. Harry has succumbed to the temptation *not* to work at his hard trade. Now his time is over, and possessive death moves in.

The story gains further point and poignancy from another obsession of Harry's, the deep sense of his loss of artistic integrity. Despite the difference between London and Tanganyika and the lapse of time between the rule of Edward VII and that of Edward VIII, Hemingway's position is that of Henry James in "The Lesson of the Master." Harry's

[5] Hemingway once told Roger Linscott that he regarded "The Snows" as "about as good as any" of his work in short fiction. "On the Books," *New York Herald Tribune Book Review,* December 29, 1946. The story was finished April 7, 1936. Hemingway to Maxwell Perkins, 4/9/36.
[6] The principal alkaloid of ipecac, used as a specific in the treatment of amoebic dysentery.
[7] *Green Hills of Africa,* p. 27.

dying self-accusations are well summarized in the words of Henry St. George, the sold-out novelist in James's novelette. "Don't become in your old age what I have in mine," he tells his young admirer, "—the depressing, the deplorable illustration of the worship of false gods . . . the idols of the market; money and luxury . . . everything that drives one to the short and easy way." [8] The dying writer in Hemingway's story has followed that route, and his creeping gangrene is the mark he bears. He knows that he has traded his former integrity for "security and comfort," destroying his talent by "betrayals of himself and what he believed in." Henry or Harry, England or Africa, the lesson of the master is the same: Thou shalt not worship the graven images of false gods, or acquiesce in the "life of pleasant surrender." [9]

Although the setting of "The Snows of Kilimanjaro" is as completely un-Jamesian as one could possibly imagine, the themes which the story engages are, on the contrary, very close to those regularly employed by James. "I wonder," Hemingway once ruminated, "what Henry James would have done with the materials of our time." One answer might be that a modern James would simply have altered the costume, the idiom, and certain of the social customs which appear in his novels. The themes, which were matters of greatest interest to him, would scarcely need to be changed at all. The close reader of "The Snows of Kilimanjaro" easily recognizes and responds to its theme of confrontation. The dying writer is far different from the ghost of his former self, the young, free, unsold writer who took all Europe as his oyster and was seriously devoted to his craft. As he listens to the self-accusations with which Harry tortures himself, the reader acquainted with James may be reminded of "The Jolly Corner." In this long story, an American expatriate, returning to his old and empty house at the corner of the American city street, finds himself beleaguered by the ghost of his other self, the ravaged man he might have been had he not followed his aesthetic ambitions to Europe. Although the situation is obviously quite the opposite of the one detailed by Hemingway, the strategy is exactly the same: the face-to-face confrontation of an ego by an alter ego. The corner of the tent in which Harry finally dies might well be called, in an echo of Jamesian irony, the jolly corner.

The story is technically distinguished by the operation of several natural symbols. These are non-literary images, as always in Hemingway, and they have been very carefully selected so as to be in complete psychological conformity with the locale and the dramatic situation. How would the ideas of death and of immortality present themselves in the disordered imagination of a writer dying of gangrene as he waits for the plane which is supposed to carry him out of the wilderness to the Nairobi hospital? The death symbols were relatively easy. Every night beasts of

[8] James, *Works* (New York: 1907-17, Scribner), XV, 36.
[9] *First Forty-Nine Stories*, pp. 158, 160, 162.

prey killed grazing animals and left the pickings to those scavengers of carrion, the vultures and the hyenas.

It is entirely natural that Harry, whose flesh is rotting and noisome—is, in fact, carrion already—should associate these creatures with the idea of dying. As he lies near death in the mimosa shade at the opening of the story, he watches the birds obscenely squatting in the glare of the plain. As night falls and the voice of the hyena is heard in the land, the death image transfers itself from the vultures to this other foul devourer of the dead. With the arrival of his first strong premonition of death, which has no other form than "a sudden, evil-smelling emptiness," Harry finds without astonishment that the image of the hyena is slipping lightly along the edge of the emptiness. "Never believe any of that," he tells his wife, "about a scythe and a skull." His mind has been far away in the days of his former life in Paris, and now it has come back to Africa. "It can be two bicycle policemen as easily, or be a bird. Or it can have a wide snout like a hyena." Death has just come as if to rest its head on the foot of the cot, the direction from which the infection will rise up towards the vital center. Presently it moves in on him, crouching on his chest so that he cannot breathe.

Harry's dying directive, "Never believe any of that about a scythe and a skull," is an important commentary on Hemingway's own habitual approach to the development of natural symbols. He is prepared to use, where they conform to the requirements of an imaginary situation, any of the more ancient symbols—whether the threes and nines of numerology, or the weight of the Cross in Christian legend. But the scythe and the skull, though ancient enough, simply do not fit the pattern of Harry's death and are therefore rejected in favor of the foul and obscene creatures which have now come to dominate Harry's imagination.

Like the death-symbol, the image for immortality arises "naturally" out of the geography and psychology of the situation. When the weight leaves his chest, Harry finds that morning has brought the rescue plane to carry him to Nairobi. Helping him aboard, Old Compton says that they will have to refuel at Arusha. Everything happens as if it were actually happening—the take-off, the long view of the plain and its moving animals, the hills and forests to the east passing in slow majesty under the belly of the plane—until it dawns on Harry that for some reason they have by-passed Arusha. At first he does not know why. But as the plane emerges from a rain-squall, he suddenly sees ahead of them the square top of Kilimanjaro, "wide as all the world," incredibly white in the sun. "Then he knew that there was where he was going."

While he was in Africa Hemingway learned that the Masai name for the western summit of Kilimanjaro is Ngàje Ngài, which means "House of God." The association between mountainous terrain and the idea of home was, however, already an old one in his mind. He had used it symbolically in the Burguete section of *The Sun Also Rises* and also,

far more extensively, in the Abruzzi and the Montreux locale-images of
A Farewell to Arms. "I will lift up mine eyes to the hills," runs the
Psalm, "from whence cometh my help." But there is no psalm-quoting
in the back-to-earth dénouement of Hemingway's story. There is only
Harry's wife Helen, waking in the middle of the night down in the
flat plains-country, far from Kilimanjaro, and calling to a husband who
does not answer.[10]

Anyone interested in the methods by which the patterns of experience
are translated to the purposes of art should find abundant materials for
study in the three stories—nonfiction and fiction—which grew out of
Hemingway's African expedition. The foreword to *Green Hills of Africa*
contains an implicit question. Given a country as interesting as Africa,
and given the shape of a month's hunting-action there, and given
the author's determination to tell only the truth, the question then
becomes this: Can such a book possibly compete on equal terms with a
work of the imagination? The answer is that it certainly can *compete,*
provided always that the narrative is managed by a very skilled writer
who takes both truth (the truth of "the way it was") and beauty (the
extremely careful formal construction) as his watchwords. Yet the experiment proved also that the narrator who takes no liberties with the
actual events of his experience, who tells things exactly as they were,
who invents nothing and suppresses nothing important, will place himself at a real disadvantage in the competition. He gives the opposition
too large a handicap. Good as *Green Hills of Africa* is in two respects
(verisimilitude and architectonics), it lacks the intensities which Heming-

---

[10] Psalm 121 might do as a motto for Hemingway's collected works. In this connection one might suggest the relevance of the leopard whose enigmatic history is given
in the epigraph of "The Snows." "Close to the Western summit of Kilimanjaro there
is the dried and frozen carcass of a leopard. No one has explained what the leopard
was seeking at that altitude." Professor C. C. Walcutt (*Explicator* 7, April 1949, item
43) sees that the conflict in Harry's life is between a "fundamental moral idealism"
and an "aimless materialism." When Harry looks at Kilimanjaro, he sees it as a
symbol of Truth, the "undefined ideal for which he has struggled." The leopard is
then a symbol for Harry's moral nature. It is not logical that Harry "should continue
to believe in man and search for meanings and values"; neither is it logical that "a
purely predatory leopard" should have reached that snowy height. What drove the
leopard there "is the same sort of mystery as the force that keeps idealism alive in
Harry. All reason, in a predatory world, is against it, but there it is." Following this
line, Professor E. W. Tedlock, Jr. finds that both leopard and mountain symbolize
the preservation of integrity for Harry. "In contrast to the leopard's dried and frozen
carcass," writes Tedlock, "Harry lies dying of a gangrenous leg amid heat and glare."
The physical infection is the result of carelessness—"the typical analogue of a spiritual
infection also resulting from carelessness." Thus we have both physical and spiritual
decay, while leopard and mountain represent those things which do not decay.
Professor Tedlock calls attention to how often Harry's thoughts "revert . . . to experiences in high altitudes and snow." Physically, this can be explained as the
"feverish man's desire for coolness and relief"; spiritually the reversions represent a
longing for "the good life" of the past. (See *Explicator* 8, October 1949, item 7).

way was able to pack into "The Short Happy Life of Francis Macomber," and it cannot possibly achieve anything like the genuine pathos of "The Snows of Kilimanjaro." The experience of wrestling with the African book, followed as it was with the writing of the two short stories, undoubtedly established one aesthetic principle very firmly in Hemingway's mind. The highest art must take liberties, not with the truth but with the modes by which the truth is projected. This was no new discovery for Hemingway. But for any serious writer it is a useful maxim.

The Death of Love in *The Sun Also Rises*

by Mark Spilka

> She turns and looks a moment in the glass,
> Hardly aware of her departed lover;
> Her brain allows one half-formed thought to pass:
> "Well now that's done: and I'm glad it's over."
> When lovely woman stoops to folly and
> Paces about her room again, alone,
> She smoothes her hair with automatic hand,
> And puts a record on the gramophone.
>
> T. S. Eliot, *The Waste Land*

One of the most persistent themes of the Twenties was the death of love in World War I. All the major writers recorded it, often in piecemeal fashion, as part of the larger postwar scene; but only Hemingway seems to have caught it whole and delivered it in lasting fictional form. His intellectual grasp of the theme might account for this. Where D. H. Lawrence settles for the shock of war on the Phallic Consciousness, or where Eliot presents assorted glimpses of sterility, Hemingway seems to design an extensive parable. Thus, in *The Sun Also Rises*, his protagonists are deliberately shaped as allegorical figures: Jake Barnes and Brett Ashley are two lovers desexed by the war; Robert Cohn is the false knight who challenges their despair; while Romero, the stalwart bullfighter, personifies the good life which will survive their failure. Of course, these characters are not abstractions in the text; they are realized through the most concrete style in American fiction, and their larger meaning is implied only by their response to immediate situations. But the implications are there, the parable is at work in every scene, and its presence lends unity and depth to the whole novel.

Barnes himself is a fine example of this technique. Cut off from love by a shell wound, he seems to suffer from an undeserved misfortune. But as most readers agree, his condition represents a peculiar form of emotional impotence. It does not involve distaste for the flesh, as with Lawrence's crippled veteran, Clifford Chatterley; instead Barnes lacks

---

the power to control love's strength and durability. His sexual wound, the result of an unpreventable "accident" in the war, points to another realm where accidents can always happen and where Barnes is equally powerless to prevent them. In Book II of the novel he makes this same comparison while describing one of the dinners at Pamplona: "It was like certain dinners I remember from the war. There was much wine, an ignored tension, and a feeling of things coming that you could not prevent happening." This fear of emotional consequences is the key to Barnes' condition. Like so many Hemingway heroes, he has no way to handle subjective complications, and his wound is a token for this kind of impotence.

It serves the same purpose for the expatriate crowd in Paris. In some figurative manner these artists, writers, and derelicts have all been rendered impotent by the war. Thus, as Barnes presents them, they pass before us like a parade of sexual cripples, and we are able to measure them against his own forbearance in the face of a common problem. Whoever bears his sickness well is akin to Barnes; whoever adopts false postures, or willfully hurts others, falls short of his example. This is the organizing principle in Book I, this alignment of characters by their stoic qualities. But stoic or not, they are all incapable of love, and in their sober moments they seem to know it.

For this reason they feel especially upset whenever Robert Cohn appears. Cohn still upholds a romantic view of life, and since he affirms it with stubborn persistence, he acts like a goad upon his wiser contemporaries. As the narrator, Barnes must account for the challenge he presents them and the decisive turn it takes in later chapters. Accordingly, he begins the book with a review of Cohn's boxing career at Princeton. Though he has no taste for it, college boxing means a lot to Cohn. For one thing, it helps to compensate for anti-Semitic treatment from his classmates. More subtly, it turns him into an armed romantic, a man who can damage others in defense of his own beliefs. He also loves the pose of manhood which it affords him and seems strangely pleased when his nose is flattened in the ring. Soon other tokens of virility delight him, and he often confuses them with actual manliness. He likes the idea of a mistress more than he likes his actual mistress; or he likes the authority of editing and the prestige of writing, though he is a bad editor and a poor novelist. In other words, he always looks for internal strength in outward signs and sources. On leaving Princeton, he marries "on the rebound from the rotten time . . . in college." But in five years the marriage falls through, and he rebounds again to his present mistress, the forceful Frances Clyne. Then, to escape her dominance and his own disquiet, he begins to look for romance in far-off countries. As with most of his views, the source of this idea is an exotic book:

He had been reading W. H. Hudson. That sounds like an innocent occu-
pation, but Cohn had read and reread "The Purple Land." "The Purple
Land" is a very sinister book if read too late in life. It recounts splendid
imaginary amourous adventures of a perfect English gentleman in an in-
tensely romantic land, the scenery of which is very well described. For a man
to take it at thirty-four as a guidebook to what life holds is about as safe as
it would be for a man of the same age to enter Wall Street direct from a
French convent, equipped with a complete set of the more practical Alger
books. Cohn, I believe, took every word of "The Purple Land" as literally as
though it had been an R. G. Dun report.

Cohn's romanticism explains his key position in the parable. He is
the last chivalric hero, the last defender of an outworn faith, and his
function is to illustrate its present folly—to show us, through the ab-
surdity of his behavior, that romantic love is dead, that one of the great
guiding codes of the past no longer operates. "You're getting damned
romantic," says Brett to Jake at one point in the novel. "No, bored,"
he replies, because for this generation boredom has become more plau-
sible than love. As a foil to his contemporaries, Cohn helps to reveal why
this is so.

Of course, there is much that is traditional in the satire on Cohn.
Like the many victims of romantic literature, from Don Quixote to Tom
Sawyer, he lives by what he reads and neglects reality at his own and
others' peril. But Barnes and his friends have no alternative to Cohn's
beliefs. There is nothing here, for example, like the neat balance between sense and sensibility in Jane Austen's world. Granted that Barnes
is sensible enough, that he sees life clearly and that we are meant to
contrast his private grief with Cohn's public suffering, his self-restraint
with Cohn's deliberate self-exposure. Yet, emasculation aside, Barnes has
no way to measure or control the state of love; and though he recognizes
this with his mind and tries to act accordingly, he seems no different
from Cohn in his deepest feelings. When he is alone with Brett, he wants
to live with her in the country, to go with her to San Sebastian, to go
up to her room, to keep her in his own room, or to keep on kissing her
—though he can never really act upon such sentiments. Nor are they
merely the yearnings of a tragically impotent man, for eventually they
will lead Barnes to betray his own principles and to abandon self-respect,
all for the sake of Lady Ashley. No, at best he is a restrained romantic,
a man who carries himself well in the face of love's impossibilities, but
who seems to share with Cohn a common (if hidden) weakness.

The sexual parade continues through the early chapters. Besides Cohn
and his possessive mistress, there is the prostitute Georgette, whom
Barnes picks up one day "because of a vague sentimental idea that it
would be nice to eat with some one." Barnes introduces her to his friends
as his fiancée, and as his private joke affirms, the two have much in
common. Georgette is sick and sterile, having reduced love to a simple

monetary exchange; but like Barnes, she manages to be frank and forth-
right and to keep an even keel among the drifters of Paris. Together
they form a pair of honest cripples, in contrast with the various pre-
tenders whom they meet along the Left Bank. Among the latter are
Cohn and Frances Clyne, the writer Braddocks and his wife, and Robert
Prentiss, a rising young novelist who seems to verbalize their phoniness:
"Oh, how charmingly you get angry," he tells Barnes. "I wish I had
that faculty." Barnes' honest anger has been aroused by the appearance
of a band of homosexuals, accompanied by Brett Ashley. When one of
the band spies Georgette, he decides to dance with her; then one by one
the rest follow suit, in deliberate parody of normal love. Brett herself
provides a key to the dizzy sexual medley. With a man's felt hat on her
boyish bob, and with her familiar reference to men as fellow "chaps,"
she completes the distortion of sexual roles which seems to characterize
the period. For the war, which has unmanned Barnes and his contemporaries, has turned Brett into the freewheeling equal of any man. It
has taken her first sweetheart's life through dysentery and has sent her
present husband home in a dangerous state of shock. For Brett these
blows are the equivalent of Jake's emasculation; they seem to release
her from her womanly nature and expose her to the male prerogatives
of drink and promiscuity. Once she claims these rights as her own, she
becomes an early but more honest version of Catherine Barkley, the
English nurse in Hemingway's next important novel, *A Farewell to
Arms*. Like Catherine, Brett has been a nurse on the Italian front and
has lost a sweetheart in the war; but for her there is no saving interlude
of love with a wounded patient, no rigged and timely escape through
death in childbirth. Instead she survives the colossal violence, the disruption of her personal life, and the exposure to mass promiscuity, to confront a moral and emotional vacuum among her postwar lovers. With
this evidence of male default all around her, she steps off the romantic
pedestal, moves freely through the bars of Paris, and stands confidently
there beside her newfound equals. Ironically, her most recent conquest,
Robert Cohn, fails to see the bearing of such changes on romantic love.
He still believes that Brett is womanly and therefore deeply serious about
intimate matters. After their first meeting, he describes her as "absolutely
fine and straight" and nearly strikes Barnes for thinking otherwise; and
a bit later, after their brief affair in the country, he remains uncon-
vinced "that it didn't mean anything." But when men no longer command respect, and women replace their natural warmth with masculine
freedom and mobility, there can be no serious love.

Brett does have some respect for Barnes, even a little tenderness,
though her actions scarcely show abiding love. At best she can affirm
his worth and share his standards and perceptions. When in public, she
knows how to keep her essential misery to herself; when alone with
Barnes, she will express her feelings, admit her faults, and even display

good judgment. Thus her friend, Count Mippipopolous, is introduced to Barnes as "one of us." The count qualifies by virtue of his war wounds, his invariable calmness, and his curious system of values. He appreciates good food, good wine, and a quiet place in which to enjoy them. Love also has a place in his system, but since he is "always in love," the place seems rather shaky. Like Jake and Brett and perhaps Georgette, he simply bears himself well among the postwar ruins.

The count completes the list of cripples who appear in Book I. In a broader sense, they are all disaffiliates, all men and women who have cut themselves off from conventional society and who have made Paris their permanent playground. Jake Barnes has introduced them, and we have been able to test them against his stoic attitudes toward life in a moral wasteland. Yet such life is finally unbearable, as we have also seen whenever Jake and Brett are alone together, or whenever Jake is alone with his thoughts. He needs a healthier code to live by, and for this reason the movement in Book II is away from Paris to the trout stream at Burguete and the bull ring at Pamplona. Here a more vital testing process occurs, and with the appearance of Bill Gorton, we get our first inkling of its nature.

Gorton is a successful writer who shares with Barnes a love for boxing and other sports. In Vienna he has helped to rescue a splendid Negro boxer from an angry and intolerant crowd. The incident has spoiled Vienna for him, and as his reaction suggests, the sports world will provide the terms of moral judgment from this point onward in the novel. Or more accurately, Jake Barnes' feelings about sports will shape the rest of the novel. For with Hemingway, the great outdoors is chiefly a state of mind, a projection of moral and emotional attitudes onto physical arenas, so that a clear account of surface action will reproduce these attitudes in the reader. In "Big Two-Hearted River," for example, he describes Nick Adams' fishing and camping activities along a trout stream in Michigan. His descriptions run to considerable length, and they are all carefully detailed, almost as if they were meant for a fishing manual. Yet the details themselves have strong emotional connotations for Nick Adams. He thinks of his camp as "the good place," the place where none of his previous troubles can touch him. He has left society behind him, and as the story begins, there is even a burnt town at his back, to signify his disaffiliation. He has also walked miles to reach an arbitrary camp site, and this is one of the ways in which he sets his own conditions for happiness and then lives up to them. He finds extraordinary pleasure, moreover, in the techniques of making coffee and pitching camp, or in his responses to fishing and eating. In fact, his sensations have become so valuable that he doesn't want to rush them: they bring health, pleasure, beauty, and a sense of order which is sorely missing in his civilized experience; they are part of a healing process, a private and imaginative means of wiping out the damages of civilized life. When this process is described with elaborate attention to surface detail, the effect on the reader is decidedly subjective.

The same holds true, of course, for the fishing trip in *The Sun Also Rises*. As Barnes and Gorton approach "the good place," each item in the landscape is singled out and given its own importance. Later the techniques of fishing are treated with the same reverence for detail. For like Nick Adams, these men have left the wasteland for the green plains of health; they have traveled miles, by train and on foot, to reach a particular trout stream. The fishing there is good, the talk free and easy, and even Barnes is able to sleep well after lunch, though he is usually an insomniac. The meal itself is handled like a mock religious ceremony: "Let us rejoice in our blessings," says Gorton. "Let us utilize the fowls of the air. Let us utilize the produce of the vine. Will you utilize a little, brother?" A few days later, when they visit the old monastery at Roncevalles, this combination of fishing, drinking, and male cameraderie is given an edge over religion itself. With their English friend, Harris, they honor the monastery as a remarkable place, but decide that "it isn't the same as fishing"; then all agree to "utilize" a little pub across the way. At the trout stream, moreover, romantic love is given the same comparative treatment and seems sadly foolish before the immediate joys of fishing:

> It was a little past noon and there was not much shade, but I sat against the trunk of two of the trees that grew together, and read. The book was something by A. E. W. Mason, and I was reading a wonderful story about a man who had been frozen in the Alps and then fallen into a glacier and disappeared, and his bride was going to wait twenty-four years exactly for his body to come out on the moraine, while her true love waited too, and they were still waiting when Bill came up [with four trout in his bag]. . . . His face was sweaty and happy.

As these comparisons show, the fishing trip has been invested with unique importance. By sticking closely to the surface action, Barnes has evoked the deeper attitudes which underly it and which make it a therapeutic process for him. He describes himself now as a "rotten Catholic" and speaks briefly of his thwarted love for Brett; but with religion defunct and love no longer possible, he can at least find happiness through private and imaginative means. Thus he now constructs a more positive code to follow: as with Nick Adams, it brings him health, pleasure, beauty and order, and helps to wipe out the damage of his troubled life in Paris.

Yet somehow the code lacks depth and substance. To gain these advantages, Barnes must move to Pamplona, which stands roughly to Burguete as the swamp in "Big Two-Hearted River" stands to the trout stream. In the latter story, Nick Adams prefers the clear portion of the river to its second and more congested heart:

> In the swamp the banks were bare, the big cedars came together overhead, the sun did not come through, except in patches; in the fast deep water, in the half light, the fishing would be tragic. In the swamp fishing was a tragic adventure. Nick did not want it. . . . There were plenty of days coming when he could fish the swamp.

The fishing is tragic here because it involves the risk of death. Nick is not yet ready for that challenge, but plainly it will test his manhood when he comes to face it. In *The Sun Also Rises* Barnes makes no such demands upon himself; but he is strongly attracted to the young bull-fighter, Pedro Romero, whose courage before death lends moral weight to the sportsman's code.[1]

So Pamplona is an extension of Burguete for Barnes: gayer and more festive on the surface, but essentially more serious. The spoilers from Paris have arrived, but (Cohn excepted) they are soon swept up by the fiesta: their mood is jubilant, they are surrounded by dancers, and they sing, drink and shout with the peasant crowd. Barnes himself is among fellow *aficionados;* he gains "real emotion" from the bullfights and feels truly elated afterwards. Even his friends seem like "such nice people," though he begins to feel uneasy when an argument breaks out between them. The tension is created by Brett's fiancé, Mike Campbell, who is aware of her numerous infidelities and who seems to accept them with amoral tolerance. Actually he resents them, so that Cohn (the perennial Jewish scapegoat) provides him with a convenient outlet for his feelings. He begins to bait him for following Brett around like a sick steer.

Mike's description is accurate enough. Cohn is always willing to suffer in public and to absorb insults for the sake of true love. On the other hand, he is also "ready to do battle for his lady," and when the chance finally comes, he knocks his rivals down like a genuine knight-errant. With Jake and Mike he has no trouble, but when he charges into Pedro's room to rescue Brett, the results are disastrous: Brett tells him off, the bullfighter refuses to stay knocked down, and no one will shake hands

---

[1] Hemingway's preoccupation with death has been explained in various ways: by his desire to write about simple, fundamental things; by his "sado-masochism"; or more fairly and accurately, by his need to efface an actual war wound, or to supplant the ugly, senseless violence of war with ordered, graceful violence. Yet chiefly the risk of death lends moral seriousness to a private code which lacks it. The risk is arbitrary; when a man elects to meet it, his beliefs take on subjective weight and he is able to give meaning to his private life. In this sense, he moves forever on a kind of imaginative frontier, where the opposition is always Nature, in some token form, where the stakes are always manliness and self-respect, and where death invests the scene with tragic implications. In *The Sun Also Rises*, Romero lives on such a frontier, and for Barnes and his friends he provides an example of just these values.

with him at the end, in accord with prep-school custom. When Brett remains with Pedro, Cohn retires to his room, alone and friendless.

This last encounter is the highpoint of the parable, for in the Code Hero, the Romantic Hero has finally met his match. As the clash between them shows, there is a difference between physical and moral victory, between chivalric stubborness and real self-respect. Thus Pedro fights to repair an affront to his dignity; though he is badly beaten, his spirit is untouched by his opponent, whereas Cohn's spirit is completely smashed. From the beginning Cohn has based his manhood on skill at boxing, or upon a woman's love, never upon internal strength; but now, when neither skill nor love supports him, he has bludgeoned his way to his own emptiness. Compare his conduct with Romero's, on the following day, as the younger man performs for Brett in the bull ring:

> Everything of which he could control the locality he did in front of her all that afternoon. Never once did he look up. . . . Because he did not look up to ask if it pleased he did it all for himself inside, and it strengthened him, and yet he did it for her, too. But he did not do it for her at any loss to himself. He gained by it all through the afternoon.

Thus, where Cohn expends and degrades himself for his beloved, Romero pays tribute without self-loss. His manhood is a thing independent of women, and for this reason he holds special attractions for Jake Barnes.

By now it seems apparent that Cohn and Pedro are extremes for which Barnes is the unhappy medium. His resemblance to Pedro is clear enough: they share the same code, they both believe that a man's dignity depends on his own resources. His resemblance to Cohn is more subtle, but at this stage of the book it becomes grossly evident. Appropriately enough, the exposure comes through the knockout blow from Cohn, which dredges up a strange pre-war experience:

> Walking across the square to the hotel everything looked new and changed. . . . I felt as I felt once coming home from an out-of-town football game. I was carrying a suitcase with my football things in it, and I walked up the street from the station in the town I had lived in all my life and it was all new. They were raking the lawns and burning leaves in the road, and I stopped for a long time and watched. It was all strange. Then I went on, and my feet seemed to be a long way off, and everything seemed to come from a long way off, and I could hear my feet walking a great distance away. I had been kicked in the head early in the game. It was like that crossing the square. It was like that going up the stairs in the hotel. Going up the stairs took a long time, and I had the feeling that I was carrying my suitcase.

Barnes seems to have regressed here to his youthful football days. As he moves on up the stairs to see Cohn, who has been asking for him, he still carries his "phantom suitcase" with him; and when he enters Cohn's room, he even sets it down. Cohn himself has just returned from the fight with Romero: "There he was, face down on the bed, crying. He had on a white polo shirt, the kind he'd worn at Princeton." In other words, Cohn has also regressed to his abject college days: they are both emotional adolescents, about the same age as the nineteen-year-old Romero, who is the only real man among them. Of course, these facts are not spelled out for us, except through the polo shirt and the phantom suitcase, which remind us (inadvertently) of one of those dreamlike fantasies by the Czech genius, Franz Kafka, in which trunks and youthful clothes are symbols of arrested development. Yet there has already been some helpful spelling out in Book I, during a curious (and otherwise pointless) exchange between Cohn and another expatriate, the drunkard Harvey Stone. After first calling Cohn a moron, Harvey asks him to say, without thinking about it, what he would rather do if he could do anything he wanted. Cohn is again urged to say what comes into his head first, and soon replies, "I think I'd rather play football again with what I know about handling myself, now." To which Harvey responds: "I misjudged you. . . . You're not a moron. You're only a case of arrested development."

The first thought to enter Cohn's mind here has been suppressed by Barnes for a long time, but in Book II the knockout blow releases it: more than anything else, he too would like to "play football again," to prevent that kick to his head from happening, or that smash to the jaw from Cohn, or that sexual wound which explains either blow. For the truth about Barnes seems obvious now: he has always been an emotional adolescent. Like Nick Adams, he has grown up in a society which has little use for manliness; as an expression of that society, the war has robbed him of his dignity as a man and has thus exposed him to indignities with women. We must understand here that the war, the early football game, and the fight with Cohn have this in common: they all involve ugly, senseless, or impersonal forms of violence, in which a man has little chance to set the terms of his own integrity. Hence for Hemingway they represent the kinds of degradation which can occur at any point in modern society—and the violence at Pamplona is our current sample of such degradation. Indeed, the whole confluence of events now points to the social meaning of Jake's wound, for just as Cohn has reduced him to a dazed adolescent, so has Brett reduced him to a slavish pimp. When she asks for his help in her affair with Pedro, Barnes has no integrity to rely on; he can only serve her as Cohn has served her, like a sick romantic steer. Thus, for love's sake, he will allow her to use him as a go-between, to disgrace him with his friend, Montoya, to corrupt Romero, and so strip the whole fiesta of significance. In the next book he will even run to her rescue in Madrid, though by then he can at least recognize his folly and supply his own indictment: "That was it. Send a girl off with one man. Introduce her to another to go off with him. Now go and bring her back. And sign the wire with love. That was it all right." It seems plain, then, that Cohn and Brett have given us a peacetime demonstration, postwar style, of the meaning of Jake's shell wound.

At Pamplona the demonstration continues. Brett strolls through the fiesta with her head high, "as though [it] were being staged in her honor, and she found it pleasant and amusing." When Romero presents her with a bull's ear "cut by popular acclamation," she carries it off to her hotel, stuffs it far back in the drawer of the bed-table, and forgets about it. The ear was taken, however, from the same bull which had killed one of the crowd a few days before, during the dangerous bull-run through the streets; later the entire town attended the man's funeral, along with drinking and dancing societies from nearby communities. For the crowd, the death of this bull was a communal triumph and his ear a token of communal strength; for Brett the ear is a private trophy. In effect, she has robbed the community of its triumph, as she will now rob it of its hero. As an *aficionado,* Barnes understands this threat too well. These are decadent times in the bull ring, marred by false aesthetics; Romero alone has "the old thing," the old "purity of line through the maximum of exposure": his corruption by Brett will complete the de-cadence. But mainly the young fighter means something more personal to Barnes. In the bull ring he combines grace, control and sincerity with manliness; in the fight with Cohn he proves his integrity where skill is lacking. His values are exactly those of the hunter in "Francis Macomber," or of the fisherman in *The Old Man and the Sea.* As one of these few remaining images of independent manhood, he offers Barnes the comfort of vicarious redemption. Brett seems to smash this as she leaves with Pedro for Madrid. To ward off depression, Barnes can only get drunk and retire to bed; the fiesta goes on outside, but it means nothing now: the "good place" has been ruined.

As Book III begins, Barnes tries to reclaim his dignity and to cleanse himself of the damage at Pamplona. He goes to San Sebastian and sits quietly there in a cafe, listening to band concerts; or he goes swimming there alone, diving deep in the green waters. Then a telegram from Brett arrives, calling him to Madrid to help her out of trouble. At once he is like Cohn again, ready to serve his lady at the expense of self-respect. Yet in Madrid he learns to accept, emotionally, what he has al-ways faintly understood. As he listens to Brett, he begins to drink heavily, as if her story has driven home a painful lesson. Brett herself feels "rather good" about sending Pedro away: she has at least been able to avoid being "one of these bitches that ruins children." This is a moral triumph for her, as Barnes agrees; but he can scarcely ignore its implications for himself. For when Brett refuses to let her hair grow long for Pedro, it means that her role in life is fixed: she can no longer reclaim her lost womanhood; she can no longer live with a fine man without destroying him. This seems to kill the illusion which is behind Jake's suffering throughout the novel: namely, that if he hadn't been wounded, if he had somehow survived the war with his manhood intact, then he and Brett would have become true lovers. The closing lines confirm his total disillusionment:

> "Oh, Jake," Brett said, "we could have had such a damned good time together."
> Ahead was a mounted policeman in khaki directing traffic. He raised his baton. The car slowed suddenly pressing Brett against me.
> "Yes," I said, "Isn't it pretty to think so?"

"Pretty" is a romantic word which means here "foolish to consider what could *never* have happened," and not "what can't happen now." The signal for this interpretation comes from the policeman who directs traffic between Brett's speech and Barnes reply. With his khaki clothes and his preventive baton, he stands for the war and the society which made it, for the force which stops the lovers' car, and which robs them of their normal sexual roles. As Barnes now sees, love itself is dead for their generation. Even without his wound, he would still be unmanly, and Brett unable to let her hair grow long.

Yet according to the opening epigraphs, if one generation is lost and another comes, the earth abides forever; and according to Hemingway himself, the abiding earth is the novel's hero. Perhaps he is wrong on this point, or at least misleading. There are no joyous hymns to the seasons in this novel, no celebrations of fertility and change. The scenic descriptions are accurate enough, but rather flat; there is no deep feeling in them, only fondness, for the author takes less delight in nature than in outdoor sports. He is more concerned, that is, with baiting hooks and catching trout than with the Irati River and more pleased with the grace and skill of the bullfighter than with the bull's magnificence. In fact, it is the bullfighter who seems to abide in the novel, for surely the bulls are dead like the trout before them, having fulfilled their roles as beloved opponents. But Romero is very much alive as the novel ends. When he leaves the hotel in Madrid, he "pays the bill" for his affair with Brett, which means that he has earned all its benefits. He also dominates the final conversation between the lovers, and so dominates the closing section. We learn here that his sexual initiation has been completed and his independence assured. From now on, he can work out his life alone, moving again and again through his passes in the ring, gaining strength, order, and purpose as he meets his own conditions. He provides no literal prescription to follow here, no call to bullfighting as the answer to Barnes' problems; but he does provide an image of integrity, against which Barnes and his generation are weighed and found wanting. In this sense, Pedro is the real hero of the parable, the final moral touchstone, the man whose code gives meaning to a world where love and religion are defunct, where the proofs of manhood are difficult and scarce, and where every man must learn to define his own moral conditions and then live up to them.

The Biological Trap

by Ray B. West, Jr.

I

Ernest Hemingway's first three important works were *In Our Time*, a collection of curiously related short stories; *The Sun Also Rises*, his first serious and successful novel; and *A Farewell to Arms*. All three deal with the same subject: the condition of man in a society upset by the violence of war. The short stories, while complete (almost idyllic) within themselves, take on an added dimension when viewed against the animal-cruelty of the connecting war scenes. *The Sun Also Rises*, although set in the postwar period, is conditioned by the wartime disability of its principal figure, Jake Barnes. But the setting for *A Farewell to Arms* is the war itself, and the romance of Frederic Henry and Catherine Barkley, their attempt to escape the war and its resulting chaos, is a parable of twentieth-century man's disgust and disillusionment at the failure of civilization to achieve the ideals it had been promising throughout the nineteenth century. While the relation of one story to another in *In Our Time* is more or less arbitrary, while the meandering action of the ex-patriots' excursion into Spain in *The Sun Also Rises* is at most emblematic, the sequence of events in *A Farewell to Arms* is ordered and logical to an extreme which (outside of Henry James) is the exception in the American novel.

As a matter of fact, the physical form of *A Farewell to Arms* more nearly resembles the drama than it does the majority of American works of fiction. It is composed of five separate books, each composed of a series of scenes, and each scene broken into sections which might be likened to stage direction and dialogue. Thus, in section one we have the introduction of all major characters, the general war setting, and a statement of the problems involved; in section two the development of the romance between Frederic and Catherine; in section three, the retreat

"The Biological Trap." (Originally titled "Ernest Hemingway: *A Farewell to Arms*.") From *The Art of Modern Fiction* by Ray B. West, Jr. (New York: Holt, Rinehart & Winston, Inc., 1949). Copyright © 1949. First published in *The Sewanee Review*, LV (Winter, 1945), 120-135. Reprinted by permission of the author, Holt, Rinehart & Winston, Inc., and *The Sewanee Review*.

at Caporetto and the decision of Frederic to escape the chaos of war; in section four, the supposed escape, the rowing of Frederic and Catherine across the lake into Switzerland; and in section five, the hope of sanctuary which, through a reversal reminiscent again of the drama, comes to a climax in the ironic scene of Catherine's death while giving birth to their child.

As Robert Penn Warren has pointed out (*Kenyon Review*: Winter, 1947), *A Farewell to Arms*, while not a religious book in the usual sense, depends upon a consciousness of the religious problems of our time. Its subject is the search for truth—for ethical standards to replace those which seemed impossible under the wartime conditions which it depicts. The use of the Christian religion is not, however, confined to the conventional uses of the ordinary religious novel, in which the characters are evaluated according to their acceptance or rejection of orthodox views. Rather, it is ironically implied, for instance, that Catherine, who is repeatedly portrayed as one with no orthodox religious sense, is really on the side of the priest, whose orthodoxy is beyond question. It is implied, too, that the priest's religious sensibility, like the sensibility of all of the participants in the novel's action, is heightened by the events of the war. After the difficult summer, during which Frederic was confined in the hospital, all of the men in his group have been softened. "Where are all the good old priest-baiters?" Rinaldi asks. "Do I have to bait this priest alone without support?" Frederic could see that the baiting which had gone on earlier did not touch the priest now. In talking with the priest he makes a distinction which is important to our interpretation of all the characters: even the priest is now not only technically a Christian, he is more like Our Lord. "It is," Frederic says, "in defeat that we become Christians."

On the other hand, it is not merely the humility of defeat, but the result of active participation (a firsthand acquaintance with the objective facts instead of the abstract theories of warfare) which makes all the difference. Outward forms divorced from action do not suffice, as when the soldier under Frederic refuses to believe that the Austrians were going to attack, because, as he said, "What has been done this summer cannot have been done in vain." Frederic thinks:

> I was always embarrased by the words sacred, glorious, and sacrifice and the expression in vain. We had heard them, sometimes standing in the rain almost out of earshot, so that only the shouted words came through, and had read them, on proclamations that were slapped up by billposters over other proclamations, now for a long time, and I had seen nothing sacred, and the things that were glorious had no glory and the sacrifices were like the stockyards at Chicago if nothing was done with the meat except to bury it. There were many words that you could not stand to hear and finally only the names of places had dignity.

When the words became separated from the acts they were meant to describe, then they meant nothing; the slaughter of war was less than the slaughter of animals in the stockyard. The names of places had dignity because the places still had some objective reality. Likewise, the acts of Rinaldi when he is practicing his craft, of Dr. Valentini (but not of the incompetent physicians), have dignity because they are done surely and skillfully—to some purpose. The early stages of Frederic and Catherine's courtship were like moves in a chess game or a game of bridge; later it became something different, so different that even the outward form of marriage could make no difference. Catherine asks: "What good would it do to marry now? We're really married. I couldn't be any more married." Even the war, when Frederic was no longer participating, "seemed as far away as the football games of some one else's college." No activity has meaning unless the participant is emotionally involved; this is the real test, like the names of places. There is Christianity and there are true Christians. There is incompetence and competence. There is marriage and there is true love. In a story in *In Our Time*, we have the picture of a bullfighter who is defeated and derided by the crowd, but he is really "The Undefeated" (the title of the story), because he is only outwardly not inwardly defeated. As we have seen, in "The Short Happy Life" even death does not defeat Francis Macomber, for it is in death that he triumphs.

But what is the real distinction between the failures—the defeated—and the *genuine* men and women in the novel—what critics have come to call "the initiated"? Rinaldi (who is one of them) says to Frederic at the time when Frederic returns to the front: "You puncture me when I become a great Italian thinker. But I know many things I can't say." Frederic, when he is talking to the priest after his return from the hospital, says: "I never think and yet when I begin to talk I say the things I have found out in my mind without thinking." There are times when Catherine "feels" immoral, but most of the time she "feels" that her love is sanctified. The peasants and the defeated soldiers have wisdom because they are not misled by the empty forms. Hemingway seems to be saying, like William Wordsworth, that such men are by circumstance closer to reality—and thus to wisdom. In the book which followed *A Farewell to Arms—Death in the Afternoon*—Hemingway says, "Morals are what you feel good after." Brett Ashley in *The Sun Also Rises* decides to give up a love affair because it makes her *feel* good "deciding not to be a bitch." The test of morals is the unadulterated sensibility—the sensibility not misled by the empty forms of patriotism, religion, and love: the sensibility of Rinaldi when he does not attempt to be a great Italian thinker; the sensibility of Dr. Valentini, who knows at once what is to be done and does it without quibble and consultation; the sensibility of the peasants; the sensibility of Catherine, who learns from

her love for Frederic that it is all right, who says: "Everything we do
seems so innocent and simple. I can't believe we do anything wrong."
Even the sensibility of Frederic, which is the developing moral sense of
the novel, is superior to Rinaldi's because it has greater scope—the
surgeon is happy only when he is working. "I know more than you,"
Rinaldi says, and Frederic agrees with him. "But you will have a better
time. Even with remorse you will have a better time."

It is this limiting quality in Frederic's character which points to the
principal problem of the novel. Rinaldi calls it remorse. Frederic cannot
completely escape the forms of his early training, though he makes a
systematic progress throughout the book. Before he was wounded he had
attempted to accept Catherine's philosophy that death is the end, but his
experience seemed to prove otherwise, for in her antireligious position
Catherine is as orthodox as the priest. Frederic says: "I felt myself rush
bodily out of myself and out and out and out and all the time bodily in
the wind. I went out swiftly, all of myself, and I knew I was dead and
that it had all been a mistake to think you just died." This is Hemingway's mysticism which triumphed in *For Whom the Bell Tolls* and which
was at its lowest ebb in his curious little essay "A Natural History of the
Dead." Frederic does not love God, but he is afraid of him in the night
sometimes. Because he does not "belong," he and Catherine cannot find
sanctuary in the church the evening they are waiting for the train, though
an Italian couple does. Yet Frederic is much more anxious about the
absence of the marriage ceremony than Catherine, and when the child
is born dead he is disturbed because it had not been baptized. The
limitations of Frederic's religious sensibility (a symbol for the religious
sensibility of our time) are depicted in two scenes, the first in his failure
to visit the home of the priest at Abruzzi, where "You would like the
people and though it is cold it is clear and dry"; the second is the incident at the church:

There were streetcar tracks and beyond them was the cathedral. It was
white and wet in the mist. We crossed the tram tracks. On our left were the
shops, their windows lighted, and the entrance to the galleria. There was a
fog in the square and when we came close to the front of the cathedral it
was very big and the stone was wet.
"Would you like to go in?"
"No," Catherine said. We walked along. There was a soldier standing with
his girl in the shadow of one of the stone buttresses ahead of us and we
passed them. They were standing tight up against the stone and he had put
his cape around her.
"They're like us," I said.
"Nobody is like us," Catherine said. She did not mean it happily
"I wish they had some place to go."
"It mightn't do them any good."

"I don't know. Everybody ought to have some place to go."
"They have the cathedral," Catherine said.

(XXIII, 157)

Catherine and Frederic have a hotel room (the "lost generation"), while the Italian soldier and his girl have the cathedral; the priest has his cold, clear, dry country; the atheists have their houses of prostitution. The priest's country appeals to Frederic, and he is sorry he did not visit it while he was on leave:

> I had wanted to go to Abruzzi. I had gone to no place where the roads were frozen and hard as iron, where it was clear cold and dry and the snow was dry and powdery and hare-tracks in the snow and the peasants took off their hats and called you Lord and there was good hunting. I had gone to no such place but to the smoke of cafés and nights when the room whirled and you needed to look at the wall to make it stop, nights in bed, drunk, when you know that that was all there was, and the strange excitement of waking and not knowing who it was with you, and the world all unreal in the dark and so exciting that you must resume again unknowing and not caring in the night, sure that this was all and all and all and not caring.

III, 13)

Here is the symbol of Frederic's predicament, a key passage, since it represents the religious contrast. The priest's religion is his clear, cold country; Catherine's religion is her love, which, as Count Greffi says, "is a religious feeling," or, as Catherine tells Frederic: "You're my religion. You're all I've got." Frederic is the modern hero, lost between two worlds, the world of tradition and certainty which he cannot wholly relinquish, and the exciting but uncertain world of the twentieth century, where you only occasionally find something substantial to look at to make everything stop whirling, where you live for the moment, giving yourself up to sensations, for it is through the senses that you discover truth: the strong man giving equal odds to his weaker opponent, the boxer, the hunter, the bullfighter, the soldier, and the lover; the strong man aware that the only order in the universe is that which he himself can supply, but aware, too, that such order is transitory, that perhaps the highest possible values consist in pure sensation which seeks out new order and a stoicism which transcends physical defeat.

II

At the beginning Frederic wavers between reason and sensibility, between formal religion and "true" Christianity, between the empty forms of love and true love. He has been thrust into a world of violent action in which choice is eventually to become necessary. An English critic has called Frederic "a uriously passive hero," but this is true only in the sense that Thomas Mann's Herr Friedemann was passive. The Hemingway hero is, theoretically, passive, because he is allied to nature through his unreason, but his particular dilemma usually has all the appearances of active seeking.

Frederic's relationship to Catherine in Book I is like a game of bridge where you pretend to be playing for stakes, but do not know what the stakes are. At the end of the section Frederic is wounded, but not seriously. It is the first hint that what he had called "the picturesque front" was capable of becoming something else. It is a foreshadowing of the retreat at Caporetto.

In Book II the action takes place in the American hospital at Milan, and almost at once we know that the formal relationship (love like a bridge game or a game of chess) has ended. Frederic thinks:

> God knows I had not wanted to fall in love with her. I had not wanted to fall in love with any one. But God knows I had and I lay on the bed in the room of the hospital in Milan and all sorts of things went through my head but I felt wonderful . . .
>
> (XIV, 100)

We are introduced to the incompetent doctors and to the professional patriots like Ettore. Frederic, although he cannot reject Ettore as completely as Catherine, does reject his own decoration, because he knows that he is not a hero. The silver medal repeats the pattern of the empty form. A new action is suggested in this book by Catherine's fear of death. She is afraid of the rain, she says, and when pressed by Frederic for an explanation, admits that it is because she sometimes sees herself dead in it. Frederic is unbelieving. "And sometimes I see you dead in it," she adds. "That's more likely," Frederic says. "No it's not, darling. Because I can keep you safe. I know I can. But nobody can help themselves." Here is one of the secrets of the passivity of Hemingway's characters. Later in the section, when Catherine admits that she is going to have a baby:

> "You aren't angry are you, darling?"
> "No."
> "And you don't feel trapped?"
> "Maybe a little. But not by you."
> "I didn't mean by me. You must be stupid. I meant trapped at all."
> "You always feel trapped biologically."
>
> (XXI, 148)

"Biologically," in the Hemingway world, convers just about everything; there is nothing you can do about life but accept it with stoicism.

This is an anticipation of the final scenes in the novel, but Frederic, fortunately, did not realize how final the trap was:

> Poor, poor dear Cat. And this was the price you paid for sleeping together. This was the end of the trap. This was what people got for loving each other.
>
> (XLI, 341-342)

In this book, however, the threat is taken only seriously enough to provoke discussion of death and the conditions of man's dying. Frederic has quoted the line, "The coward dies a thousand deaths, the brave but one"; Catherine replies: "The brave dies perhaps two thousand deaths if he's intelligent. He simply doesn't mention them."

There is an indication that Frederic is very little different from Catherine in his fear of death. They are in a café and it is raining. He quotes Andrew Marvell: "But at my back I always hear/Time's wingéd chariot hurrying near." He wants to talk facts. Where will the baby be born? Catherine refuses (stoically) to discuss it. "Then don't worry, darling," she tells him. "You were fine until now and now you're worrying."

The tone of this section suggests death, but the reader does not know, any more than do Catherine and Frederic, whose death it is to be. Frederic returns to the front, where there are rumors of a new attack by the Austrians. Catherine awaits the time when she will have her baby. Both are, in a sense, trapped—trapped by the war, by their love, and (though they are unaware of it) by death.

At the very beginning of Book III we are introduced to the town of Caporetto. Frederic "remembered it as a little white town with a campanile in a valley. It was a clean little town and there was a fine fountain in the square." This is where the summer fighting has ended. One of Hemingway's most constant symbols of the goal which his heroes seek is—to utilize the title of one of his stories—a "Clean, Well-Lighted Place." War has undoubtedly destroyed the "clean little town," but this is just an additional indication of war's ugliness. Caporetto is the point where the Austrians succeed in breaking through and turning Frederic's "picturesque front" into a machine of destruction. There are only isolated examples of decency and order in the retreat; the whole atmosphere is one of anarchy and confusion.

Malcolm Cowley has likened Frederic's plunge into the river to escape execution as a baptism—a symbol of Frederic's entering the world of the initiated, but this is true only in so far as it refers to his decision (his rebirth) concerning the war. The chapters preceding, where Frederic returns to the front and meets his old comrades, indicate both how much he had learned through his stay at the hospital (the baptism of love) and how much the members of his company have learned through the difficult fighting of the summer (their baptism of fire), but the final consecration does not come until later when Frederic is confronted by love and death at the same time. The retreat does, however, represent a major phase in his initiation. Frederic is in the position of the fat gray-haired little lieutenant-colonel whom the carabinieri were questioning at the bridge:

> The questioners had all the efficiency, coldness and command of themselves of Italians who are firing and are not being fired on.
> "Your brigade?"
> He told them.
> "Regiment?"
> He told them.
> "Why are you not with your regiment?"
> He told them.
> "Do you not know that an officer should be with his troops?"
> He did.
> That was all. Another officer spoke.
> "It is you and such as you that have let the barbarians onto the sacred soil of the fatherland."
> "I beg your pardon," said the lieutenant-colonel.
> "It is because of treachery such as yours that we have lost the fruits of victory."
> "Have you ever been in a retreat?" the lieutenant-colonel asked.
>
> (XXX, 239)

The military police are firing but are not being fired on. They are like religious persons who have never been tempted, condemning the sinner who has succumbed; the police have the hollow shell of patriotism, using such phrases as "the sacred soil of the fatherland" and "the fruits of victory," but it is punctured by the lieutenant-colonel's simple question: "Have you ever been in a retreat?" The carabiniere's brave words have no relation to the reality of the situation, while the condemned man's question goes right to the heart of it. Frederic rationalizes his own situation as follows:

> You had lost your cars and your men as a floorwalker loses the stock of his department in a fire. There was, however, no insurance. You were out of it now. You had no more obligation. If they shot the floorwalker after a fire in the department store because they spoke with an accent they had always had, then certainly the floorwalkers would not be expected to return when the store opened again for business. They might seek other employment; if there was any other employment and the police did not get them.
> Anger was washed away in the river along with any obligation. Although that ceased when the carabiniere put his hands on my collar. I would like to have had the uniform off *although I did not care much about the outward forms* [our italics] I had taken off the stars, but that was for convenience. It was no point of honor. I was not against them. I was through. I wished

them all the luck. There were the good ones, and the brave ones, and the calm ones, and the sensible ones, and they deserved it. But it was not my show any more and I wished this bloody train would get to Mestre and I would eat and stop thinking. I would have to stop.

(XXXII, 248)

The fighter obeys the rules until they are suspended or no longer enforced; then he gets out of the ring (cf. Margot Macomber in "The Short Happy Life"). With the retreat at Caporetto, the Austrian front ceased to be "the picturesque front"; it is no longer subject to the traditional rules of "honorable" warfare. Frederic, too, for the time being ceases to be the "curiously passive hero." He cannot escape the war until he escapes from Italy with Catherine, and to escape is to struggle.

Yet according to the standards of Frederic Henry's world, such a decision is in itself dangerous. His reasoning is too pat, his assurance too great. The determination to struggle becomes a kind of "tragic flaw"— a brash modern pride which tempts fate as the occupants of Stephen Crane's little boat tempt the seven mad gods of the sea. Hemingway hints at this in the beginning of Book IV. In the hotel at Stresa, where Frederic went to find Catherine, the barman asks him questions about the war.

"Don't talk about the war," I said. The war was a long way off. Maybe there wasn't any war. There was no war here. Then I realized it was over for me. But I did not have the feeling that it was really over. I had the feeling of a boy who thinks of what is happening at a certain hour at the schoolhouse from which he has played truant.

(XXXIV, 262)

The war is not over. Even after the successful effort to leave Italy and enter Switzerland, the war (which is really a symbol for the chaos of nature—the biological trap) catches up with Frederic and Catherine. It is significant that Frederic's reason tells him he can escape—that he *has* escaped; his sensibility suggests that he is only playing truant. Frederic felt like a masquerader in his civilian clothes. That is to say, in the modern sense, all happiness is a form of truancy. The months in Switzerland were idyllic. Even the snow came late, almost as though Frederic had ordered nature's cooperation.

The trap is sprung in Book V. Catherine's confinement is difficult, and the birth when it does come is finally performed through a Caesarean operation. The child is born dead. Catherine herself dies soon afterward. Yet, though it is Catherine who dies, *A Farewell to Arms* is not her tragedy. Unlike Francis Macomber and unlike Manuelo in "The Undefeated," she does not *become* admirable in her dying; she *remains* admirable according to the rules of decorum which Hemingway has set up:

The nurse opened the door and motioned with her finger for me to come. I followed her into the room. Catherine did not look up when I came in. I went over to the side of the bed. The doctor was standing by the bed on the opposite side. Catherine looked at me and smiled. I bent down over the bed and started to cry.

"Poor darling," Catherine said very softly. She looked gray.

"You're all right, Cat," I said. "You're going to be all right."

"I'm going to die," she said; then waited and said, "I hate it."

I took her hand.

"Don't touch ‚me," she said. I let go of her hand. She smiled. "Poor darling. You touch me all you want."

"You'll be all right, Cat. I know you'll be all right."

"I meant to write you a letter to have if anything happened, but I didn't do it."

"Do you want me to get a priest or any one to come and see you?"

"Just you," she said. Then a little later, "I'm not afraid. I just hate it."

(XLI, 353-354)

Catherine had had the perception of death early, but it had come to Frederic only since learning of the doctor's fears. During the operation he thought she was dead: "Her face was gray." Catherine knows intuitively that she is going to die. Frederic senses it, but his reason will not allow him to accept it, as she does, as "just a dirty trick."

I knew she was going to die and I prayed that she would not. Don't let her die. Oh, God, please don't let her die. I'll do anything for you if you won't let her die. Please, please, please, dear God, don't let her die. Dear God, don't let her die. Please, please, please don't let her die. God please make her not die. I'll do anything you say if you don't let her die. You took the baby but don't let her die. That was all right, but don't let her die. Please, please, dear God, don't let her die.

(XLI, 353)

Frederic's hope that he could prevent her from dying is as illusory as his belief that he could escape the war by signing a separate peace. In a sense, Frederic is a depiction of the narrator's figure in "The Open Boat," who, when he realizes that there is no tangible thing to hoot, feels the desire to confront a personification and indulge in pleas. It isn't until he has accepted the terrible reality of Catherine's death that he is truly initiated: "It was like saying good-by to a statue." This is the biological trap—sprung. Catherine has been right from the beginning. Early in the novel, in speaking of her English lover who was killed in France, she says: "I thought perhaps he couldn't stand it and then of course he was killed and that was the end of it." "I don't know," Frederic said. "Oh, yes," Catherine emphasizes. "That's the end of it."

These are the limits, then, as circumscribed by nature: death is the end of life. After death there is only the lifeless statue. It was this conclusion (or something like it) which caused Gertrude Stein to say of Ernest Hemingway that he belonged to the "lost generation," lost because the comfortable morality of the nineteenth century had been denied them after 1914. Frederic Henry attempts to believe in the validity of warfare, but even the peasant soldiers under him know better. When he puts his trust in religion or in his love for Catherine he is also defeated. He reasons it out as follows:

> That was what you did. You died. You did not know what it was about. You never had time to learn. They threw you in and told you the rules and the first time they caught you off base they killed you.
>
> (XLI, 350)

In "The Short Happy Life of Francis Macomber" the emphasis was upon man's final victory over death. That view is represented here in the stoical death of Catherine, but the emphasis is upon futility. In a striking image which represents the key scene in the novel, we have Frederic thinking about an experience he has had:

> Once in camp I put a log on top of the fire and it was full of ants. As it commenced to burn, the ants swarmed out and went first toward the centre where the fire was; then turned back and ran toward the end. When there were enough on the end they fell off into the fire. Some got out, their bodies burnt and flattened, and went off not knowing where they were going. But most of them went toward the fire and back toward the end and swarmed on the cool end and finally fell off into the fire. I remember thinking at the time that it was the end of the world and a splendid chance to be a messiah and lift the log off the fire and throw it out where the ants could get off onto the ground. But I did not do anything but throw a tin cup of water on the log, so that I would have the cup empty to put whiskey in before I added water to it. I think the cup of water on the burning log only steamed the ants.
>
> (XLI, 350)

The relationship of this parable to Catherine's predicament is unmistakable. For her there is likewise no messiah to come to the rescue. Death is the end of it, and the only value in death is man's knowledge of it. In Ernest Hemingway's novels, those who live well die like heroes. They are the initiated. But the initiation of Frederic Henry comes gradually. He learns about war, love, and finally death. Catherine's death is the final stage in his initiation.

III

If this conclusion is true, we might ask: "Why the title: *A Farewell to Arms*"? The title suggests in its obvious implications that the author saw his subject concerned primarily with the war. In that case, we might say either that we are wrong in our conclusions or that the author was wrong in his selection of title. This raises the question of Ernest Hemingway's method—his style. Hemingway's sensibility, when it is functioning at its highest point, has always worked upon an immediate objective level which translates ideas into terms of concrete things: life as a baseball game where each error is punished by death or compared to the struggle of ants on a burning log, the comparison of a hero's death with the slaughter of animals at a stockyard. In each case we are aware of the double implication, the idea and the image; and the emotional force of the idea is intensified by the shock supplied by the image. This is the more complicated form of Hemingway's noted "understatement." At the time of Catherine's operation, while the doctor has gone to make his preparations, Frederic is left to administer the anesthesia. He has been told that the correct amount would register upon the dial at number 2, but when Catherine is in extreme pain, he says, "I turned the dial to three and then four. I wished the doctor would come back. I was afraid of the numbers above two." The statement "I wished the doctor would come back" is understatement. The use of the machine-image suggests Catherine's immediate danger. Another author might have examined in great detail both Catherine's illness and the emotion which Frederic was experiencing at that time; but from the simple, quiet statement, reinforced by the dial registering the numbers above two, we get the full force of Frederic's terror in a few strokes.

That Hemingway was aware of this quality is evidenced by the statement which he once made that what he was attempting to get was a "fifth dimension" in his prose; not the ordinary dimensions of exposition and description, but the full quality of the emotional experience. This is not an unusual characteristic of a work of art; it is merely Ernest Hemingway's means of explaining his own intention; but it suggests the caution a reader should exercise in taking the author's words or sentences at their most obvious level of meaning. Perhaps this is true also of the title, *A Farewell to Arms*. Someone has suggested somewhere that the "Arms" referred not to the war, but to the arms of Catherine; thus suggesting that what the novel was about, really, was Frederic's loss of his love. This is as limited an interpretation as that which sees the novel as only a "war novel." A more valid interpretation would see the title as completely ironic. Frederic has attempted to escape from the obligations which life imposes. He did not wish to fall in love, but he did. He attempted to escape the war, but he felt like a schoolboy who was playing truant. His life with Catherine in Switzerland and the life which they anticipated after the war were relatively devoid of conflict. Catherine and Frederic had said farewell to the life of action and struggle, but ironically their greatest test—the attempt to save the life of Catherine—came at the very moment when they seemed to have achieved a successful escape.

What the novel says, finally, is that you cannot escape the obligations of action—you cannot say "farewell to arms"; you cannot sign a separate peace. You can only learn to live with life, to tolerate it as "the initiated" learn to tolerate it.

The Later Hemingway

by Nemi D'Agostino

I

The impulse toward autobiography, which Hemingway had hitherto so wisely restrained, thrusts itself to the fore at the beginning of the Thirties, at the time of his great wave of popularity and the journalistic build-up of the Hemingway legend. The inner lyricism of works like *A Farewell to Arms* gives way to a manifest regression into sensationalism and melodrama in the two biographical books on bullfighting and African big-game hunting. The clear-cut presentation becomes blurred by the impulse to confession and exhibitionism, is marred by rhetoric and sentimentality, and dimmed by a new sophisticated attitude. Under the absurd Byronic pose which Hemingway could strike so effectively, a crisis was taking place. It was a crisis in his fundamental romanticism, which the very nature of his talent and his cultural background forced toward an accentuated aestheticism. He had been the poet of a complex of emotions which had sprung from the atmosphere of war. But within the violent frame of that world Hemingway had emerged as the upholder of the only humanism which seemed possible at the time. His art, penetrated by a tragic sense of loss, seemed to represent the dilemma of all contemporary humanity. Now the world which had been so desperately lost to his heroes, suddenly appeared to be well lost to him. From extreme disillusion and distrust of all values he swung round to the exaltation of daring, of the beauty of violence and of the beauty of death; and in adopting himself the code of behavior which was so convincing and humane in his heroes, he turned it into a preposterous and unironical search for excitement for its own sake. While his youthful rebellion sprang from a vivd consciousness of the collapse of a moral order in a precise historical moment, now he seemed to want to cut himself off from historical development, taking refuge in irresponsible and self-complacent isolation. Tied up to his lost generation, he was now beginning to live in a time whose issues he was no more able to grasp.

"The Later Hemingway." Translated by Barbara Arnett Melchiori. From *The Sewanee Review* LXVIII (Summer, 1960), 482-493. Copyright © 1960 by The University of the South. Reprinted by permission of the author, the translator, and *The Sewanee Review*.

Death in the Afternoon, the "treatise" in which he collected in 1932
his experiences as a lover of Spain and *aficionado* of the bull ring, was
striking in its implicit (and certainly unconscious) denial of that fundamental postulate of his art, the search for the "exact sequence," the real
thing, the inflexible fidelity to the dry and concrete evidence of the
senses. It was really surprising that the Hemingway who had looked at
the war with such a disillusioned eye should now be taken in to such an
extent by the tragic masquerade of the bullfight. In an exhibition of that
kind, a frame-up playing on the bravado of danger, exploiting the cruelty
and the brutality of the crowd, there is certainly nothing that can be
called art, any more than in the risks run by the acrobat or the lion
tamer. And of course these activities, whose end is the exhibition of their
own technique, lack the ethical and intellectual basis of art. The limi-
tation of Hemingway's "spiritual diary" lies in his sentimental conception
of Spain, a literary interpretation utterly lacking in Manzoni's demand
for reality, so that he can see in that violent display a form of tragic
poetry and a ritual symbolizing a profound conception of human destiny.

This passion for the bull ring, this over-subtle primitivism, this craving
for sensation which finds vent in moments of morbid and bloodthirsty
ecstasy, actually springs from a cultured and detached pleasure in the
primitive and the barbaric. As Geismar and other critics have suggested,
the Hemingway who gazes in fascination at the sight of the indescribable
whiteness of bone in the bullfighter's torn thigh, and who describes the
disembowelling of the horse as the comic scene in the tragedy, is at heart
an intellectual driven to a renunciation of culture and of that conquest
essential to human progress, the suppression of the blood instinct. Hemingway, in the belief that he is getting at the very heart of Spain, and
communing in spirit with its people, is merely exalting his own decadence
into a canon of refinement: a "philosophy" we can only see as an abdi-
cation from maturity.

Behind the stylized killing that links the two strange "lovers" of the
"tragedy," the hunter and its victim, some critics have described the real
hero of the book, Death. But what we find in the "treatise" is not the
emotion of death as the profound, inspiring, and infinitely human
phenomenon that it is, but only the celebration of that sordid post-
prandial slaughter, with its cruel and mannered ritual. The whole book
is debased by the incomprehension implied in this impoverished idea of
death. The style is verbose, crammed with wedges of rhetoric and fake
lyricism, becoming the vehicle now of polemic, now of petulance, and
now of private grudges. It is decked out in the trappings of magic, but
unable to transform into the true substance of poetry its basic concepts,
which are easily shown up for commonplaces and sentimental frippery.
The most genuine passages are the objective accounts of the lives of
bullfighters, which bring us back to the mournful poetry of the "unvan-
quished," the commentaries to the photographs: here a coolly tragic

camera has picked out the squalid corners of the arenas, the livid faces of the gladiators, the heavy and desperate shadow of the beasts, or certain anguished faces of the dead among indifferent onlookers—and here at last it seems to us that we catch the solid and painful reality which belies Hemingway's whole literary travesty of Spain.

But after all, the book on bullfighting should be seen as one of those unpleasant but useful outlets which sometimes serve to purify an author's talent. From *Death in the Afternoon* to *Green Hills of Africa*, another book which, as Aldridge says, was written not by Hemingway but by his legend, the pursuit of excitement becomes less convinced, nearer to the point of crisis. The second is certainly the least important and most untidy of Hemingway's books. But from amongst the medley of shots and oaths, irrelevant details and purple passages, emotions which leave us cold and irrational outbursts of happiness, we can already catch the obscure dissatisfaction which in the same year finds vent in "The Short Happy Life of Francis Macomber" and "The Snows of Kilimanjaro," and which was to lead up to the tentative change in Hemingway's attitude reflected in his abortive novel of 1937, *To Have and Have Not*.

In the meanwhile, the world of "Macomber" had a dramatic immediacy and a living rhythm not to be found in the real world of *Green Hills*. The characters were once again felt and objectified, violent figures from out of the young world without hope of the early novels and tales, that world in which the relation between man and woman is torture and a *safari* is only another drug for the conscience, a costly anaesthetic. It is a pity that in the second of the two stories, where the crisis of the intellectual hero is still more intense, the desire for renovation should find a fictitious outlet in a sentimental sublimation, which breaks up and dilutes the crisp language into confused lyricism and technical virtuosity in a mannered "metaphysical" style and in pursuit of rather banal effects. In spite of the sincerity of its motives and the skilful plot, "The Snows of Kilimanjaro" is spoiled by rhetoric, and more than "Macomber" it remains one of Hemingway's most static and literary stories.

The crisis which was to break down some at least of the pales of Hemingway's aestheticism and its "poetics" (set out in a well-known passage of *Green Hills*), coincided with the development in America, in the years after the Slump, of a rather naïve and doctrinaire Marxist culture, and with the establishment of Fascism in Europe, leading up to its try-out in the Spanish Civil War. For a time the liberal and democratic propensities in Hemingway had the upper hand and pushed him towards a socialist position, even though cautious and wary. Although in his article on Tolstoy in *Men at War* he declared that he wished to remain true to his nature as a narrator of effects and not of causes, his new novel shows a programmatic intention, a thesis as ill-defined and as full of anger. His short, intense, and angry book *To Have and Have Not*

was actually the outcome of the imperfect piecing together of two stories
of derangement and violence (written in 1933 and 1936) and of a third
part dashed off out of a sense of social duty to the sound of the first
guns of the Spanish war. Hemingway had certainly neither the talent
nor the training necessary to create a work of art *engagé* in the deepest
sense, to write the epic of ideological and social conflicts in a tragic
epoch. The result was perforce a novel in which his old individualistic
postulate and the new social urge met and clashed without fusing. His
fierce and tormented hero, Harry Morgan, was but a vacuous intensi-
fication of his standard protagonist, the solitary heir of the Frontier
spirit, and Hemingway's fresh burst of rage only swelled his character of
Giaour and romantic rebel to the limits of parody and grotesque. Nor
did Hemingway succeed in welding into a moral and artistic whole the
aspects of violence, corruption and social disintegration against which
Morgan should be seen as struggling. The meanness and turpitude of
the middle-class world form in the background a heap of meaningless
horrors, and are set out in a series of unrelated scenes, which the thread
of the main plot links together only externally, and which are filled with
figures that are more or less abstractions; while the alternation of various
narrative techniques, mostly borrowed and alien to Hemingway's genius,
is more the fruit of critical calculation than of inner necessity. Even in
the most authentic passages the language seems to be in an acute stage
of crisis: at the one end, through an exaggerated desire to "express," it
falls into documentary naturalism, at the other it scales heights of a
lucid intensity, but it does not succeed in creating a continuous and
pregnant rhythm for a new grasp of reality, or in giving full expression
to the sense of pity, bitterness, and indignation from which the novel
sprang.

II

It has been said that Morgan's last words ("a man alone ain't got no
bloody chance") open a new period in Hemingway's art, that now should
be seen as imbued with a fresh faith in the social destinies of man, with
that fervid sense of the human community reflected in the Donnean epigraph of *For Whom the Bell Tolls*. In the midst of the rage and suffering
of a new war this novel was the product of a tumult of experience and
emotions: the overthrow of the author's non-political attitude in the
face of a pressing need for action, the hate of Fascism and sympathy for
the Loyalist Republic, a romantic love of old Spain, and the enthusiasm
and anxiety for the future of the world which flung many artists into the
international brigades as if to fight a decisive crusade for human liberty.
All these feelings surge through the book, in the very urgency and com-
pactness of its structure, in the fervor of its language which now accepts
and sweeps into its ardent eloquence the reasoning, the meditations, the

search for explanations and causes of which Hemingway had been so impatient in the past. It was unquestionably subject matter which had been almost religiously felt by the author, and the book was written with a brusque tenderness and compassion which touches the heart, and which assured it the sympathetic reception it deserved.

On the other hand, the critics were right to point out that the novel had certain basic weaknesses. Its language was intended to be in part the intimate expression of the intellectual protagonist, and in part to shape itself around the simple heroes of the guerilla, and to throw an epic light on the events. It is instead dim and turgid in the long meditations of the hero; and in the passages of dialogue, where Hemingway tried to create a Platonic language composed of the Spanish idiom, the Bible, and the Elizabethans, it is overloaded with dialectal quotations (which is a critical transfer and not an artistic solution), weighed down with over-much local color, and often forced into melodramatic effects. The element of melodrama found its way also into the tension of the plot, into the structure of the various "scenes" (including the improbable expedient of Pilar's long story), and into the confused and ill-defined character of the hero himself.

In spite of all this *For Whom the Bell Tolls* is in many respects a very interesting work. It is, first of all, a work in which Hemingway's story-telling broke free from its aesthetic *impasse* of the Thirties and re-entered a zone of deeply human feeling, even though the experience represented was no longer new. What we find in the book is another lost young man, another individual failure, a solitary drama that is symbolic of all the individual dramas of all times and places. The only difference is that now the individual failure is overtly seen as part of a collective failure, a common drama in which the new ideals and hopes one by one prove fruitless, and in the end the only thing which remains is the unbroken chain of pessimism and despair. As Kazin rightly noted, the novel was written in the same spirit as the fine short story "Old Man at the Bridge" of 1938: it was born out of pity for the hopeless drama of each single man; it was again a picture of a fatalistic world, centering round the drama of the individual. Not an epic of the war, nor even the story of Robert Jordan's education in the war, but almost an elegy sung in praise of the lonely rebel, serving in a foreign country with a foreign army, though now with the illusion of a "cause": a lost man whom the war overwhelms without changing him. In the face of this central feeling of the impossibility of belief, the Marxist ideal, like every other ideal, can only be the opium of the people, an austere façade hiding deceit. Actually each new faith frightens and unsettles the writer, and Jordan-Hemingway is the old tormented individualist divided between his need for the community and the scorn and fear it excites in him. And the novel is not so much imbued with history as impregnated by the confused attitude of that no-man's party to which Hemingway belongs.

An elegy on a dying man, a symphonic study of suffering and dissolution, a triumph of death: here lies the true feeling which shapes
the book. It has been rightly pointed out that it opens with the theme of
awaited death (the image of the man lying full length which is one of its
leitmotivs, and with which it also closes), and immediately introduces
the theme of fatalism (the hopeless and ironic fatalism of the frequent
interjection: *Qué va!*), while the theme of dissolution is interwoven with
that of destruction in the very structure of the four *movements,* and the
whole, in the end, is only an interval stretching between two supine
postures. The utter uselessness of the attempt on the bridge, upon which
the future of the human race might depend, is made clear from the
start, as is the uselessness of the pathetic heroism of that group of solitary
eccentrics which Hemingway selects as his chief characters. The sky
overhanging the sierra is without depth and beyond the mountains there
is no crusade but only the confused movements of heterogeneous crowds,
a massacre in a betrayed land. Jordan is a new Frederic Henry, who
finds a code of behavior by which to endure life in the exact fulfilment
of his mission, and in the end is driven to "sacrifice" more by desperation
than by any certainty. Even his improbable sentimental idyl (and those
scenes of love in the face of death are among Hemingway's most inadequate, naturalistic, and yet abstract writing) only serves to emphasize the
self-centeredness and irresponsibility of his character. His drama is too
oppressive and restricted to reflect the so much wider and more complex
tragedy of Spain.

Nevertheless we are moved as we reread this novel, born out of a new
and bitterer disenchantment—a melodrama perhaps, but ennobled, in
its naïve solemnity, by the breath of poetry. Hemingway has attempted a
freer and broader narrative rhythm, which is not always successful, but
which touches at times moments of true intensity and genuine dramatic
power: the wiping out of El Sordo's band, Andrés journey behind the
republican lines and the moving close of that episode. And he has tried
to create varied and trenchant characters, succeeding in setting beside
the somewhat inadequate protagonist and the conventionally picturesque
portraits of Pilar and Maria such fierce and poetic figures as El Sordo,
Joaquin and Anselmo.

Hemingway had to wait for another war, and live in it through another
of his eccentric adventures, before writing another book, which turned
out to be the most autobiographical and weakest of all his novels. His
standard hero, grown old in a world torn by constant war, and more
lonesome and tormented than ever, goes in *Across the River and Into the
Trees* toward the death beautiful, indulging for the last time in his
favorite occupations: hunting, love-making, and the pursuit of precious
sensations. And for once fortune favors him: in the exquisite and slightly
decayed beauty of Venice in the wintertime, surrounded alike by the
affection of aristocrats and of the people, and loved by his dream-princess,

he can finally indulge his weakness for self-confession and his longing to arouse admiration and pity. Hemingway wanted to transfigure his eternal hero, making him a pathetic and solemn figure, a creature of bitter passions and childish goodness, whose solitary experience has brought wisdom, nobility, and peace. But the character he actually portrays is that of an embittered and bad-tempered old man, querulous and self-conceited to the point of parody, full of boring and depressing boasts. Indeed, there had never been such a striking contrast between Hemingway's intention and his results. Tied still to his world of desperate young men, he has only been able to fall back on his old type, in a mannered and senile version. Linked to the brittle and laconic language of his vanquished heroes, he has been unable to create an idiom of the upper classes and aristocracy: the characters of *Across the River* speak in a conventional and literary style frozen into tired Alexandrine cadences, spun out by a flow of repetitions. His youthful gift for intensity has failed him.

"I want you to die with the grace of a happy death," Renata, the unconvincing character who is both mistress and nurse, tells the hero. But the good death fails to find poetic fulfilment. From beneath the golden and musical idyl that Hemingway has built up to lead his hero into a safe port, the old desperation breaks through. What the writer really felt was the anguish of Cantwell's lonely march towards extinction: the despair behind the kisses, the funereal thoughts at the moment of love-making, the cold wind blowing over worn and decaying things, the death of all certainty, the turning of his thoughts in "a movement without hope," like the neck of the wounded mallard drake in the jaws of the dog.

Certainly the exotic and primitive setting of the tropics in *The Old Man and the Sea* is better suited to Hemingway's aged hero than is the new Europe. The main theme of the story is absolute failure in life and the irrational sublimation of the defeat. The saintly Santiago goes back in the end to his dreams, his head almost encircled with the halo of holiness. The old man is certainly not the brother of the great realistic heroes of Tolstoy or Verga, nor is he, on the other hand, a fully convincing character in the tradition of symbolism. The story leaves the realistic level as soon as Hemingway tries to make it something more than an immediate objective reality, the moment the strange old man begins to accompany the action with a lyrical commentary, using a refined oratorical language, emphasizing its symbolical substratum, its nature as a projection of the poet's consciousness. As soon, that is, as the chase itself stands revealed as an exploit springing from *un élan d'infini, un amour de l'impossible*. The fable contains a subtle anagogy, which unfortunately is more imposed from without than an intrinsic part of it. Whatever the old man is intended to symbolize (and he seems to be a biblical and Melvillean version of the usual Hemingway hero) he simply does **not** come poetically true; the symbolism remains a fictitious disguise, and the religious or mystical implications are forced in so far as they want to be more than the religion and morality of aestheticism.

Actually the rhythm and idiom of the tale are a clue to its essential emotion. The rhythm is the cadence of the lyrical paragraph, which proceeds with a sumptuous and solemn fall. The language is rich in suggestive and exotic words, in rich and sensuous imagery, in highly literary expressions, in bright and exquisite touches, and is consciously regulated by a love of verbal magic. It is, in short, the rhythm and language of a decadent *poème en prose*, which, however suggestive and intense, must always remain an artificial and minor form, incapable of full historical and moral significance. Within these limits *The Old Man* is certainly a refined work, with its admirable linear development and its brilliant "imagistic" style. A late work by a tired writer who belives more than ever in the religion of beauty, its subtly mannered idiom, its elegant and frozen rhythms, are separated by the space of a whole lifetime from the lucid movement, the fresh and crystalline clarity, the poignancy and the shock-power of the language of the young Hemingway.

III

In spite of all his brave restlessness, Hemingway's basic attitude to reality remained unchanged from *In Our Time* to *The Old Man and the Sea*. Life is a solitary struggle, a desperate fever of action, conscious of having no sense or reason beyond itself. Nothing in it that can be justified, bettered or saved, no problem that can really be set and solved. In this fundamentally non-religious world man can rage and die—and the writer, the defender of humanity, looks sadly and impotently on over the fence. For he too must cling to his own rigid code, in cultivating his small golden garden. Art, as Goethe said in another context and in another time, is the attempt of the individual to save himself from the destructive power of the All.

Hemingway is not of course an easy writer. In his personality are concealed romantic, puritanical, irrationalistic elements. He felt the crisis of romantic individualism in all its complexity, and his characters are also engaged in living out the deep and tormenting problem of liberty of which Mann speaks in *Meine Zeit*. It is true that only the characters in his youthful works are fully symbolic of their own time, while his later heroes are figures in a myth which grows more and more rigid, artificial and poetically ineffective.

It is also true, although Hemingway's effort toward the ideal of the great European novel yielded noble results, so that even his failures are not devoid of dignity and interest, his true genius tended to express itself in an elementary narrative form, in the limpidity of a lyrical and subjective "imagism," which apparently simplifies the context of life, but in effect contrives to include, in the sort of essential emotion it presents, a wide range of connotations. He is at his best in *A Farewell to Arms*, in *The Sun also Rises* and in his early short stories. These works, springing from the climate of war and its aftermath, will certainly continue to hold a very important place in American literature. The vast influence they had until the Forties on the young novelists both of America and Europe has many negative and ephemeral aspects, but has also been seriously constructive: in helping for instance young European writers to break away from narrow literary zones, to seek rejuvenation in greater closeness to present life, to revitalize their language, and also to turn back to certain forgotten lessons of the past.

Confiteor Hominem:
Ernest Hemingway's Religion of Man

by Joseph Waldmeir

In recent years, critics have become increasingly suspicious that it is necessary to read Ernest Hemingway's work on the symbolic as well as on the story level in order to gain a full appreciation of its art.[1] Since the publication of *The Old Man and the Sea*, the suspicion has become first an awareness, then a certainty. Of all Hemingway's work, this one demands most to be read on both levels; and the story, its details, its method of presentation, are sufficiently similar to the balance of his work as to suggest strongly the possibility of a similar reading and perhaps a similar interpretation.

The Old Man and the Sea is, as story, very good Hemingway. It is swiftly and smoothly told; the conflict is resolved into a struggle between a man and a force which he scarcely comprehends, but which he knows that he must continue to strive against, though knowing too that the struggle must end in defeat. The defeat is only apparent, however, for, as in "The Undefeated," it becomes increasingly clear throughout the story that it is not victory or defeat that matters but the struggle itself. Furthermore, *The Old Man and the Sea*, while reasserting the set of values, the philosophy which permeates all of Hemingway, is built upon the great abstractions—love and truth and honor and loyalty and pride and humility—and again speaks of the proper method of attaining and retaining these virtues, and of the spiritual satisfaction inevitably bestowed upon their holder.

The Christian religious symbols running through the story, which are so closely interwoven with the story in fact as to suggest an allegorical intention on Hemingway's part, are so obvious as to require little more

"Confiteor Hominem: Ernest Hemingway's Religion of Man." From *PMASAL*, XLII (1956), 277-281. Reprinted by permission of The Michigan Academy of Science, Arts, and Letters and of The University of Michigan Press.

[1] The two most recent comprehensive examinations of Hemingway symbolism are: Carlos Baker, *Hemingway: The Writer as Artist* (Princeton: Princeton University Press, 1952), and Philip Young, *Ernest Hemingway* (New York: Rinehart, 1952).

than a listing of them here. The Old Man is a fisherman, and he is also
a teacher, one who has taught the boy not only how to fish—that is, how
to make a living—but how to behave as well, giving him the pride and
humility necessary to a good life. During the trials with the great fish and
with the sharks his hands pain him terribly, his back is lashed by the line,
he gets an eyepiercing headache, and his chest constricts and he spits
blood. He hooks the fish at noon, and at noon of the third day he kills
it by driving his harpoon into its heart. As he sees the second and third
sharks attacking, the Old Man calls aloud " 'Ay,' " and Hemingway comments: "There is no translation for this word and perhaps it is just such
a noise as a man might make, involuntarily, feeling the nail go through
his hand and into the wood." [2] On landing, the Old Man shoulders his
mast and goes upward from the sea toward his hut; he is forced to rest
several times on his journey up the hill, and when he reaches the hut
he lies on the bed "with his arms out straight and the palms of his hands
up." [3]

The Christian symbolism so evident here shifts from man to fish—a
legitimate symbol for Christ since the beginning of Christianity, as it
was a legitimate religious symbol before Christianity—and back to man
throughout the story. This apparent confusion is consistent not only
within the Hemingway philosophy as an example of the sacrificer-sacri-
ficed phenomenon (a point which I will discuss later in this paper) but
within formal Christianity as well, if the doctrine of the Trinity be
accepted. Furthermore, the phenomenon itself closely parallels the Roman
Catholic sacrifice of the Mass, wherein a fusion of the priest-man with
Christ takes place at the moment of Transubstantiation.

Along with the Christ symbols, reinforcing them, but depending on
them for its importance, is a rather intricate numerology. It is not
formalized—neither is the numerology of Christianity—but it is carefully
set forth.

Three, seven, and forty are key numbers in the Old and New Testa-
ments, and in the religion, and Hemingway makes a judicious use of
them. The Old Man, as the story opens, has fished alone for forty-four
famine days and with the boy for forty more. The Old Man's trial with
the great fish lasts exactly three days; the fish is landed on the seventh
attempt; seven sharks are killed; and, although Christ fell only three
times under the Cross, whereas the Old Man has to rest from the weight
of the mast seven times, there is a consistency in the equal importance of
the numbers themselves.

But, once it has been established that *The Old Man and the Sea* may
be read on the symbolic as well as on the story level, a new problem
presents itself, a problem which grows out of the nature of the symbolic

---

[2] Ernest Hemingway, *The Old Man and the Sea* (New York: Scribner, 1952), p. 118.
[3] *Ibid.*, p. 134.

level and out of the disturbing realization that the two levels exist harmoniously in the work. I think that the problem may best be expressed by two questions which the discerning reader must have asked himself as he put *The Old Man and the Sea* down: Is the story, as it appears at first glance to be, a Christian allegory? Has the old master tough guy decided, in the words of Colonel Cantwell, "to run as a Christian"? If neither of these questions can be answered with an unqualified affirmative—and I submit that they cannot—then a further question must be asked: Just what is the book's message?

The answer assumes a third level on which *The Old Man and the Sea* must be read—as a sort of allegorical commentary by the author on all his previous work, by means of which it may be established that the religious overtones of *The Old Man and the Sea* are not peculiar to that book among Hemingway's works, and that Hemingway has finally taken the decisive step in elevating what might be called his philosophy of Manhood to the level of a religion.

Two aspects of the total work, including *The Old Man and the Sea*, must be considered at this point in order to clarify the above conclusion on the one hand, and to answer the questions concerning Hemingway's Christianity on the other.

The first of these aspects is Hemingway's concern with man as man, with man in his relation to things of this world almost exclusively. The other world, God, does not often enter into the thoughts, plans, or emotions of a Hemingway character. God exists—most of the characters are willing to admit His existence, or at least, unwilling to deny it—but not as an immanent Being, not ever benevolent or malevolent.

God is sometimes prayed to by the Hemingway hero at moments of crisis, but His aid or succor are never depended upon, never really expected. Thus we have Jake Barnes in the Cathedral at Pamplona, on the eve of his great trial, praying for everybody he can think of, for good bullfights and good fishing; and as he becomes aware of himself kneeling, head bent, he

> was a little ashamed, and regretted that I was such a rotten Catholic, but realized that there was nothing I could do about it, at least for awhile, and maybe never, but that anyway it was a grand religion, and I only wished I felt religious and maybe I would the next time. . . .[4]

And thus, too, we have the Old Man, who, after twenty-four hours of his monumental struggle have passed, prays for heavenly assistance mechanically, automatically, thinking, "I am not religious," and "Hail Marys are easier to say than Our Fathers." And after forty-five hours, he says:

[4] Hemingway, *The Sun Also Rises* (New York: Scribner, 1926), pp. 99-100.

"Now that I have him coming so beautifully, God help me to endure. I'll say a hundred Our Fathers and a hundred Hail Marys. But I cannot say them now."

Consider them said, he thought, I'll say them later.[5]

But when the struggle is ended and the full ironic impact of his "victory" is clear, he asks himself what it was that beat him, and answers, "Nothing . . . I went out too far." [6]

He who depends too heavily on prayer, or for that matter on any external aids when faced with a crisis, is not very admirable to Hemingway. In *Death in the Afternoon*, when he wants to describe the unmanliness of a "cowardly bullfighter" girding himself for action, Hemingway places him in church

in his bullfighting clothes to pray before the fight, sweating under the armpits, praying that the bull will embiste, that is, charge frankly and follow the cloth well; oh blessed Virgin that thou wilt give me a bull that will embiste well, blessed Virgin, give me that bull, blessed Virgin, that I should touch this bull in Madrid to-day on a day without wind; promising something of value or a pilgrimage, praying for luck, frightened sick. . . .[7]

A man must depend upon himself alone in order to assert his manhood, and the assertion of his manhood, in the face of insuperable obstacles, is the complete end and justification of his existence for a Hemingway hero. The Old Man *must* endure his useless struggle with the sharks; Manuel, in "The Undefeated," *must,* in spite of his broken wrist and a terrible goring, go in on the bull six times and accept the horn at last; Jake *must* continue to live as "well" and "truly" and "honestly" as he is able in spite of his overwhelming frustration. And each must face his struggle alone, with no recourse to otherworldly help, for only as solitary individuals can they assert their manhood.

And significantly they must go it alone without regard to otherworldly blame. As far as sin is concerned, Jake would probably say along with the Old Man, "Do not think about sin. It is much too late for that and there are people who are paid to do it. Let them think about it." [8] And Manuel would probably nod agreement.

[5] *The Old Man and the Sea*, p. 96.

[6] *Ibid.,* p. 133.

[7] Hemingway, *Death in the Afternoon* (New York: Scribner, 1932), p. 90.

[8] *The Old Man and the Sea*, p. 116. Hemingway has always had a deep respect for Christians—provided they *live* like Christians. His great abstractions are also great Christian virtues; and when he finds a believer, such as the priest in *A Farewell to Arms* or Anselmo in *For Whom the Bell Tolls*, who lives in accord with the abstractions, he praises him as "a Christian," and adds, for the benefit of the hypocritical, "something very rare in Catholic countries."

There is no evidence of intentional blasphemy in any of his work; the deeply religious are frequently exalted, not in the terms of Christianity, but in Hemingway's own terms. In the one-act play, "Today is Friday," Christ's Manhood is given far

However, in spite of such obvious rejections of otherworldly Christianity in his affirmation of Manhood, Hemingway has formulated as rigid a set of rules for living and for the attainment of Manhood as can be found in any religion. These rules, along with the detailed procedure for their application, constitute the second aspect of Hemingway's total work to be considered in this paper.

The rules are built upon the great abstractions mentioned above. They are so bound up with the procedure for their application that the procedure itself might be considered to be a rule—or better, that neither rules nor procedure exist without one another. Hemingway's philosophy of Manhood is a philosophy of action; a man is honest when he acts honestly, he is humble when he acts humbly, he loves when he is loving or being loved. Thus, taking an awareness of the rules as he has taken an awareness of the abstractions for granted, Hemingway concerns himself primarily with the presentation of procedure. The procedure is carefully outlined; it is meticulously detailed. If no part of it is overlooked or sloughed off, it must result in a satisfying experience almost in and of itself.

This procedure, this ritual—for such is what the procedure actually amounts to—is most clearly evident in Hemingway's treatment of the bullfight. *Death in the Afternoon* is devoted to an evaluation of the manhood of various bullfighters on the basis of their ability to abide by the rules, and to a description of the ritual by means of which they prove possession and communicate the satisfaction to be gained from a proper performance of function to the spectator. War, the prize ring, fishing, hunting, and making love are some of the other celebrations by means of which Hemingway's religio-philosophy of Man is conveyed. But the bullfight is the greatest because, besides possessing, as the others do also, a procedure inviolate, intimately related to the great abstractions, it always ends in death. It assumes the stature of a religious sacrifice by means of which a man can place himself in harmony with the universe, can satisfy the spiritual as well as the physical side of his nature, can atone for the grievous omissions and commissions of his past, can purify and elevate himself in much the same way that he can in any sacrificial religion. The difference between Hemingway's religion of man and formal religion is simply—yet profoundly—that in the former the elevation does not extend beyond the limits of this world, and in the latter, Christianity for example, the ultimate elevation is totally otherworldly.

---

greater importance than His Godhead with no blasphemous overtones. The First Soldier, speaking for Hemingway and offering the highest praise he is capable of, answers, "He was pretty good in there today," each time the cynical Second Soldier minimizes Christ's manliness. The words are not only directly addressed to the cynic, but indirectly to the emotionally disturbed Third Soldier as well, who has had a religious experience which the First cannot share, but which he comprehends and sympathizes with.

The bullfighter is in a sense a priest, performing the sacrifice for the sake of the spectator as well as for his own sake, giving each that "feeling of life and death and mortality and immortality" which Hemingway described in *Death in the Afternoon*, and, as does the Roman Catholic priest on the ideal level, the bullfighter actually places his own life in jeopardy. This curious phenomenon of the sacrificer gambling on becoming the sacrificed serves to clarify the terms of Hemingway's system, rather than, as at first glance it might seem, to confuse them. The bullfighter recognizes the possibility and immanence of death when he steps into the ring, and he must face it bravely. He must perform the sacrifice cleanly, with one true stroke, preserving both his honor and the bull's dignity. If he kills out of malice or out of fear his actions will show it, and the spectator will be distracted from concentration upon the sacrifice to awareness of the man, and no satisfaction will result.

There must be a cognizance of death both from the standpoint of killing and from that of being killed; there must be more than a cognizance actually; there must be an acceptance. Knowledge of death's inevitability so that he does not react to its immediacy, coupled with unconcern for the possibilities of life after death, are necessary attributes of the ideal bullfighter. His aim can extend no further than the great abstractions themselves, how he earns them and how he communicates them. He must realize that it is not *that* one dies but *how* one dies that is important. And equally important, that it is not *that* one kills but *how* one kills.

It is not only in his treatment of the bullfight that this second aspect of Hemingway's total work is evident, though there it may be most immediately apparent. The abstractions, the rules, the ritual, the sacrifice dominate the details of *The Old Man and the Sea* as they dominate those of "The Undefeated" and *The Sun Also Rises*.[9] We are told carefully, painstakingly, how the Old Man performs his function as fisherman; how he prepares for the hoped-for struggle:

[9] With the possible exception of sacrifice, they dominate the details of *Across the River and Into the Trees* as well. If examined in terms of the religion of Manhood, this is not as unsuccessful a book as most critics have claimed. It gives those members of the Order who realize that they will die a natural death a way to meet the problem of dying. Colonel Cantwell still enjoys many of the things that have contributed to the happiness of his life—the beauties of nature and art, the taste of good food and drink, the pleasures of hunting, the give and take of sexual love—and in memory he can experience again the pleasure of fulfilling a soldier's duties.

The reviewers have looked upon this preparation for dying as little more than nostalgic sentimentalism; but even granting that the story tends in this direction, it still fits neatly into the Hemingway religio-philosophical mold. At its climax there is the usual refusal to turn to the supernatural, a more pointed refusal than ever: "You going to run as a Christian?" the Colonel asks himself, and answers, "Maybe I will get Christian toward the end. Yes, he said, maybe you will. Who wants to make a bet on that?" (p. 291)

Before it was really light he had his baits out and was drifting with the
current. One bait was down forty fathoms. The second was at seventy-five
and the third and fourth were down in the blue water at one hundred and
one hundred and twenty-five fathoms. Each bait hung head down with the
shank of the hook inside the bait fish, tied and sewed solid and all the projecting part of the hook, the curve and the point, was covered with fresh
sardines. Each sardine was hooked through both eyes so that they made a
half-garland on the projecting steel.

. . . Each line, as thick around as a big pencil, was looped onto a green-
sapped stick so that any pull or touch on the bait would make the stick dip
and each line had two forty-fathom coils which could be made fast to the
other spare coils so that, if it were necessary, a fish could take out over three
hundred fathoms of line.[10]

We are told how he hooks the fish and secures the line, waiting sus-
pensefully for the fish to turn and swallow the bait, then waiting again
until it has eaten it well, then striking, "with all the strength of his
arms and the pivoted weight of his body," three times, setting the hook;
then placing the line across his back and shoulders so that there will
be something to give when the fish lunges, and the line will not break.
We are told specifically, in terms reminiscent of such descriptions of the
bullfight, how the kill is made:

The old man dropped the line and put his foot on it and lifted the harpoon as high as he could and drove it down with all his strength, and more
strength he had just summoned, into the fish's side just behind the great
chest fin that rose high in the air to the altitude of a man's chest. He felt
the iron go in and he leaned on it and drove it further and then pushed all
his weight after it.[11]

The immanence of death for the sacrificer as well as for the sacrificed,
and his total disregard of its possibility, are made clear at the climax of
the struggle when the Old Man thinks: "You are killing me, fish . . .
Come on and kill me. I do not care who kills who." [12]

It is at this point I think that the questions asked earlier in this paper
can be answered. Has Hemingway decided to "run as a Christian"? I
think not; the evidence in *The Old Man and the Sea*, with the exeception
of the Christian symbolism, indicates that he is no more Christian now
than he was when he wrote *The Sun Also Rises*. But the Christian
symbolism *is* in the book, and it *does* appear to constitute a Christian
religious allegory. Yes, but on a superficial level. The religious allegory,
attached to the two aspects of the total body of Hemingway's work **as**

[10] *The Old Man and the Sea*, pp. 33-34.
[11] *Ibid.*, pp. 103-104.
[12] *Ibid.*, p. 102.

they appear in *The Old Man and the Sea,* which have been the subject of most of my discussion thus far, actually constitute a third level on which *The Old Man and the Sea* must be read—as the allegorical interpretation of the total body of the work.

I said above that Hemingway is no more Christian now than he was thirty years ago; it has been my intention in this paper to show that he was *no less religious* thirty years ago than he is now. The evidence which I have presented adds up to something more than a philosophy or an ethic, the two terms which have most often been used to describe Hemingway's world view; it adds up to what I would call a Religion of Man. Hemingway did not turn religious to write *The Old Man and the Sea.* He has always been religious, though his religion is not of the orthodox, organized variety. He celebrates, he has always celebrated, the Religion of Man; *The Old Man and the Sea* merely celebrates it more forcefully and convincingly than any previous Hemingway work. It is the final step in the celebration. It is the book which, on the one hand, elevates the philosophy to a religion by the use of allegory, and on the other, by being an allegory of the total body of his work, enables us to see that work finally from the point of view of religion.

The Art of Evasion

by Leon Edel

I would like to offer a mild dissent amid the current cheering for our poet of big-game hunting and bullfighting. Doubtless we rejoice, as Americans, that our literature has been honored once again by the Swedish Academy; and it is pleasant to feel that a writer as swash-buckling and myth-making as Ernest Hemingway should have been selected. Nevertheless the Swedish Academy has not been very brilliant, on the whole, in its choice of Nobel prize winners; the list, going back to the beginning of the century, is filled with forgotten names, redolent with omissions. They gave the prize to Kipling, but when the time came they did not give it to James Joyce. As Hemingway himself pointed out, they passed over Mark Twain and Henry James and, we might add, Edwin Arlington Robinson. Of the Americans who have received it, only Faulkner, O'Neill, and T. S. Eliot (an American turned Englishman) have had the world stature envisaged when the prize was created.

Ernest Hemingway, I hold, belongs to the second shelf of American fiction, not the first: he can safely be placed beside Sinclair Lewis rather than beside Hawthorne, Melville, or James. But my dissent at this moment is not in matters of classification. It stems from the Academy's bestowing of the prize on the grounds of Hemingway's Style—his "mastery of the art of modern narration." I am not, of course, sure what the Swedish Academy means by "modern narration"—unless indeed it is thinking of brisk journalism, the most characteristic form of narration of our time. But the award has generally been interpreted as an award for Style.

Now Style, I agree, is virtually everything in literature. The writer who forges a Style places himself, in the very nature of things, in the forefront of his period, and provides himself with a shining passkey to the future. But we must be careful here—both myself and critics who have been embalming Hemingway—to be sure we speak of the same thing. A Style involves substance as well as form. No writer has received his key for swaddling meager thought in elegant flowers. Such flowers fade easily. I would argue that Hemingway has not created a Style: he

"The Art of Evasion." From *Folio*, XX (Spring, 1955), 18-20. Copyright 1955 by the Department of English, Indiana State University. Reprinted by permission of the author and *Folio*.

has rather created the artful illusion of a Style, for he is a clever artist
and there is a great deal of cleverness in all that he has done. He has
conjured up an *effect* of Style by a process of evasion, very much as he
sets up an aura of emotion—by walking directly away from emotion!

What I am trying to suggest is that the famous Hemingway Style is
not "organic." And any style worthy of the name must be, as the much-
worn, but nevertheless truthful *mot, that Style is the man,* testifies. Is
Hemingway's Style the man? At the risk of a pun, I would answer no, it
is the mannerism! It is an artifice, a series of charming tricks, a group of
cleverness. Gertrude Stein taught Hemingway that one can obtain wry
effects by assembling incongruities, and Hemingway really learned how
to juxtapose these with high skill. "There were many more guns in the
country around and the spring had come." Now the coming of spring
is, strictly speaking, a *non sequitur.* It has nothing to do with the guns.
Spring occurs in many parts of the world where there are no guns. And
yet this juxtaposition underlines the ironic effect that in spring, and in
this particular time and place, men could still shed blood, at the very
season of the year when everything around us is re-born. This is very
good, and there are many such examples in Hemingway. There are
others which are mere incongruity, as when he writes "The river ran
behind us and the town had been captured very handsomely." This is
quite simply hodge-podge. It is easily imitated, as a whole school of
junior Hemingways has demonstrated. It's a fine trick. But it is hardly
a Style. Neither can certain of his long tagged-together sentences, reminiscent of Molly Bloom's internal monologue, be regarded as "organic"
prose.

What of the substance? In Hemingway's novels people order drinks—
they are always ordering drinks—then they drink, then they order some
more; they make love, and the love-making is "fine" and "nice" and
it is "good" and it is sufficiently romantic, as in the pulps, that is,
sufficiently adolescent. There is some killing. There is some fine riding
and shooting and sailing. It is a world of superficial action[1] and almost
wholly without reflection—such reflection as there is tends to be on a
rather crude and simplified level. It will be argued that all this is a
large part of life and thus has validity in fiction. Of course. It is my
contention merely that such surface writing, dressed out in prose mannerisms, does not constitute a Style and that the present emphasis on this
quality in Hemingway tends, in effect, to minimize the hollowness of
his total production. Hemingway has created a world of Robinson
Crusoes, living on lonely islands, with bottle and gun for companions,
and an occasional woman to go with the drinks.

I have said that Hemingway belongs to the second shelf of our literature, or at least that is where I would put him, and it would be precisely on this ground: that he has not written an "adult" novel. He has

[1] See footnote in Mr. Young's reply.

contrived, with great cleverness, some very good novels. He is at his happiest, in reality, in the short story. The short story by its very nature demands simplification; characters need not be developed, plot and drama need not be created—a mood, a nostalgia, a moment of experience, suffice. Hemingway is an artist of the small space, the limited view. And I am not sure that what I have called "evasion" in his work will not be borne out if we search for its roots in his life, from which, after all, an artist's work always springs. To be able to cope with emotion only by indirection, or to write prose which seeks surface expressly to avoid texture—is this not a little like escaping from life by big-game hunting or watching violence in a bull ring or daydreaming through long hours of fishing? These are all fascinating pursuits for our hours of leisure or when given a proper perspective and taken in proper proportion (unless indeed one earns one's living by fighting bulls or is a career-fisherman). When they become a substitute for other forms of life—and granted that they themselves are part of life and partake of it—they can become an evasion of life.

But Hemingway is not as old as his Old Man. There have been striking examples in the history of literature of artists in whom, only at the end, is there a great fusion of experience and of expression that culminates in a large, mature, and durable work. And a Style. We must not at all exclude the possibility that Hemingway may yet write a book for the top shelf of our literature. But let us not put him there until he does.

Hemingway: A Defense

by Philip Young

It comes as a bit of a surprise to be defending Hemingway where he is usually thought to be strongest. Even the most abject of his devotees are ordinarily prepared to make concessions on other matters, but as for style—this is where his foes generally do the conceding.

And it is hard to know how to justify that style without undertaking a long, and probably tedious, analysis of it. Surely it is not possible to demonstrate in a short space that the style *is* organic, *is* the man, or that its "evasions" are a meaningful part of the style. Nor is it feasible to distinguish both quickly and effectively between "Style" and an "*effect* of style," or between stylistic "tricks" and "Style." (But are these things really so different from each other—different in *kind?* Isn't it mostly that the term "tricks" is pejorative? What if we called them "aesthetic devices"?) So I restrict myself to the two instances that have been singled out in the dissent as objectionable, although they do seem to me unrepresentative.

The first of these, the "hodge-podge," would be only a most minor trick in a formidable repertoire if it were a trick at all, that is, if it were a *non sequitur.* But it is not, and I do not think it takes any expert in military tactics to see why it is not: "The river ran behind us and the town has been captured very handsomely . . ." Clearly, these people have been attacking, and when you have been doing this it makes quite a lot of difference whether you have crossed a river or have yet to cross it. The coordinated clauses, then, are roughly equivalent features of a soldier's satisfaction in a victory, and there's not a *non sequitur* in sight. (This would seem fairly obvious even out of context; in context, the beginning of Chapter Two of *A Farewell to Arms,* it is patent.)

As for the Molly Bloom passage, I concur: it does not constitute a style. But that is rather beside the point. The point is that this wayward echo of Joyce, which closes *To Have and Have Not,* is not *characteristic* of Hemingway; he had never tried that kind of thing before, and never did again.

Well, "What of the substance?" On the drinking, hunting and fishing,

"Hemingway: A Defense." From *Folio,* XX (Spring, 1955), 20-22. Copyright 1955 by the Department of English, Indiana State University. Reprinted by permission of the author and *Folio.*

I would agree, a little. These are relatively superficial activities. But it seems to me that at his best Hemingway has treated them, from *The Sun Also Rises* to *The Old Man and the Sea*, as means for saying *other* things—things about life in general. In the earlier books, he was saying things especially about life in that time; he wrote about people who drank and fished and watched bullfights. But the point was that they did these things because in the famous collapse of values that followed the First War they did not know what else to do. In a later book a man again goes fishing, and *his* story is a means of saying things about life in any time—true and rather stirring things, thought many people, including the prize committee and me.

However, the notion that love-making and war-making are "superficial activities" finds me with no defense at all.[1] I might just as well admit that I have been under the impression that sex and killing were, in the personal and social spheres, respectively, the foremost problems of our age, and had never questioned their validity as proper subject matter. I cannot change overnight, so let them go as regrettable preoccupations—probably more signs of Hemingway's adolescence, and my own.

There are often places where it is possible to agree with criticisms of Hemingway. Surely he does have a somewhat "limited view," and this fact does indeed have its roots in his life. Yes, he has often been in escape; yes, there are many aspects of existence which he has consistently evaded. There is a whole book in print on these matters, and I have always thought it a remarkably persuasive one.

But it is not possible to agree all the way. First, Hemingway's view of things is much more limited on the surface than anywhere else; it might be better to call him narrow; he *is* narrow, compared, for instance, to Tolstoi. But his view is also rather deep: why else are his books, and not just his life, "myth-making"? Second, if Hemingway has often escaped to the bullfights, he has escaped oftener into wars, which, by common consent (I take it), may well prove our undoing—making this a very odd sort of escapism indeed. Nor, third, is it possible to go so far as to say that his evasions constitute an "evasion of life," for this too much begs the question of what life is. (I am certain it is not what it was in the nineteenth century, and I suspect it is largely *that* life he is said to evade.)

And so I must agree with the Nobel people. The citation was proper, however belated. For me Hemingway is, next to Thoreau, the greatest prose stylist in our literature. That's at the most. At the very least, he is the writer of some of the cleanest, freshest, subtlest, most brilliant and most moving prose of our time. There are passages in three of the four

---

[1] *"Perish the thought! I have at no time wanted to suggest that love and war are not important. My whole quarrel with Hemingway's style is that it makes them seem unimportant."—Leon Edel.*

novels I have mentioned here, and in a few of his stories, that can never
go bad. (There is no need to specify which passages; I mean the famous
ones.)

Thus it seems incongruous to say that Hemingway, even at his worst,
belongs with Lewis, who was at his best a brilliant mimic and journalist,
and not a truly creative writer at all. I am not so sure about Hemingway
in relation to Hawthorne, Melville and James; mainly it's that he is very
different from them, just as our world is from theirs. But if Eliot and
Faulkner belong up there on that first shelf, and I gather that they do,
then they ought to move over and make room.

Chronology of Important Dates

1899	Born in Oak Park, Illinois, second of six children of Clarence Edmunds Hemingway, M.D., and Grace Hall Hemingway.
1917	Graduates from Oak Park High School; rejected by Army because of eye injured in boxing; works as cub reporter on Kansas City *Star*.
1918	Goes to Italy as Red Cross ambulance driver. Legs severely injured by mortar fragments and heavy machine gun fire midnight July 8, two weeks before nineteenth birthday, near Fossalta di Piave.
1920-24	Reporter and foreign correspondent for Toronto *Star* and *Star Weekly*.
1921	Marries Hadley Richardson; leaves for Europe.
1923	*Three Stories and Ten Poems* published in Paris. Contains "Up In Michigan," "Out of Season," and "My Old Man."
1924	*in our time*, thirty-two pages of miniatures published in Paris.
1925	*In Our Time*, U.S. edition, published by Boni & Liveright. Fourteen short stories plus miniatures of Paris edition, which are used as interchapters.
1926	*The Torrents of Spring* published in May by Charles Scribner's Sons, New York, publisher of all subsequent works. *The Sun Also Rises* published in October.
1927	Divorces Hadley Richardson; marries Pauline Pfeiffer. Publication of *Men Without Women*, fourteen short stories, ten of which had appeared in magazines.
1928-38	Lives mostly at Key West, Florida.
1929	*A Farewell to Arms*, Hemingway's first commercial success: 80,000 copies sold in first four months.
1932	*Death in the Afternoon*.
1933	*Winner Take Nothing*, fourteen stories. Publishes first of thirty-one articles and stories to appear in *Esquire* during next six years.

1935	*Green Hills of Africa.*
1936-37	Writes, speaks, and raises money for Loyalists in Spanish Civil War.
1937	In Spain covering Civil War for North American Newspaper Alliance. Appearance of *To Have and Have Not,* three interconnected stories, two of which had been published separately.
1938	*The Fifth Column and the First Forty-Nine Stories.* Contains the play, the short stories in the three previous collections, plus seven previously published stories.
1940	*For Whom the Bell Tolls,* Hemingway's best-selling book. Pauline Pfeiffer divorces him; he marries Martha Gellhorn.
1942	*Men at War.* A collection of war stories and accounts edited and with an introduction by Hemingway.
1942-45	Covers European theater of war as newspaper and magazine correspondent.
1944	Divorced from Martha Gellhorn; marries Mary Welsh.
1950	*Across the River and Into the Trees.*
1952	*The Old Man and the Sea* published in *Life,* September 1.
1954	Wins Nobel Prize. Cited for "forceful and style-making mastery of the art of modern narration."
1961	Dies of self-inflicted gunshot wound July 2 in his Ketchum, Idaho, home.

Notes on the Editor and Contributors

ROBERT P. WEEKS, editor of the anthology, is a professor of English at the University of Michigan, editor of *Commonwealth vs. Sacco and Vanzetti*, and author of several critical essays on Hemingway.

CARLOS BAKER is a professor of English at Princeton University and the author of *Hemingway: The Writer as Artist*.

CLEANTH BROOKS, a professor of English at Yale University, was among the first and most perceptive of the New Critics to turn to fiction. He is coauthor—along with Robert Penn Warren—of *Understanding Fiction*.

MALCOLM COWLEY knew most of the writers responsible for the brilliant resurgence of American letters during the 1920's—Fitzgerald, Hemingway, Faulkner, Anderson, and others—and has written about them and their times.

NEMI D'AGOSTINO is a professor of English literature at the University of Trieste.

LEON EDEL, author of *The Psychological Novel: 1900-1950* and a biography of Henry James, is a professor of English at New York University.

LESLIE FIEDLER is the author of *Love and Death in the American Novel* and *An End to Innocence*, a collection of essays. He is a professor of English at Montana State University.

E. M. HALLIDAY is the author of *The Ignorant Armies* and an editor of *American Heritage*.

D. H. LAWRENCE (1885-1930), British poet, essayist, and novelist, was also a first-rate critic, as his *Studies in Classic American Literature* testifies.

HARRY LEVIN is a professor of comparative literature at Harvard and the author of numerous distinguished scholarly essays, most of them concerned with Elizabethan drama, literary criticism, or the modern novel.

SEAN O'FAOLAIN, who lives in County Dublin, Eire, is well-known as a novelist, short story writer, critic, and interpreter of modern Irish life.

LILLIAN ROSS has been a writer on the staff of *The New Yorker* for more than fifteen years. She has written mostly Profiles and other long articles.

MARK SPILKA is the author of *The Love Ethic* of D. H. Lawrence and is a professor of English at the University of Michigan.

JOSEPH WALDMEIR is a professor in the Department of Communication Skills at Michigan State University.

ROBERT PENN WARREN, distinguished novelist and critic, is a professor of English at Yale University.

RAY B. WEST, JR., professor of English at San Francisco State College, is coeditor with Robert Stallman of *The Art of Modern Fiction.*

PHILIP YOUNG is a professor of American literature at Pennsylvania State University and the author of *Ernest Hemingway,* a psychobiographical study.